STRATEGIC INTERVENTIONS FOR PEOPLE IN CRISIS, TRAUMA, AND DISASTER

Revised Edition

Diana Sullivan Everstine and Louis Everstine
Foreword by Paul Watzlawick

Routledge
Taylor & Francis Group
New York London

Routledge is an imprint of the
Taylor & Francis Group, an informa business

D1441336

Routledge
Taylor & Francis Group
711 Third Avenue
New York, NY 10017

Routledge
Taylor & Francis Group
2 Park Square
Milton Park, Abingdon
Oxon OX14 4RN

First issued in paperback 2013

International Standard Book Number-13: 978-0-415-95071-8 (Hardcover)
International Standard Book Number-13: 978-0-415-86113-7 (Softcover)

Library of Congress Cataloging-in-Publication Data

Everstine, Diana Sullivan, 1944-
    Strategic interventions for people in crisis, trauma, and disaster / Diana Sullivan Everstine and Louis Everstine.-- Rev. ed.
        p. cm.
    Includes bibliographical references and index.
    ISBN 0-415-95071-6 (hb : alk. paper)
    1. Crisis intervention (Mental health services) 2. Victims of family violence. 3. Post-traumatic stress disorder. 4. Psychic trauma. I. Everstine, Louis, 1933- II. Title.

RC480.6.E913 2006
362.2'04251--dc22   2005028146

Visit the Taylor & Francis Web site at
http://www.taylorandfrancis.com

and the Routledge Web site at
http://www.routledge-ny.com

For Paul Watzlawick, our source and inspiration.

Contents

Acknowledgments

One of the joys of writing a book is meeting the people who read it. In this respect, *People in Crisis* (1983) brought us in contact with many wonderful people, whose enthusiastic reception of the book was, of course, a contributing factor to the current revision. Not the least of these supporters was Margaret Singer, whose recent death was a loss both for us and psychology; we shall never forget her humor, breadth of knowledge, and courageous spirit.

In 1991, the Crisis Intervention Centre in Kraków, Poland, was founded by Dr. Wanda-Badura-Madej, who had read our book in English. The Centre is still providing 24-hour emergency psychological services to this city of nearly a million people. We salute this remarkable achievement.

With time, the book was translated into German, French, Spanish, Dutch, Swedish, Polish, and Hebrew, bringing us a veritable new world of colleagues and friends. They became our hosts at workshops and seminars in their countries, and gave us the gift of broadened horizons. There were Bert Van Luyn and Herman Vergouwen in Holland, Pierre and Sylvie Angel and Anne Ancelin-Schützenberger in France, Mony Elkaim in Belgium, Bjorn Reigstad and Knut Sørgaard in Norway, and Delilah Esposito and Rocio Gomez in Mexico. We thank them for their hospitality and for their insights as caring persons and skilled practitioners. In our dialogues with them and their students and assistants, we learned that everyone in the world is our brother or sister, and that crisis is a part of life.

Closer to home, we are grateful to Louis Arcarese for his insights into the suffering of veterans who live with trauma born of going to war in the service of their country. We thank our many colleagues in the law enforcement community of California who have assisted us in our work with victims of abuse and violent crime. In particular, Chief Scott Vermeer of Mountain View, Sheriff Don Horsely of San Mateo County, Sheriff Laurie Smith of Santa Clara County, Chief Wes Bowling (ret.) of East Palo Alto, Chief Lucy Carlton (ret.) and Chief Bob Lacey of Los Altos, Commander Teri Molakides of Menlo Park, Chief Carlos Bolanos of Redwood City, Chief Tom Hitchcock of Brisbane, and Chief S.D. Lodge of the City of Santa Clara.

Lastly, we thank Bessel van der Kolk, whose groundbreaking research on the neurobiology of trauma brought trauma from the shadows of weakness and pathology into the reality that the body, as well as the mind, can suffer psychological injury.

Foreword

The interactional view of human behavior guides and informs the analyses of crisis and trauma that are presented in this book. This view holds that the behavior of one person affects, influences, motivates, sets in motion, or controls the behavior of another person. The process is reciprocal, in that each person, in turn, has a causal effect on the behavior of the other. This causal sequence is most evident in the dyad or two-person system. Many years ago, this interactional paradigm was applied to explain the etiology of schizophrenia; more recently, it has been applied to the etiology of suicidal behavior (see Chapter 9).

In bringing the related but different subjects of psychological crisis and trauma together in one volume, the authors have targeted the most difficult situations into which a therapist can intervene. Trauma and crisis incorporate the most profound psychological experiences that people can endure, from grief to terror, from abuse to self-loathing, from sexual assault to divorce and warfare over custody, to helplessness in the face of the depredations of Nature. And while not every dangerous experience is traumatic, and not every dilemma is a crisis, these extremes of the human condition are those that most cry out for attention and care.

Everyone reaches points of crisis in life, when one's modus vivendi cannot accommodate yet another source of stress. Our life patterns are found to be inadequate to cope with a situation that has just now "come to a head." Even though we may have seen it coming or have suspected that it would happen eventually, we often find ourselves ill-prepared. An example would be when the youngest child moves on to college and "empty nest" is at hand; it may involve more than the loss of a child, as when it is no longer economically feasible to maintain a family home, and the parents are made to feel like displaced persons. No amount of anticipation or planning can fully prepare a parent for so drastic a lifestyle change.

Circumstances such as these are worsened when problem-solving is hampered by old patterns of interaction. In the example cited, the parents may clash about the best way to proceed when the nest is empty: the mother may see it as an opportunity to move out of the city to a rural area, because she was raised on a farm and has always yearned to adopt a more tranquil way of living. The husband, for his part, may feel that he must stay in the city because of an obligation that he owes to his job; for him, a move to the country is a dream that must be deferred to retirement years

Some couples will, of course, avert a crisis by negotiation and compromise. For other couples, the issue may become suppressed indefinitely, leaving an undercurrent of conflict that can affect even the most trivial disagreement. In time, their mutual resentment may escalate to the point at which they will need the intervention of a counselor to avoid World War III.

In sharp contrast to this slow-boiling stew, the experience of a traumatic event is instantaneous and irrevocable. At one end of the spectrum of such an experience is the shock of being taken unawares; at the other end is sheer terror and potential death. The unfathomable logic of the event takes over rational thinking in a surreal surge of denial, whose only expression becomes "This can't be happening." One's environment has spun out of control, leaving the person feeling helpless and alone. Whether surviving a car crash, rape, a natural disaster, or war, the sense of being the unluckiest person alive is not easily dispelled

This book describes what it feels like to be in the grip of forces such as these, and how people can be helped to recover from traumatic wounds that were never deserved. The process is much like microsurgery, in that symptom after symptom must be isolated, examined, and worked-through by the trauma therapist and survivor. The unique point-of-view brought by this book is that trauma is not evidence of psychopathology, and that "disorder" in the term "PTSD" is a misnomer. It follows that trauma treatment departs from the traditional forms, to represent a wholly new speciality within the mental health disciplines.

The need for a fresh approach to therapy for trauma is manifest in daily headlines of victims of war, violent assaults, and sexual crimes, not to mention the capriciousness of nature. A government official, remarking on the damage done by hurricane and flood in Louisiana, said "This was not a disaster, it was a catastrophe." To think that, each day, somewhere in the the world people are suffering cataclysms of this magnitude must give us pause. Books such as this one will enable helpers to assist survivors recover and get on with their lives.

Overview

A "crisis," as the word implies, is a situation that has reached a critical point. Its origin lies in a sequence of events evolving over time. A "life crisis," for example, is the outcome of a process begun long before in the course of the person's development, brought to an acute condition by events such as a change in health or a significant anniversary or the death of a contemporary, that is, an intimation of mortality. One way to conceptualize causal factors in the experience of crisis is to think of one's history as "catching up" with the person. For instance, a man comes to the realization that he is not going to be promoted by the company he has served for years; a young person is discovering his or her sexual identity and is terrified of "coming out" to the parents; a wife reaches the limit of her endurance with an alcoholic husband, whom she may have to leave unless he stops drinking.

A crisis may occur at any stage in one's lifetime—adjusting to school, choosing a career, coping with marriage, the empty nest, beginning to feel old. These are natural processes, as described by the metaphorical Seven Ages of Man. They are crossroads in life's journey. Decisions must be made; the consequences of whatever path is chosen must be faced. Part One of this book suggests methods for helping people weather crises such as these.

A "trauma," by contrast, is a state of mind engendered by a singular event in the life of a person. The event itself—unforeseen, overwhelming, like a bolt of lightning—must be distinguished from the experience of trauma per se. The reason is that, often, two people react differently to a shared event. One man's terror at having been in a car accident could be another man's feeling of gratitude for staying alive. Trauma waits upon the vagaries of Mother Nature—floods, earthquakes, heart attacks, and so on;

or, human error—as in a car crash; or, human intention—as in rape, acts of terrorism, being held hostage, public humiliation, being sent to prison, and so on. These are the "slings and arrows of outrageous fortune," and each represents a singular event, once thought unlikely or impossible to happen, that becomes one's living horror.

A traumatic event can be prolonged over time, as when a person is held captive or when an act of abuse is repeated again and again throughout childhood; the people of London were traumatized almost daily by German bombs in the Battle of Britain, or the recent series of terrorist bombings that, for some, reawakened old traumatic memories. A person may experience trauma without having been harmed by a traumatic event, as when witnesses to the My Lai massacre or emergency service workers who work at disaster scenes, are haunted for years by what they had seen.

As will be shown in the pages to follow, trauma is not pathology, but, rather, a normal response to an extraordinary, inescapable, horrific stimulus or recurring stimuli. It results from an assault on the person's sense of self, and tests the strength of the defense mechanisms that protect a person's ego. The degree of trauma varies with the intensity and duration of the causal event and the personality of the survivor of the event. Its most prominent consequences are variants of feelings of helplessness and failure, paradoxical guilt, and a general sense of having been punished by Fate. This book proposes specific interventions for undeserved shocks to the system such as these.

The way to differentiate crisis and trauma is best shown by example. A child is the victim of incest by her father, the assault continuing many times through her early years. She is afraid to tell anyone about these traumatic events, even after they have ceased. Years later, she feels compelled to reveal what happened to her mother, because of a current situation in her life (perhaps the divorce of her parents or her fear that it will happen to her younger sister). She is afraid of telling her mother what happened, both because she might be thought complicit in some way, and because she had kept the matter secret from her mother for so long. This fear precipitates a crisis. Even though the symptoms of trauma (e.g., flashbacks, intrusive thoughts, sleep disturbance, etc.) have diminished or faded away, she must now cope with confusion, indecision, guilt, potential loss of love, or even fear of retaliation by the father for disclosing the crime. Another example would be of that of a family in which a sixteen-year-old son is killed in an accident when driving the family car. This would traumatize everyone who knew him, and the parents would be left with everlasting feelings of guilt. Four years later, a younger son becomes sixteen and asks for permission to drive. The parents have reached a moment of crisis. Should they forbid him to drive until he is older? Should they insist that he be accompanied by a parent when he drives? Should they buy an old car for him, one that can't be driven at high speed? These parents are truly on the horns of a dilemma, as are the protagonists in any crisis situation.

Naturally, crisis does not always have roots in trauma, but an *unresolved* trauma often portends some moment of crisis later in life. In fact, a necessary step in helping a person through a time of crisis is to find out whether or not he or she has been traumatized previously. And part of helping a person to recover from trauma is to ensure that it will not provoke another crisis down the road.

PART ONE

CRISIS

CHAPTER 1

Introduction to Crisis

Introduction

When the ancient Greeks made myths, their gods were drawn to such human scale that they experienced problems just as ordinary mortals do. Moreover, their problems seemed inevitably to escalate into crises. Crisis was a way of life for these figments of the imagination, and how they would cope was an ever-renewable source of entertainment. Down here in the real world, there are many moments of crisis in the course of any ordinary life, nonetheless humbling for being godlike.

A person in crisis encounters a situation or series of situations that cause the person to alter his or her patterns of living. The circumstances that lead to each person's crisis moment are unique to the person, but the experience of *being-in-crisis* is universal—from the cabinet minister to the cabinet-maker. The key element in everyone's crisis is disruption in the normal conduct of one's affairs, of change being required of the person by forces beyond control, by the feeling that "things might never be the same."

The Chinese character for the word "crisis" is a combination of the characters for "danger" and "opportunity." The danger part of the equation is well known, but the sense of opportunity is difficult to convey. This book intends to describe the experience of crisis in considerable detail, in both its positive and negative aspects. The book's prime objective is to aid those who work in the helping professions to guide people through the stages from crisis onset to resolution, to the epiphany that they are stronger for having had the experience.

When a person has become so ill that he or she should be in a mental hospital, the people who care for him or her face a crisis. When potential dangerousness is feared, or when child abuse or domestic violence must be stopped, a crisis moment has been reached. Similarly, crisis occurs when a family discovers that incest has occurred, or when a threat of suicide has been made. These are the subjects of chapters comprising Part One.

Crises are, in the acute stage, emergencies and must be given immediate attention. This book contains a lot of information about how to intervene in psychological emergency situations. An experience that differs both qualitatively and quantitatively from the larger category of crisis is that of trauma. The traumatic experience will be analyzed thoroughly here, and therapy for trauma will be fully described in Part Two.

Background

Part One is the revised edition of a book that drew on and celebrated the establishment and subsequent work of a mental health program called the Emergency Treatment Center (ETC). ETC, a nonprofit corporation, was neither an agency nor a clinic in the true sense. It was a group of psychologists and a psychiatric nurse who received a local government grant to provide twenty-four-hour intervention to persons or families in emergency situations. Calls came into our crisis line (292-HELP) or from local police agencies that had been called by citizens for assistance. A team of two therapists were dispatched to the scene of the crisis, whether to a home, a motel, or a street corner. In many instances, the police arrived first and assessed the situation before calling us. After the emergency intervention, some of the people involved were seen in our offices for follow-up treatment. The rapport established at a time of dire need meant that many of these new clients could derive rapid and lasting benefits from the therapeutic experience.

Role of the Police

Many of the case studies used to illustrate emergency work in this book make reference to collaboration between clinicians and police officers. This variation in the procedures of most private practices may seem awkward, but there are practical considerations worth noting. When a call is received by a 911 operator, it will most likely be forwarded to a police agency; even if, as in cases of injury or severe illness, paramedics are dispatched or the fire department is dispatched to a fire, the police will probably arrive at the scene of an emergency. And, as will be obvious from some of the cases that you will read about here, they can be valuable allies at various stages of an intervention.

For the police, going to the home where an incident is in progress is often a source of both concern and annoyance, for two reasons: (1) family disturbances can be dangerous, as when family members turn against them as a common enemy; (2) officers see the family disturbance as a distraction from their primary mission, namely (in their words), "catching bad guys." Yet, even with those deterrents, the police will nearly always be available to help a clinician defuse a crisis. This is a resource that cannot be overestimated.

For the clinician who would like to connect with this resource, a useful first step is to call the local police headquarters and ask if the department has a "ride-along" policy. As part of their community outreach services, many departments arrange for citizens to ride in a patrol car during a shift, usually in an evening. This is a perfect way to learn something about police procedures, the concerns of officers, the terms that they use, and so on. Rarely does an experience such as this fail to produce a greater appreciation of an officer's role and the work that they do.

When a clinician has begun a relationship with a local department, he or she may wish to establish contact with officers who have special assignments, for example, one who works with juvenile cases, one who works with domestic violence, and one who specializes in sexual assault cases; some departments combine these functions in a single assignment, and others subsume them within a Detective Bureau. With the passage of time, it is probable that a clinician will make use of some part of this network as an aid to client care.

A Perspective

The reader will find, in this book, reference to human tragedies of every kind and severity. Rape, incest, battering, threats of murder, and suicide are routine topics here. For all their poignancy, events such as these are relatively rare, and a mental health professional could abide for an entire career without being called on to intervene in one of them. The fact remains that clinicians are much needed to help people in crisis moments such as these. Here is a responsibility that, at least intellectually, any therapist can accept. It behooves them to have an understanding of crisis dynamics, should they encounter people in crisis in the course of clinical work.

Why do most people think of calling 911 when they can't cope? One reason is that many who are experiencing an emergency do not define it as being "mental" or psychological in nature. When a referral to a mental health clinic is suggested, it is ignored more often than it is accepted. The fact is that many people are still fearful of mental health systems. They are afraid of the stigma of being labeled as "crazy" or "mentally ill" or as having a "disorder," and they fear the social or occupational repercussions that may follow should someone find out about it.

To our discredit, mental health professionals still do much to mystify themselves and their methods to the public. Most people feel that they at least understand the motives and methods of the police, and so are more inclined to turn to them when they are in crisis, especially when they are afraid. But, when the help they need to solve their problems is not forthcoming from this, the only source they know and trust, a cycle of dysfunction or violence may be set in motion or prolonged.

Emergencies or Crises: Terms and Definitions

We conceptualize an acute emergency as an extremely unstable situation that has escalated out of control. There is the potential risk that someone may die, as in the case in which a person has become suicidal or homicidal. As well, there could be imminent physical danger such as occurs:

- When a person is psychotic or agitated or manic
- In domestic violence
- In stalking situations
- In child abuse
- In child molestation
- With out-of-control behavior such as in anorexia
- With high-risk behavior of any sort
- In natural disasters
- In states of war or terrorist attacks

The primary goal for an intervention in an acute emergency is to ensure people's safety and to stop the escalation process. Most interventions in an acute emergency involve the creation of some sort of external structure or restraints to contain the escalation. Typical interventions in acute emergencies are:

- Immediate medical care
- Separation of participants
- Medication
- Temporary shelter
- Disaster relief
- Vigiling or supervision by a trusted person
- Hospitalization

We view a crisis (as do James and Gilliland, 2001, and Myer, 2001) as an unstable situation, but one that has not yet escalated out of control. Without immediate intervention, the crisis will have the potential of developing into an acute emergency.[1]

CHAPTER 2

Communication Principles for High-Stress or Dangerous Situations

This chapter discusses aspects of communication that pertain when dealing with extremely agitated or angry people, as well as communicating with people under highly stressful conditions. Even though many of these methods are drawn from our experience in hostage negotiation, the communication principles discussed here are applicable to a wide range of problem situations, for example, working with a violent family or with a person who is threatening to commit suicide. Some of these principles may seem simplistic because it is the clinician's own language that is being discussed, but it is easy *not* to notice how language is used. It is easy to relax and become sloppy, and to fall into language patterns that would probably go unnoticed in everyday life but might cause problems should a therapist become involved in a high-stress situation.

To begin with, some basic rules of communication will be reviewed, the first of which is the famous observation of Paul Watzlawick, that a person "cannot NOT communicate" (1964, p. 2). When one person says "Hello" and the other person says nothing and turns away, the second person has communicated something quite clearly.

The second basic rule is that *human communication is a multilevel phenomenon* (Watzlawick, 1964, p. 3; confirmed by Birdwhistell, 1970; Hackney and Cormier, 1999; Myer, 2001). In fact, an attempt at communication may prove meaningless when it is reduced to one level. When a person speaks in a way that ignores the *context* of the communication, what is said can very likely be meaningless. Should a person say, "I am not the person who is speaking to you," the paradox sounds odd because it doesn't fit within the context in which it was uttered. Thus, communication has content, which is the information that the individual is conveying, and also communication can only occur in a specific context. For example, when someone enters a store and a salesperson walks up and says, "May I help you?," that remark is seldom prefaced with, "I am a salesperson and my job in this store is to sell you something." That fact is understood and the relationship of employee to prospective customer is already established. In general, disagreement about the *content* of communication may be resolved quite easily. That is, if someone walks up to a person and says, "You're blue," the person can say, "No, I'm not. My sweater is blue, my face is flesh-colored, and my hair is brown;" both can then appeal to a third party to settle the disagreement. And, if someone says that the earth revolves around the moon, the hearer can verify or disqualify the assertion. However, in respect to *context,* disagreements can become more complicated and much more emotionally charged, as will be shown in this chapter.

Contextual disagreements arise in respect to how one person in a conversation misperceives the other, or how one has managed to misunderstand what the other said. Although we may like to think that we live in a world of reality, the reality is that *we live in a world of personal opinion* (Watzlawick, 1976). Much of what each of us considers to be reality consists of the sum total of our personally arrived-at, and absolutely unique, set of opinions. This fact is vitally important when a therapist is engaged in a crisis situation. In such a situation, it is highly probable that the clinician will be attempting to communicate with a person who does not share his or her reality or perceptions of the world. The other person may inhabit a totally different value system, may come from a totally different socioeconomic background, and may represent a different ethnic group; moreover, he or she may not have grown up in this culture. The issues of relationship, and how another person thinks that he or she is perceived, may become critical in communicating with people in psychological emergencies and other high-stress situations.

One of the clinician's primary tasks is to understand the "worldview" of the person in crisis and to communicate with him or her in a way which is consonant with that view. When this worldview is examined carefully, the clinician will probably discover a discrepancy between the conception of present reality of the person in crisis and the clinician's own conception (For a detailed discussion of how world images may be discrepant from reality, see Watzlawick, 1978, Chapter 5.) When contradictions of this type are observed, a clinician has essentially two options: (1) change the reality conditions that pertain to the person, for example, by attempting to "make deals," give practical advice, or persuade people whom the person in crisis has mentioned as being significant to come to the scene; or (2) work toward changing the worldview of the person in crisis. Although the latter course of action may seem an impossible task, it is often the first choice of a skilled therapist and the wiser course of action in most instances. By contrast, changing reality conditions may be very difficult indeed; in fact, any rapid change in those conditions may be disbelieved by the person in crisis, in which case it will not have the desired effect. Instead, a clinician usually tries to help the person in crisis to change his or her perceptions of reality in such a way that the person can see alternative, beneficial means of resolving current problems.

A third basic rule of communication is that *message sent is not necessarily message received* (Watzlawick, 1964, p. 4). Just because one person has said something does not mean that the other person has understood what was said. Often, we assume that the people to whom we are speaking share our views, our values, and our feelings, and we assume that certain words have the same connotations for others as for us. It is helpful to imagine a series of events such as the following: a therapist says something to a person in crisis. The therapist assumes that the person understood what was said, that is, understood both the denotative meaning and the connotations of the words in the message. But, actually, the person in crisis has, in some way, misunderstood what the clinician said, and the reply is based upon that misunderstanding. Next, the therapist replies to what the person in crisis replied, which was based on misunderstanding in the first place, and so it goes back and forth.

A case example to which this rule of communication applies is that of a couple who were being seen for counseling. It was not a seriously disturbed relationship, although the two had trouble in communicating because of their very different ethnic backgrounds (she was Scandinavian and he was from a second-generation Latin family). One of their main problems concerned a woman friend of the wife, about whom they had been arguing for at least six months. Although the husband hated his wife's friend, the wife felt that she should defend her. The husband's view was that the friend was immature, loud, and inconsiderate of her own husband.

In counseling, one of the first things each was asked to do was to give a detailed description of the woman in question, with this instruction: "I want to make sure that I hear both sides of the story. I want you to take turns in describing the person to me." When they described her, it seemed as though they were both saying similar things about this woman, and for that reason the counselor asked for more details from each, for example, "Did you mean such-and-such?" After some time had been devoted to this form of translation from one person's English to the other's, they realized that some of the words that each had been using were being perceived as inflammatory by the other. Apparently, because of their different cultural backgrounds, the same words had acquired differing connotations (in effect, differing meanings). Thus ended the misunderstanding. When the session was over, the partners had become aware that they shared a mutual dislike for the woman friend. This example shows how misunderstandings can arise when two people forget that the message sent is not necessarily the message received. The tendency to forget that rule is enhanced when a therapist is under marked stress and is trying to communicate with a total stranger, by definition a person who is probably very different from the therapist.

Connecting with the Person in Crisis

People begin to structure and to set rules for their relationship, as soon as they first meet. This is very important in working with people in high stress or emergency situations because a clinician will want to be in control of the development of this relationship while therapy is proceeding. The therapist will seek to guide the relationship in such a way that the person in crisis will be so comfortable with the relationship that he or she may form an attachment with the therapist. Establishing a strong attachment may make it possible to induce the person in crisis to be a helpful participant in resolving the emergency. What is said (content) by the therapist will be particularly vital, because he or she may not always have the luxury of employing other channels of communication such as the nonverbal, or time to indulge in meta-communication (discussion about the communication itself) in the heat of the moment. In many cases, a therapist may be talking on the telephone with a potentially suicidal person who cannot see facial expressions or the subtle gestures which often accompany speech; for example, the other person will not know when the clinician smiles or looks worried or concerned (context). Each will "read" the other only by means of sounds conveyed by a telephone.

In point of fact, English is a very difficult medium for the establishment of relationships. Many other languages have a relationship "code" built into them. For example, French has a familiar mode of addressing another person, the "tu" or informal mode, and a formal mode in which the word "vous" is used (both words mean "you"). Many other languages employ the two-mode system, but these mutually exclusive modes do not exist in English. Considerable social information is built into the structure of languages other than English, and many Europeans who visit here think that we are rude because we are seldom sensitive to social factors in the way we speak. To some degree their judgment is correct, because it is very easy to make mistakes in respect to matters of relationship, especially along the dimension of formality versus intimacy. The French expression "tu-toi" means that a close or intimate relationship has been formed between two persons, such as when a man and a woman are getting close romantically. The grammatical structure of language (as opposed to the actual content) is being used, in this instance, to describe certain qualities of an interaction. Because English lacks this distinction, it provides more opportunities to make a mistake, overlook a "boundary," or get too intimate too soon with another person.

Establishing a relationship through language is a very subtle process, but one whose importance cannot be overemphasized. For example, this process is especially important when attempting to reason with a psychotic person in crisis, because many psychotics are terrified by close relationships and feel extremely threatened when people try to establish closeness early in a relationship. Thus, making this kind of mistake in the relationship aspect of language can serve to rapidly accelerate the other person's level of anxiety. What is required is restraint, sensitivity, and clarity of expression.

Disagreements about the relationship aspect of communication are often painful and difficult to resolve. The reason is that when two people disagree about the relationship aspect of their communication, it may signify that one person's wish to be seen in a certain light is not being fulfilled. In effect, one person may be interpreting the other's behavior as containing the message: "I don't see you as a person worthy of respect or value; I see you as someone with whom I have a right to take liberties." That kind of approach would be especially dangerous when applied to someone who is struggling with inner feelings of impotence or helplessness. One of the reasons why he (or she) is acting-out is to force others to see him (or her) in the way he (or she) wishes to see himself (or herself), namely, as a powerful person. If a clinician makes some slip that could lead the person to think that the clinician does not view him or her as powerful, the person may become enraged. People such as these, beneath their outward grandiosity, may feel deeply inadequate, and anything a therapist may do to reinforce this feeling of inadequacy can lead to an escalation of violence.

Complementary and Symmetrical

Two basic kinds of human relationships are called "complementary" and "symmetrical" (see Chapter 5). The classic complementary relationship is that of mother and child. In a complementary relationship, one person is dominant or superior and one person is submissive or inferior; one person defines the relationship and the other accepts the definition. (This does not have anything to do with strength or weakness per se and, in fact, the "weaker" or submissive person may powerfully affect the relationship.) A symmetrical relationship exists between two equals or two people who view each other with equality.

The most common disagreement about any relationship occurs when one person defines the relationship as symmetrical and the other person defines it as complementary. One person asks to be treated as an equal and the other responds by treating the person as inferior (or even as superior). If the therapist treats someone as superior and the person is uncomfortable about that (i.e., is afraid of being treated as superior), he or she may become hostile.

A clinician should be quite cautious about how the relationship is worked out with someone in a high-risk situation such as hostage negotiation. Because the clinician should strive to be extremely flexible in the kinds of positions taken, patience is recommended in these circumstances. It is important to listen for clues that will tell how the person in crisis wants or needs to define the relationship. For example, if the therapist is negotiating with a hostage-taker who is a known criminal and who may view himself or herself as a loser, that person may become very uncomfortable if the clinician treats him or her with deference. He or she may be more comfortable if the clinician takes a relatively more superior position when defining the relationship for the purpose of communication.

A common error that people make when they are frightened and are trying to be friendly is speaking to someone whom they don't really know in a manner that is too familiar—for example, by first name or nickname. People's names are very important to them, and they have deeply rooted and highly emotional feelings about their names. When first meeting someone named "Peter," the clinician may not know that his mother, whom he hated, had been responsible for giving him that name, or that he may have resented that name all his life. Because he always wanted to be named "Tony," it may be that his friends call him that; using his real name, or a nickname such as "Pete," may be a source of great embarrassment to him.

When asking about the person's name, it is important to find out what he prefers to be called; for example, "Do you like to be called 'Pete' or is there another name that you prefer?" Most people will respond to that kind of question because it is a courtesy that they respect. When in doubt, it is wise to avoid the presumption of an intimacy that does not, or cannot, exist. In many cultures, first names are not used unless the people have known each other for a long time. For example, it shocks most people of Latin extraction when, within minutes after they have been introduced, Americans use their first names when speaking to them.

The same principles apply to establishing a relationship with someone who is being treated in a crisis situation. If a therapist is talking to a person who has a very low sense of self-esteem—someone who is acting out in sudden rage, holding hostages, or suicidal—this person may be wielding power for the first time in his or her life. Thus, referring to such a person by a first name or nickname could challenge his or her illusion of power; worse yet, there may be no awareness of doing this, so that efforts could be made to ameliorate it. (Relationship nuances such as these are discussed in detail in Everstine and Everstine, 1983; Myer, 2001.) In the authors' experience, when faced with an unfamiliar culture or lifestyle, it is wise to admit lack of knowledge. Ask the person in crisis or someone from the culture about how to address or respond to the person with sensitivity.

First Steps

A basic first step would be to introduce oneself and to ask the person in crisis what he or she would like to be called. If the person refuses to reply, it is best to give up on that point and simply refer to the person as "you." If the therapist has been talking with the person for a long time and begins to feel awkward, he or she may wish to ask something like this: "I am uncomfortable calling you 'you'; would you mind telling me your name, or a name that we can use for the time being?" If there is considerable reluctance, the question should not be pursued. The person may be either terribly frightened or psychologically disturbed, and may wish to hide his or her identity for now. The best tactic is to "take what is there," trying to understand the person's psychological state in that precise moment and trying to get a "feel" for the person as an individual. This approach is particularly vital when dealing with someone who is psychotic—that is, someone who may be thinking in a very primitive way, with an undercurrent of magical thinking. Even though what the person says and does may be very bizarre, the therapist should not assume that the person is insensitive or stupid; on the contrary, he or she is probably listening most carefully to *every word*, with each subtlety it may contain.

There are other aspects of the way in which people communicate that may facilitate or hinder successful negotiation under stress. A common error is to use the royal "we." Even when attempting to be friendly, "we" usually sounds condescending unless the speaker is referring to something that the speaker and the other person have in common. What is more important is to focus on, and try to understand, the other person's world—to be "in his place" for a moment. In this context, Weakland and Jackson's (1958) concept of the "illusion of alternatives" is especially relevant. Milton Erickson describes a situation that occurred when he was a young boy, growing up in a family that kept hogs and chickens (Erickson et al., 1976). He noticed that his father would ask him whether he would like to feed the chickens or the hogs first. The son was being given the illusion that he had a choice, when in fact he did not, because he did not have the choice of whether or not to work at all. His father had conveniently omitted the third possible option, which was to refuse to feed both the hogs and the chickens and, in effect, to loaf.

An extension of this concept can be found in the art of political sloganeering. Watzlawick cites the example of a Nazi slogan that was phrased as a question, namely, "National Socialism or Bolshevik chaos?," which omitted alternative choices (1978, p. 68). In order to make use of this concept successfully, it is necessary for the person who would use it to have a clear understanding of the other person's worldview, and to fit the choices (however illusory) carefully to the template provided by that worldview.

In order to understand other people's world image fully, it is necessary to listen carefully to their use of language to describe this personal "world." Do they speak in terms of abstract ideas or emotions and feelings? What do they select from their environment to pay attention to or ignore? As a clinician gains knowledge of a person's image of the world, he or she realizes that, out of millions of possible choices, only a few choices will fit within that particular person's worldview. The next task is to discover what this person's choices are, and whether or not they were made under the illusion of a free choice among alternatives. (In Chapter 3, this concept will be discussed further, especially as it pertains to actual clinical intervention in crisis situations.)

Early in this process, it is important to get the person to agree with something, that is, to say "yes," by inducing him or her to answer trivial questions in the affirmative. The therapist should see how frequently he or she can be led to say "yes" or "okay" by means of verbal feelers—for example, "Will you think about that for a while?" "Does that make sense to you?" or "Can we agree about that?" When the person begins to respond favorably to seemingly trivial requests, the therapist may be getting somewhere. Positive language has much more influence than negative language (Watzlawick, 1978).

Another important nuance of negotiating with a stranger is to focus on behavior. This strategy can help the therapist avoid doing something that can cause people to become very angry—namely, "mind-reading." This presumptuous behavior implies, to the other person, that one knows what the other is thinking or feeling. For example, if a therapist says, "You are afraid, aren't you?," he or she gives the impression of knowing what the other person is feeling. Instead, the clinician may say, "What you said just now makes me think that you are afraid. Are you?" In that way, he or she gives the other person psychological "room" to explain or deny a feeling. In the same way, these two utterances may sound similar but are quite different: "You're hostile" differs from "What you said sounded hostile. Did I say something to make you angry?" The first utterance implies "You are a hostile person" (i.e., "You are bad; there is something in you that is not right"). The second says: "Your words [not something that I am 'reading into' your words] sound angry, and I am trying to understand why you said them." It is a subtle but important difference.

A therapist should try not to assume intimacy or friendship when he or she doesn't know a person. It is best to avoid making statements like: "You're a nice guy." The therapist may mean well and want to reassure an angry, frightened person by saying that, but the other person may think: "How do you know I'm a nice guy? You don't know me." Among those who may be acting-out in a crisis, many do not think of themselves as nice people; many have a low sense of self-esteem. For that reason, the clinician should avoid giving the impression of judging the other person's character or figuring out his or her intentions. The clinician should also avoid projecting his or her own wishes onto another but, rather, focus on behavior. For example, "What you did for that person was really kind" or "What you said made sense" are credible statements because they have a basis in reality as opposed to personal assumptions or fantasies.

When describing or explaining something (an event or an action or a statement), it is important to keep the presentation simple and avoid words such as "always," "never," "any," or "all"—for example, "You *always* say that" or "That's *all* I'm asking you to do." The reason is that "always" seldom happens and "never" is rare, and exaggerated statements of this kind have a patronizing tone to them. It's easy for the therapist to slip into speaking in this manner, particularly when he or she is excited, wants to make a telling point, or is under pressure and not thinking about how he or she sounds.

This also applies to making a request: keep it very simple and direct. For instance, asking, "Would you mind giving me the gun?" may prompt the person to respond by saying, "That's right, I would mind giving you the gun," which is a logical, and probably an honest, response to the question that was asked. In this case, poor communication has caused a delay in solving the main problem, namely, that the clinician wants that gun. The therapist is scarcely concerned about whether or not the person would "mind" handing over the gun. Another condescending way of making a request is the following: "Would you like to open that door?," which implies that the person should (1) open the door and (2) enjoy doing so (like a "good child"). A final example of a well-intentioned question that confuses the issue is: "Why don't you tell me why you are angry?" The person may tell you why he or she won't tell you, rather than saying why he or she is angry. "Please tell me why you are angry" is simple and direct and does not get the conversation sidetracked onto absurd issues.

Points of Caution

When talking with disturbed persons, it is important to avoid some of the demeaning ways in which some parents speak to their children. Many such persons have had poor relationships with their parents, and when a therapist phrases a comment or question in ways that are parental, he or she may provoke the person to become angry or to "project" onto the clinician a role as substitute for his or her parent. Most people do things for specific reasons, and an acutely disturbed person may be no exception. The disturbed person's system of logic may differ considerably from the therapist's, but *there is a system,* and it is the task of a therapist to discover what that system is. When it is discovered, the person's behavior may make much more sense. Most people, even when agitated, will follow a request as long as the request is presented in a polite and reasonable way, for example, "Please give me the gun." "Please" is a word that many people in authority are afraid of, or one whose usefulness they have forgotten. Many people in crisis feel trapped and don't know what to do. If a clinician can propose a reasonable way for the person to get out of the situation and save face in the bargain, the person may take it. This process may, however, take considerable time.

When asking questions, a clinician should try not to challenge the ability of the person in crisis to perform a task; for example, he or she should avoid asking: "Could you do that?" or "Can you give me the gun?" The questioner wants to know whether or not the person *will* do something, not whether the person *can* or *cannot*. To question someone's ability is insulting and puts the person questioned into a child's position. Questions like that often make an adult (particularly an adult who has low self-esteem) feel angry or insulted without being aware of why it is happening. Another important point to be aware of when communicating with someone in a crisis situation is not to say things that guarantee or promise, unless one is sure that one can do what has been promised. If the guarantee fails or the promise is not performed, credibility will have vanished. A humble stand is preferable, that is, "I'm going to try to do what I can."

Whenever limits must be set with a person in crisis, they should be framed in the way suggested by this example: a therapist who is trying to convince an agitated, psychotic patient to surrender a weapon and agree to go to the hospital might say, "I want to help you, but you need to go to the hospital for me to do so. I don't think the police out here are going to let you shoot anyone, and I don't think they are going to let you go. So, what are you going to do?" In this way, the interaction does not remain one-up/one-down or superior/subordinate anymore, and this approach can be used in many situations. This manner of speaking conveys to a person in crisis that the clinician is concerned and will try to help; but, at the same time, the person should not think the clinician so "involved" that he or she can be manipulated.

Suicidal people can be manipulative in this way, if they think that a person is very concerned about them. They will threaten self-destructive things to make the other person feel guilty or sorry, so that he or she will do what they want. The clinician can respond to a suicidal person with this basic message: "I am concerned; I don't want you to hurt yourself, but it is really your business if you want to do that." It is an honest and a credible statement, and it is also one that the person cannot use for manipulative purposes. The same idea applies to other potentially violent situations because, if the therapist overreacts and shows too much concern when someone acts-out and threatens to harm another person, that overreaction can reinforce the prior threat. If someone is hurt and a clinician hears a scream and overreacts, the person who is acting-out may have decided that the best way to put pressure upon the clinician is to harm the person again. In this sort of situation, the therapist should try to take the focus off the injured person and, instead, place the focus on what the acting-out person wants and needs. The reason is that keeping the focus on the person who has been hurt, and reacting primarily when something has happened or when a threat is made, can make the acting-out person *even more reluctant* to release or stop hurting the other. A therapist can inquire concerning the health of the injured person, but it is better to do that at a time when the acting-out person is not interacting with the victim if possible, or at a moment when the stress level is relatively low.

Effective communication in emergency situations often demands time in abundance, and with it considerable patience and careful thought. These requirements may be difficult to meet, especially because many people who do emergency work are oriented toward action. But, the slower the pace of communication in such a situation, the longer it will last and the more likely it is to be successful. Waiting and listening carefully to what is said will give a therapist more time to frame responses precisely. A response can either stimulate more acting-out behavior or encourage calm behavior and thus lower the stress level of the situation. When deliberate and thoughtful, a therapist's own behavior gives this subtle but important message: "I want to listen to you; what you say is important."

When communicating, the therapist should try to avoid predicting future events and making promises but, rather, talk only about what is known. If it is necessary to talk of the future, it is preferable not to sound optimistic because the acting-out person knows that his or her future prospects are probably not bright, and thus the clinician will not be believed. Do not give guarantees. When speaking of something the therapist is planning to try in the future, he or she should always acknowledge that there will probably be a measure of difficulty in getting it done. In case a significant positive change in the situation occurs, it is better to try to plan it so that the person in crisis can be given credit for the change. In that way, he or she can feel responsible for the eventual successful outcome of the negotiation, and the therapist can avoid being seen as someone who has the power to make things happen. The correct position of the clinician is neutral, not that of a person who possesses power. If the clinician is seen as having power, the acting-out person is going to try to manipulate the clinician into doing what he or she wants done; for example, making concessions or granting favors. This neutral position is sometimes difficult for an action-oriented person to take, but it is of vital importance in potentially violent situations.

The power of praise is too often misused in high-stress interactions. Praise should be formulated thoughtfully and expressed with care. Self-reflection will confirm that it is very, very hard to accept praise from someone whom one does not know and does not trust, particularly when frightened or angry. In fact, there are times when praise can make a person angrier than either a neutral statement or criticism—if the person does not trust or believe the praise. Because most of us have at least potentially successful careers and positive life scripts, it is easy for us to forget how threatening praise can be to some people in certain contexts. A therapist is probably not someone who has been in and out of clinics or hospitals or jails repeatedly, nor someone whose life has meant continual humiliation, failure, and loss. When communicating with a person whose own sense of self-esteem is obviously low, the therapist may wish to insert a compliment between two neutral or two negative statements—for example, "You've had a rough life and you are in a very bad spot, but it's amazing that you have managed as long as you have. You're probably a strong person, but I don't know if you are ready to hear that right now." Embedded in those statements is a compliment. By framing or embedding praise in this way, the clinician can compliment a person in crisis in a way that is compatible with the negative view that the person has of himself or herself. By contrast, lavishing a person who is really insecure with praise will cause the other to become uncomfortable in short order.

A related point is to avoid the common error of trying to cheer up a depressed person. It is well known that many people in crisis are suffering from acute depression at the time. By trying to cheer that person up and get him or her to "see the bright side," the therapist is disqualifying his or her view of reality, and acting as if the person's problems are small or are nothing to worry about. On the contrary, those problems are so important that the person may hurt someone or himself or herself because of them. So, the first thing for the therapist to do is to let the person know that he or she hears what the problem is, acknowledge it as a problem, and then let the person talk about some of the things that he or she is hurt or angry about. A therapist can even give the person some credit for "standing it" for so long, by saying something like this: "I don't know if I could have taken it as long as you have." Thus, the clinician shows recognition that there is a problem and that the person has worth in his or her eyes. At this point, the person in crisis may be more willing to start communicating in an active, positive way.

It is vitally important that the person in crisis feel that he or she is understood, or at least that the clinician is willing to try to understand his or her view of reality. In short, a therapist wants someone to trust enough to take a great risk, the risk of stopping his or her pathological behavior and trying a new approach to problem resolution.

CHAPTER 3

Clinical Interventions in Emergency Situations

When someone calls for help in an emergency, no matter who that person is—a police officer, a mental health professional, a rape victim, the parent of a psychotic adolescent, a suicide threatener, or a woman who has been beaten by her husband—the person has already defined that situation as beyond his or her resources to control. Too often, emergencies have been dismissed or mishandled because the person who received the call for help was not sensitive to the needs or feelings of the caller (Everstine and Everstine, 1983; Myer, 2001). A professional person may be concerned or fearful that a situation may be in process of escalating beyond the possibility of establishing control, but because these encounters with persons in emergency situations are extremely critical, they must be met with considerable sensitivity. As a general rule, it is wise to look on the caller as a person who is experiencing a true emergency—simply by virtue of the fact that the person has spoken of the situation as such, assessing it as being beyond his or her ability to cope.

The beginning of this chapter reviews some basic telephone procedures for this first contact. It describes the kinds of information that it is advisable to gather when first talking by telephone with a person who is involved in an emergency situation. How to ask for and make use of police assistance in a potentially dangerous situation is also discussed.

Collecting Information

On receiving an emergency call, the first priority is to try to get the name and telephone number from the caller. This may seem trivial, but on several occasions obtaining a phone number has saved a person's life. Many people who are extremely upset may panic and hang up suddenly: for example, suicidal persons often change their minds about talking and hang up, and the therapist may find him- or herself knowing full details of the sad story but not knowing who the person is or how to recontact the person. Usually, people will provide their names and telephone numbers fairly easily in an automatic way, if it is requested early enough in the conversation and in a matter-of-fact manner. The best method to accomplish this is to refer to a "bad connection," that is, pretending to be worried about being cut off will help to induce an agitated person to give the telephone number without thinking about what he or she is doing. Then, even if the person does hang up suddenly, the address of the person can be traced through a "reverse directory," which lists addresses by telephone numbers and is generally available through a local police department at night and on weekends, or from the telephone company. There is a commonly held misconception that telephone calls can be easily traced if the caller can only be kept on the line. Actually, calls are extremely difficult to trace, even though the advent of caller ID has made this less of a problem (with the exception of calls from a pay phone or a blocked line).

After obtaining this important information, the therapist should try to get a clear description of the problem from the caller (clear, concise information is one of the essential elements in successful crisis intervention: Everstine and Everstine, 1983; Cournoyer, 1996; James and Gilliland, 2001; Dale, 1995; Grunstone and Leviton, 1993; Myer, 2001; Hendricks and McKean, 1995). Try to find out how many people are involved in the emergency situation. How many people are there in the family and how many people are present at the moment of this call? Next, the therapist should ascertain whether or not there are weapons present and whether drugs or alcohol have been involved in the problem. It is not necessary to be blunt or obvious in asking these questions—mentioning weapons directly, for example, may frighten or make the caller suspicious. The therapist can ask, "Has anyone been hurt?" and "Are you hurt?" and, if the answer is yes, "Did someone hit you with a hand or hurt you with something?" A therapist can usually obtain this information while talking in a general way or asking questions about the problem in a conversational tone of voice, thus avoiding the implication that the person is being interrogated.

As a general rule, the therapist should try to speak briefly with each person present if possible, before responding or scheduling an appointment. This approach does not require a lengthy conversation; it is only necessary to gain each person's general consent to be seen. This step also lets everyone know that the therapist is interested in him or her and respects the family members' individual rights. Meanwhile, it is also wise to determine whether or not someone has already left the scene in anger, that is, a person who may be likely to return later and be surprised by the presence of a third party at the scene; or, a person who is angry that, without his or her knowledge, a therapist was called. Of course, this is a situation which it is best to avoid, if necessary by planning to meet the caller outside of the home or away from the scene of the emergency. The only situation in which we do not gain the consent of everyone present before making a visit is when there is a life-or-death issue: for example, when someone has attempted suicide or is going to hurt himself or herself, or when someone is behaving in an acutely psychotic manner and may be capable of hurting another person; or, in the case of a family emergency, when someone announces that a person may be severely battered at any moment if an intervention does not occur immediately. But, in most cases when making an emergency response to the home, it is vital to respect people's civil liberties—above all, their right to privacy—and to gain consent for such a visit. In short, the therapist should have the consent of each person who is present in the home when possible, unless someone's life is at stake.

In many cases, such as that of a battered spouse or a severely acting-out adolescent, one or more family members may not be pleased about someone having called a therapist. For example, an abusive husband may be most unwilling to talk with anyone about his conduct, and yet there are good reasons for trying to get his consent. By doing so, a clinician can indicate that he or she is prepared to treat the husband as a person, and thus the therapist may be seen as less of a threat. In addition, this unexpected or paradoxical approach may help to change the husband's set way of thinking about therapists, so that at least some of his resistance may be bypassed.

If consent is given and it appears to be reasonably safe, the clinician can arrange an appointment or go directly to the scene. If the husband does not consent in a battering case, it may be wiser to offer meeting the wife at some place outside the home, for example, at a friend's house, a coffee shop, or any place that is safe, neutral territory. In those instances in which there is an extremely enraged person in the home, who has been actively violent or has used a weapon recently, it may be necessary to call for police assistance.

Before a therapist does emergency work, or if the therapist often treats high-risk or potentially violent persons who may become involved in emergencies, it is wise to establish a good working relationship with the local police, the ambulance service, and the fire department. (Unfortunately, many mental health professionals have an antagonistic—or at the very least indifferent—attitude toward their local police.) If a therapist is dealing with an emergency situation that involves a young child or adolescent, and emergency police assistance is needed during the day, the department's Juvenile Officer can usually be asked for assistance. (In most police departments, there is a Juvenile Officer who has had special training in working with young people.) When a therapist is working with an adult in, for example, a battering situation, he or she can ask for someone in the Detective Bureau; and, the department may have an officer or officers who work exclusively on domestic violence cases. These officers wear plain clothes and have some special training in helping victims. If none of these specialist officers is available and it is necessary to go through dispatch, it is advisable to try to explain to the officer on duty that this is a family emergency situation and that it would be helpful if the officer who responds to the call is one who is experienced in dealing with families and doesn't mind doing family crisis work. If possible, it should be an officer in plain clothes and in an unmarked car. It is useful to recall, in such situations, that the people who called for help asked for the help of a therapist or a counselor and were *not* calling the police; also, they may have had a good reason for not asking the police to intervene. Even so, the therapist must take reasonable precautions for his or her safety, as well as that of the clients.

How a therapist coordinates the emergency response with the police is often critical, and how the police are brought into the emergency situation is of extreme importance. Of course, if the therapist is dealing with a situation in which someone is actively violent and has injured someone or is holding a person hostage, the police must be summoned immediately. But if, for example, a call has been received about a psychotic person or a violent family fight and the description of the situation is such that the therapist does not feel comfortable responding alone, in such a case it is equally appropriate to call the police for assistance with the visit. Should it not be advisable or wise to inform the family or person that the police are on their way, it will be a good idea to meet the police at a corner near the house or apartment, that is, one that is completely out of sight of the house. It is not wise simply to call the police and tell them about the incident and ask them to respond to the scene, because information about the problem may be conveyed incorrectly to police officers in the field by a dispatcher, and these officers may be the ones to arrive first, with an incorrect view of the situation. If this happens, the person or family member who called a therapist is likely to feel angry and betrayed, and any attempt to establish a therapeutic relationship will be difficult or impossible.

Whenever one person must tell another something in a hurry, confusions and distortions readily occur. One unfortunate miscommunication of this sort happened when a therapist called for help with a large, and potentially explosive, psychotic adolescent in a parking lot. The message that the police in the field received was, "Sniper with a gun at a parking lot. Dr. Everstine is in danger." Much to the clinician's surprise, the SWAT team arrived. So, when calling the police, it is important to be aware that a request for assistance often may be passed along by two or three people and can become distorted in the process. Consequently, if a situation is particularly sensitive, the therapist may ask that the officer in the field call him or her back. In this way, the therapist can speak to the officer directly before he or she responds to the call, in order to be sure that the problem is understood. The therapist should plan to meet the officer at some distance from the scene and proceed there with the officer on foot. On arrival at the scene, an explanation can be given to the person who called concerning why the police were brought in. If the situation appears to be calm, the therapist may choose to ask the officer to leave; or, the officer may be asked to remain for a while, until the problem has deescalated to the point at which the therapist feels safe without an officer present.

It is usually advisable to establish a secure communication link between the therapist(s) who are responding to the emergency scene and the office, so that they can call in for help or assistance should an unexpected problem occur. The communication system should be sufficiently discreet to enable a therapist to notify the office that he or she needs help, while at the same time the people at the scene do not know that help has been called for. We have experienced frightening moments when therapists were threatened, but fortunately the therapist was able to talk his or her way out of each situation. In one instance, a therapist responded to a call from a battered spouse; later, her husband returned, drunk and armed with a knife. The clinician was able to make a cell phone call back to the office on false pretenses and was able to convey, subtly, to the office staff that he was in serious danger and needed police assistance. The police were asked to respond to the call immediately.

After another, similar instance which involved a battered child, we decided to institute the following telephone call-in system. When therapists respond to an emergency in the field (any emergency in which there is some indication that there may have been violence or there is the potential for violence), as soon as they arrive they tell the people whom they are visiting that they will have to telephone the office. If a situation is dangerous, the counselor will first say (upon reaching the office), "This is ___ calling in. Were there any calls for me?" When that happens, the office staff (at night, the answering service) will know that a therapist in the field is in trouble and will send police assistance immediately. If, by contrast, the situation is relatively calm, the clinician will merely identify him- or herself by first name only, and that informal method of identification will let the office staff know that the staff member is all right. In puzzling or ambiguous situations, the counselor will use the first name but will add "Thank you. I'll call back in fifteen minutes" (or whatever time span is appropriate). The office staff is thus alerted that, if no call has been received fifteen minutes later, police assistance should be dispatched.

Responding to an Emergency

Before proceeding to offer some recommended procedures for the emergency response, it will be useful to reflect on considerations that cause this sort of clinical work to be somewhat unique. When a clinician responds to the scene of an emergency, there are many aspects of that kind of scene which differ from emergencies that take place in a hospital, clinic, or private office. Some of these differences are quite subtle and, if overlooked, can affect the course and outcome of treatment in a negative way. This section will review these differences, in addition to discussing nontraditional ways in which it is possible to work with people who would be resistant to the more traditional methods of psychotherapy.

In a majority of emergency incidents, clinicians are often surprised to find that people may be receptive to change if the therapist is cautious and sensitive about how he or she approaches them. In fact, those who have been struggling with a problem for a long time may be *more* receptive to change, merely because they have been in conflict longer than some others. And, no matter how angry or polarized people may appear to be on the surface, at least one person usually recognizes that outside help can be useful in resolving problems. What is critical here is that a clinician who intervenes in an emergency should be extremely sensitive to the cultural pride and self-esteem of the people involved; it is vital not to jump to conclusions or to humiliate or "corner" people, however inadvertently.

Paradoxical as it may seem, the sooner a therapist can see people in an emergency the better, even if one or more of those involved is still acting-out or is agitated. (The only exception would be if someone was too drunk to communicate coherently or was under the influence of drugs. In such a situation, it would obviously be wise to wait until each person is clearly sober and coherent.) If the clinician has this opportunity to see people while the actual emergency is taking place or very shortly thereafter, so much the better, because their resistance to intervention will be lessened. The people involved are in emotional turmoil and, because of that, are much more motivated to change or to work on their problems. After time passes and they are not experiencing as much discomfort, they may then be more reluctant to do something about a problem. Another reason for seeing a person as soon as possible is that it gives the message that someone genuinely cares and is concerned about what will happen to him or her. This point cannot be emphasized too much. Many people whom we have successfully treated would never have gone to a traditional clinic. We were able to help those people primarily because we reached out to them when they were experiencing chaos.

It is important to consider what steps must be taken by someone who is seeking help for a personal or interactional problem. First, the person must be aware (at least to some extent) that the problem is psychological in nature. Second, the person must be able to figure out what kind of agency or profession can be of help—not an easy task when one considers the declining number of social agencies and programs, both public and private, not to mention the difficulty one faces when navigating through a managed care network. After deciding which agency or practitioner is appropriate to his or her needs, the person must find and visit the agency (assuming that it is during regular working hours), a prospect that may be frightening for various reasons, such as language or cultural barriers or socioeconomic class distinctions. He or she must then explain, to a total stranger (on the phone or in what may be an intimidating setting), intimate details of his or her personal life. Under these circumstances, it is a matter of some amazement that people find help at all.

When undertaking a home visit, it is well to remember that, in essence, a therapist is entering the other person's *space*. This applies even when meeting the person in a public place, because many of the key aspects of a professional's role and authority are not present in a public or neutral place. Many assertive or confrontational interventions that can be accomplished by a therapist in the office with great ease may be misperceived as a threat or as an insult when the therapist is visiting someone's home or has met the person in a public place.

A therapist who does emergency work needs to be aware that, even though his or her self-perception is that of someone who is nonthreatening and who wishes to help others, some people in crisis may view the therapist as a very real threat. For example, accidentally sitting in someone's favorite chair may make that person uncomfortable or angry without the person knowing why. Assuming a strong authority role too quickly in a family situation may possibly offend a mother or father, who may feel that his or her role is being challenged because of not being able to solve the family's problems him- or herself. A therapist can take more liberties in the office, mainly because clients have come there (more or less) because they wanted to and have entered the therapist's domain. Even so, therapists should be very aware that social customs differ widely from culture to culture. A person might have been demeaned or treated with cultural insensitivity in the past. These issues should be taken into account at the initial crisis intervention (Prediger, 1994).

By contrast, when a clinician goes out on an emergency call, he or she is often responding to the request of someone else, for example, another family member, a neighbor, a probation officer, or the police. Because the people involved in the emergency probably did not originally intend to see a therapist, they have probably not yet defined their problems as psychological in nature. Even though they may have given their consent to see a counselor or therapist, it may have been a tentative or reluctant consent; their first reaction to the arrival of a clinician may be fear or anger or both. They may be full of misunderstandings about what a therapist is and does, and they may find such a person threatening in addition to the upset and humiliation occasioned by the emergency itself.

Consequently, it is often advisable for the therapist to move at a much slower pace than usual when working at the scene, and to set therapeutic goals much differently. Sometimes, therapists become discouraged after an emergency visit or after the second visit of a case that began as an emergency, thinking that they have not really accomplished much. But, if a therapist can get a family or family member to come into the office the next day or a week later for a follow-up session, the therapist has achieved a very large and very important goal during the first visit.

A Typical Case

The following description of a family that is typical of those seen in emergency work, will serve to illustrate some points made above in this section. Harry and Mabel have been married eighteen years and have two adolescent children—a boy, Wayne (sixteen), and a girl, Debby (fourteen). Both Harry and Mabel have drinking problems and once or twice a month they have violent fights. Harry lost control one day about a week ago and "slapped around" his daughter when she "talked back" to him. Debby is an unhappy girl who smokes marijuana and sometimes has been known to overuse pills. She has had an abortion that neither of the parents knows about. Debby's brother, Wayne, is not home very much these days, but his parents don't seem to notice. He has also used drugs and was arrested once for shoplifting, which his father dismissed as boyish fun; lately, he has been selling pot and pills. Mabel sometimes mixes tranquilizers with alcohol, and twice she had to go to an emergency room for what was called an "accidental" overdose.

The police are fairly frequent visitors to Harry and Mabel's home, because when Harry drinks too much he often loses control. Harry was laid off last year for six months and things got pretty bad at home, but Mabel was too ashamed and afraid to tell anyone about it at the time. She called a social agency once but didn't keep the appointment. The school counselors and the Probation Department are concerned about the family, but what can they do? Friends and relatives have suggested that the family needs help, but Harry and Mabel have ignored them. If someone dared to advise these people that theirs is a "mental health" problem and that they need psychotherapy, either Harry or Mabel would more than likely tell the person to "go to hell" because they are not crazy!

One day, this man and wife will have another fight. They will both be drunk and Mabel will be threatened with a beating again. When she realizes that she is in physical danger—during the most explosive phase of the struggle—Mabel may well call the police. Harry will be arrested; Mabel will refuse to cooperate. The thought of calling a mental health professional for help would not occur to her. The police, in their turn, might act to quell the marital crisis, but once that had been accomplished would have little to offer the embattled couple. If Harry and Mabel were lucky, the police would call for assistance from an agency that would reach out to them. Obviously, for people like Harry and Mabel to permit a therapist to visit their home and later agree to a second visit, considerable rapport will have to be established within a short time. In order to be able to reach out to the many people who are similar to Harry and Mabel, clinicians need to develop highly flexible and readily adaptable techniques. Many approaches taken by traditional schools of psychotherapy would tend to confuse and alienate people like Mabel and Harry. That is a good reason for the clinician to adopt therapeutic interventions that fit within Harry's and Mabel's perceptions of reality and their system of values.

When talking with people like Harry and Mabel, it generally makes more sense for a therapist to speak in terms of difficulties and problems, rather than to use traditional psychological terms. It will be understandable to talk about managing difficulties in a better way so that they do not escalate into serious problems. A clinician may reassure the person that it's normal to have difficulties in life and that no one is without them. The therapist may add that people generally mismanage difficulties in three ways: (1) they may make too little of a major problem, such as when a mother dismisses her son's drug abuse and petty thievery as just an adolescent "stage," or when a wife denies her husband's alcoholism; (2) they can make too much of a minor difficulty, thus causing it to grow out of proportion, for example, a parent's overreacting to some minor acting-out on the part of a teenager, leading the teenager to think that the magnitude of his crime should be increased to fit the magnitude of his punishment; and (3) they often mismanage a problem by applying a "commonsense" remedy that may make it worse, for example, trying to "cheer up" people who are depressed, which is exactly the wrong thing to do because it conveys the message that they have no reason to be depressed when, in fact, they think they do. In effect, it tells a depressed person that, for one reason or another, he or she has not been listened to.

In order to reach people like Harry and Mabel, a clinician needs to learn to talk with them in terms that they can understand. Emphasis needs to be placed on real issues of the here-and-now, such as Harry's temper, the substance abuse of Harry and his son, or how Mabel, in her well-intended way, maintains the problem instead of fixing it. Furthermore, a therapist needs to gain insight into the person's perceptions of reality, keeping in mind that what someone considers to be "reality" is, for the most part, his or her highly personalized concept of what reality should be. In fact, a clinician's perceptions of reality may differ greatly from those of someone who is experiencing an emergency; and, if a therapist and a person in crisis are going to communicate, the therapist needs to be aware of what differences exist in their two separate realities; one must be able to speak according to the client's point of view. It is also necessary to be cognizant of the fact that people who are experiencing the stress of an emergency tend to think in a rigid and concrete manner. That is, when they are agitated or frightened, people tend to cling more rigidly to their private reality or worldview. So, in an emergency, it is even more important to decode the perceptions of reality of the person in crisis and to frame the therapeutic intervention in terms appropriate for that person's reality—so that one can be heard.

Arriving at the Scene of an Emergency without the Police

Although most of us go through life with the awareness that life has its tragedies as well as its joys, most of us do not have to contemplate the possibility of being attacked by another person in the course of our work. For some reason, many people think that this sort of thing happens only to others, and that is particularly true of people in the helping professions, that is, too many are basically humanitarian in character and optimistic about the human spirit. We have often found that psychotherapists are reluctant to take some of the precautions necessary in responding to emergency calls. Nevertheless, this fact should not imply that all people in crisis are potentially dangerous, for many are frightened people who feel trapped and desperate because they have been hurt beyond endurance; some are people who, in other circumstances, would never dream of hurting another person. Even so, people in the heat of an emergency can more easily become inflamed and act-out in a blind, aggressive, or violent manner. Because of that, it is wise to observe certain precautions.

First, it is not advisable to go to an emergency alone, particularly at night. Even the police do not respond to violent family fights or to obviously dangerous situations alone. Police officers invariably ask for "cover" (that is, another officer or a police team) when they respond to emergencies. Therefore, if the police don't respond alone (with their radios, guns, mace, and other accoutrements) to emergencies, it stands to reason that mental health professionals who lack this kind of equipment should not respond alone.

We have found that a team of a man and a woman is best for working in emergencies. Our rationale is that it is often necessary, at first, to separate the people and talk with each person alone, for the purpose of permitting each to ventilate feelings and calm down before any kind of therapeutic intervention, with everyone present, begins. It is usually easier for a female therapist to talk with the woman who is involved in the conflict, without causing any feelings of anger or jealousy on the part of her husband or lover, and for a male therapist to talk with the man in question, also without arousing jealousy and suspicion.

When arriving at the scene of an emergency situation, it is wise to proceed in a cautious and well-planned manner. Even though what a clinician has heard on the telephone from the person calling for help may have sounded very fearful or desperate, it is important that the response is well thought through; in other words, as the saying goes, he or she is best advised not to "rush in where angels fear to tread." The following plan of action is recommended. Park a short distance away from the house and walk to the house slowly and quietly. Listen for sounds of a disturbance or active violence. Continue listening carefully while walking up to the door, and do not enter the home without being invited. Even when responding to someone who has expressed profound distress, do not rush pell-mell into that person's home; remember that it is the other person's territory and that suddenly entering someone's home may be interpreted as aggression rather than concern. In addition, the person who called for help may not have been telling the truth or may have distorted the situation to suit his or her own needs. A hurt person who has called in anger may have painted a picture of the situation that is completely inaccurate. An injured person may be unaware that he or she has distorted the facts and has misled the clinician about the behavior of the other people involved.

People who call for help in family emergencies are usually grateful that someone has come to the home, and often are pleasantly surprised that someone cared enough to respond to them in a moment of need. But, occasionally, something very unexpected and possibly dangerous may be waiting for the therapist, and so it is best to approach these situations with utmost care. When going to people's homes, as noted earlier, the therapist should concentrate on the awareness that it is *their* home or space. When waiting to be let in, it is wise to stand back a little way from the door. By doing so two things will be accomplished: (1) the person who answers the door is given "space," and doesn't feel crowded or threatened; and (2) if he or she does become angry, the person waiting will not be as much of a target and will have room to move out of the way. It is wise to bear in mind that a clinician does not have the same rights and privileges (under the law) as a police officer. If, for example, a therapist walks into someone's house without permission, the therapist is technically trespassing. Hence, legally, as well as ethically, it is wise to wait and use caution.

If a house is extremely dark, it may be necessary to enter even more slowly in order to adjust to the darkness. When first entering the home, the therapist should introduce him- or herself and give the person(s) present some form of identification. Meanwhile, it is important to look around for any signs of violence, for example, broken things on the floor or overturned furniture. Also, the clinician should be very cautious of the "space" of the person(s) with whom he is talking. Generally, in American and European cultures, under nonthreatening circumstances, about one and one-half to two feet of personal space is considered to be safe and comfortable. In an emergency situation, it is not advisable to get much closer than three or four feet, unless the person gives a clear message that he or she would be agreeable for someone to come closer.

If the emergency has calmed down enough so that it appears that the family members are ready to talk with a therapist, it will be best for the clinician to choose an appropriate room for the meeting. It is usually a good idea to avoid the kitchen because there are knives and a variety of small, dangerous objects that could be used as weapons, should things become heated. Around the dining room table or in the living room are generally good places to discuss things. If the living room is chosen, the therapist may wish to select a straight-backed chair or to bring one into the room. In that way, the therapist can avoid choosing someone's favorite place and thus inadvertently annoying that person. Also, it is a good idea for the therapist to be stationed at a fair distance from the person in crisis, without being obviously distant, until the situation can be fully evaluated. The therapist might say, "I want to move this chair so that I can see everyone," and few people will find this to be unusual or take offense. During this period, it will be possible to determine whether or not the people can discuss their problems as a family group. If it is impossible for them to talk as a family without someone becoming angry, the therapist might suggest that the group discussion stop (temporarily) and talk with each person individually to help him or her ventilate enough anger to be able to return, eventually, to the group.

In determining whether or not a family or couple can talk calmly together, the therapist may wish to use the "only one person speaks at a time" rule: that is, each person can describe his or her perception of the problem, in turn, without having another member interrupt or become agitated. When people are capable of following this rule, they can usually work together as a group. Moreover, this rule can serve to convey to each person the message that the therapist wants to hear each side of the story. It is a good idea to ask the most potentially explosive person to speak first. By doing this, the clinician will convey recognition and respect and, in addition, will find out fairly rapidly if that person can be worked-with along with the others, or will require separation and individual attention.

Basic Steps and Goals

The first important step in making an emergency response is to gain the rapport and trust of the person in crisis. This point cannot be emphasized too strongly. It means that someone who is going to be working in the field of emergency psychology needs to be able to establish rapport with many types of persons from many differing backgrounds. An emergency therapist should be able to talk with anyone from the young "street person" to the alcoholic to the fundamentalist Christian to someone who lives in a very elegant, upper-class home. In emergency work, particularly when responding to police emergency calls, a therapist must be flexible enough to respond to *anyone* who may be present at the scene. There is no selectivity in the clients accepted in a crisis situation, as often occurs in private clinics or private practice. So, the initial step is to gain rapport with the person in crisis; and, if this is the only accomplishment of the first visit, it can be considered a success. (Everstine and Everstine, 1983; Myer, 2001; Prediger, 1994).

The next step, after establishing rapport, is attempting to formulate a clear definition of the problem: what actually is the problem and how can it be described in behavioral terms? It is often surprising to realize that many people have not really thought through what their true problem is, nor what has brought it to the current status of an emergency. There may be two definitions of the problem: a clinician may define the problem one way and the person experiencing the emergency may define the problem another way. In fact, the therapist may not always wish to share his or her own definition of the problem at first. It may be wiser to propose a definition of the problem that the people can understand in clear, behavioral terms.

Next, it is important for a clinician to know what the people have done in the past, or are currently doing, to cope with or to resolve the problem. Obviously, it is a waste of time and energy to recreate a strategy for change that was unsuccessfully tried before. The therapist will then want to establish some goals for treatment. One way to obtain a behavioral description of the problem that will help in the formulation of goals is to ask the question, "What will be different when the problem stops?"—that is, how will they know that things are different, that the problem has gotten better or has gone away? Goals, like the definition of a problem, need to be stated in precise behavioral terms. Goals such as "I really want to get my head together" or "I want to be less depressed" are patently not acceptable. Less depressed, less miserable—these are vague strivings, not objective goals. Therapeutic change requires clear definitions and specific goals that can be understood and contrasted, by all parties, to the current state of affairs. The therapist needs to know what the people in crisis will be enabled to do if things change, as well as what kinds of events will no longer take place if change occurs. In particular with people who are depressed, it is essential to direct them toward thinking about concrete, behavioral changes that can be observed—in light of the goals they want to accomplish—because depressed people tend to negate what progress they make unless progress is demonstrated to them unequivocally.

Finally, it will be important to focus upon the people's perceptions of reality. When people are in a crisis state, their perceptions of reality become quite limited and rigid as a result of the intense stress that they are experiencing. This phenomenon might be described as emotional "tunnel vision." Because of this, people in crisis are more susceptible to techniques such as those of Milton Erickson (Erickson et al., 1976) and the indirect or paradoxical techniques of the Brief Therapy Center (Watzlawick et al., 1974). Some of the more traditional therapeutic approaches that require insight, reasoning, and interpretation may cause agitated or angry persons in acute crisis to become even more defensive and resistant. In other words, it is unreasonable to expect people in crisis to be reasonable. Consequently, we suggest that a therapist attempt to convert the person's perceptual rigidity into a clinical advantage, by means of methods recommended later.

Strategies for Defusing Emergencies

The therapist should try to incorporate the person's worldview and self-perception into the design of an intervention. Immensely valuable clinical information can be gained from the person's use of language, such as what his or her values are, what the person is afraid of, and what the person's perceptions of self and people in general are. Because people are tenaciously wedded to these perceptions when they are in a state of crisis, a therapist who is facile can have enormous freedom of movement in the crisis situation by redefining desired or undesired behavior according to the person's rigidly defined reality. For example, if being strong and manly is a vital part of the person's perception of himself, then restraint and self-control can be reframed (redefined) as manly, and aggressive behavior can be reframed as childish or unmanly.

Another example of reframing a person's reality is that of someone who wishes to punish a loved one for abandoning him or her, by committing suicide. A therapist may redefine the suicidal person's reality in these terms: if the suicidal person really wants to punish the former lover, he or she should try to find a new lover and establish a happy relationship with this new person. Thus, the former lover would be shown as less important and, in fact, readily replaceable. And the formerly suicidal person can have the exquisite pleasure of being present to witness this revenge.

Because reality is a subjective phenomenon, a clinician can work toward altering the person's view of reality by reframing certain components of this perception, as described by Watzlawick:

> In this changeability of subjective "realities" lies the power of those therapeutic interventions that have come to be known under the rubric of reframing. Let us remember: we never deal with reality *per se,* but rather with *images* of reality—that is, with interpretations. While the number of potentially possible interpretations is very large, our world image usually permits us to see only one— and this *one* therefore appears to be the only possible, reasonable, and permitted view. (1978, p. 119)

The description aptly pertains to people in crisis, who are especially resistant to clinical interventions and to change. Because they are frightened and confused, they cling to their habitual but neurotic behavior patterns, which usually only serve to perpetuate a problem.

Traditionally, direct or "rational" attempts to persuade the person in crisis to give up old and unsuccessful problem-solving techniques will often prove to be useless, because what is familiar—even if unsuccessful— usually feels safer. Thus, it will be wiser to accept the patient's defensiveness and to incorporate this resistance into the clinical intervention. An example of making use of resistance is the following.

A woman therapist was called to the home of a young couple for the purpose of deciding whether or not the husband would require hospitalization. On arriving, the clinician was told that the husband had been rolling around on the floor and yelling that he wanted to die because he found out that his wife had had an affair. Being a woman of fairly small stature, the therapist realized that any direct approach would be unwise and ineffectual, as the husband was quite large. Also, he was gaining considerable emotional "payoff" from his actions, which served to stimulate humiliation and grief on the part of his wife. The therapist therefore decided to accept the husband's resistance and try to "preempt" any further acting-out on his part by several means.

First, she said to the wife, in a serious tone of voice (and loud enough to be heard by the husband), that she felt that the wife had "wounded" her husband very deeply. In addition, the husband needed to roll around on the floor in order to express his deep feelings of anguish concerning what she had done to him. In fact, he would probably need to roll on the floor for another hour before he would be able to express himself fully and thus experience some relief. Then, the therapist began encouraging the husband to shout louder and to roll around more furiously. After a few moments of this intervention, the man stopped rolling and said (to the therapist), "What's the matter with you? Are you crazy?" The therapist replied that she was not crazy but knew that he was deeply hurt and needed to express to his wife the intensity of the emotional pain he was feeling. The husband agreed to the latter comment.

In this situation, if the clinician had insisted on taking a more direct approach to gaining control over the husband, the emergency would have probably had a very different outcome. In all likelihood, the police would have been called and the husband would have been sent to a psychiatric facility for observation. Although the intervention itself may sound simplistic and scarcely adequate for defusing such an emotionally charged situation, it may have been this very quality of simplicity that led to its success. In any event, the therapist was able to avoid a confrontation by accepting the husband's behavior first and then giving him a reason to change it himself.

Another concept (previously noted in Chapter 1) that is useful for defusing acute emergency situations is that of the "illusion of alternatives" as identified by Weakland and Jackson (1958), Erickson and Rossi (1975), and by Watzlawick (1978), who defined the concept as follows:

> . . . establishing a frame within which a seemingly free choice is offered between two alternatives, both of which amount to the same outcome—that is, therapeutic change. An illusion is thus created, suggesting that there are only these two possibilities, or—in other words—a state of blindness is produced for the fact that there indeed exist other possibilities outside the frame. (p. 120)

This kind of intervention can be used to therapeutic advantage in emergencies precisely because the person in crisis lacks perceptual flexibility. For example, this technique could be used in a situation in which the clinician has decided that someone should be hospitalized and the person is hesitant. In the course of negotiating this important event in the person's life, the clinician can offer to arrange transportation to the hospital either by ambulance or in a police car, and give the person in crisis free choice between the alternatives.

There will be times when a therapist will feel stymied during the initial stages of treatment and will seek to make more efficient the process of obtaining information on the nature of the problem. One way is to ask the people not to change right away—providing it is safe to do so. (This is clearly not a wise intervention technique for situations in which violence has occurred.) The therapist can ask people to take notes or keep a journal of certain kinds of behavior, between one session and the next. The subject of these records will be actions or incidents that the therapist needs to know more about, and thus during this period people's attention will be focused on observing their own behavior and their interactions more closely. In the process a certain kind of change will in fact have occurred, because their concentration will be diverted from escalating the conflict to documenting it. Admittedly, this may be only a slight change, but it will prove significant if it yields information that the clinician can use to formulate new interventions.

Should an emergency situation begin to escalate once more, the following tactics of distraction can be quite useful in bringing a crisis back under the therapist's control. He can ask a series of trivial but professional-sounding questions about the life of each person in the family—in effect, taking a quasi-psychological history by asking, for example: "How many children were there in your mother's family?," "What was your father's profession?" and "What high school did you go to?" Most of us are accustomed to visiting a physician and having him or her ask us odd but innocuous questions. They elicit automatic kinds of responses and subtly establish that the professional person is supposed to ask the questions and the client is supposed to reply. Generally, within a few minutes, the clinician will have structured the situation so that he or she is in control once more and can proceed to work out an intervention.

Another technique that may be of help in calming people is for the therapist to feign being slightly "thick" or confused, or to act as though he or she is not quite clear about what the people are trying to convey. The rationale is that most people, despite being upset or angry, want others to understand their side of an issue. If the clinician acts in a concerned but uncomprehending manner, the angry person will usually put more effort into attempting to clarify his or her point of view. Of course, caution is in order so that the person who is speaking doesn't become annoyed. The therapist could say, "I want to make sure that I understand you correctly," and then repeat to the person what he or she has just said but slightly incorrectly. As a consequence, the angry person will have to expend some effort and energy in explaining what he or she has been trying to say. This process can divert some of the person's energy away from anger into clarifying the issue for the therapist.

An additional device that may be used to calm someone or to get a person to listen in a tolerant way is to frame behavior in a more positive light. This doesn't mean "painting things rosy" or acting in a Pollyannaish manner; what it means is looking for the positive aspects of a person's behavior and calling attention to that part in order to gain his or her trust. For example, with an aggressive and possibly assaultive husband, the therapist might refer to his behavior as that of a man who is "strong," and comment on the importance of being strong. The therapist may tell him that he gives the impression of being someone who wants to control his environment, and who wishes to have some authority over what is going on around him. This tactic can point out positive aspects of the husband's behavior that he may be able to "hear," and may give the clinician some leverage toward inducing him to pay attention.

Yet another method that may be used for getting people to settle down and listen is that of paradox. Sometimes a paradoxical intervention can change the situation or a person's "set" just enough to break the escalating cycle of anger and violence. For example, the therapist may, when visiting a person's home, ask politely for a cup of coffee or a glass of water. This somewhat unusual request can immediately change the role of antagonist in a crisis to the person's more usual role of host or hostess. Such a disarmingly simple or unexpected request may often be successful because it serves to divert the person's attention long enough to de-escalate the anger. One staff member once stopped a couple in the middle of a very heated fight by saying, "Do you smell gas? I think I smell something strange." All at once their attention was focused on something other than their conflict. It gave the clinician a chance to break the escalation of anger and to move the communication in a different direction.

Finally, humor can be a marvelous way to divert, calm, or slow down angry behavior. But humor has to be used with great caution and sensitivity to the pride and dignity of others. Care must be taken so that the humor itself, as well as the manner in which it is used, will not be misunderstood or taken as making fun of the other person. Some therapists and counselors can use humor in a natural way and some cannot. If the use of humor is something that a therapist does well and easily, it can often be most valuable in an emergency situation. If it does not come naturally, a therapist will be well advised not to use it.

CHAPTER 4

Hospitalizing Persons in Crisis

One of the more critical clinical decisions that a therapist will make is the choice of hospitalizing or not hospitalizing a person in crisis. This decision, of course, is most serious when it involves involuntary hospitalization. Frequently, clinicians who are comfortable in a hospital setting forget how terrifying hospitalization can be to a client, and what hospitalization will mean to that person's life in a real or a symbolic way. Hospitalization means that, for a period of time, a person's life is being placed under the control of other people who, in most cases, are unknown to the person. The person temporarily loses his or her civil liberties—totally. Also, putting someone in a mental hospital exposes that person to the threat of a stigma that could be lasting—considering the proliferation of data banks and automated record-keeping systems, and despite the new HIPAA protection of the privacy of client records. One psychiatric hospitalization could affect someone for the rest of his or her life.

In critical situations such as those described in this chapter, considerable pressure is often placed on a therapist by the friends or family of the client to hospitalize, or not to hospitalize, the person. The therapist must weigh each consideration independently and base a decision upon what he or she believes to be the best interests of the client. This chapter is intended to be useful to a therapist in making this difficult decision on clinical grounds. The chapter reviews general procedures for preparing to hospitalize someone, either voluntarily or involuntarily, and presents some guidelines for assessing the extent of a client's potential for violence toward other people. (See Chapter 9 for information that may be helpful in assessing suicide risk, and Chapter 5 for assessing dangerousness.) Two case studies are presented to illustrate the hospitalization process. In addition, suggestions are offered on how to handle the situation when a therapist decides, contrary to the desires of the client or the family or friends, that hospitalization would *not* serve the best interests of that person.

Deciding Whether or Not to Hospitalize

Even if the therapist has had a long-term relationship with a client, the hospitalization process will not always be an easy one. Essentially, the decision should be based on considerations such as: whether or not the therapist believes that a client's condition is at serious risk of deteriorating unless he or she is placed in a protected environment; whether or not the client is so mentally ill that he or she poses a threat to self or others; whether or not the person is so gravely disabled by mental illness as to be no longer able to care for himself or herself.

This critical decision should not be made merely because the client *wishes* to enter a hospital. Some people use hospitalization to punish or manipulate those around them, and some chronically ill persons use the hospital as a refuge from the responsibilities of living. Moreover, the decision to hospitalize should not be made because a person is merely bizarre in manner or difficult to live with. It can be hard for a therapist to resist the pressure that friends, neighbors, or relatives apply in favor of putting an annoying or odd person into the hospital. In such cases, a therapist should return responsibility for the care of this kind of person to the family or friends, where it belongs. The therapist should help these "significant others" to realize that a period of hospitalization may temporarily relieve them of some pressures, but that it will not necessarily change the person nor make it easier to live with him or her. Instead, changes in their own behavior toward the client will have a better chance of altering the unacceptable behavior, eventually.

Assessment and Plan

If the person in crisis is unknown to the therapist who is assessing his or her condition to determine whether or not hospitalization will be necessary, the situation will often require considerable skill. First, it will be wise to observe the person carefully, while approaching him or her slowly. When observing his or her nonverbal behavior, it is important to be careful to allow enough personal space so that the person does not feel trapped or confronted. Disturbed or agitated people can easily feel threatened and may act out suddenly if someone gets too close to them. Also, cultural issues are involved in personal space, and are more intense in crisis situations. In some cultures, it is rude to stand close to others. Some involve touch as a form of greeting. Absent knowledge of the cultural norm about these things, a therapist should err on the side of giving the person plenty of space. He or she could ask what the custom is in respect to greetings and interpersonal distances.

As with other emergency situations, the therapist should focus first on gaining rapport, while also trying to understand what has caused the person to become agitated. The therapist should bear in mind that this person has not chosen him or her as a therapist, and quite possibly this person may not have defined the present situation as an emergency. Often the person who is being assessed was not the one who called for help, and he or she also may have been treated in an insensitive or provocative manner before the therapist arrived. Thus, a clinician may face not only the problem of gaining rapport with a disturbed person but also the added task of trying to undo the cruel or insensitive treatment of others. There is an additional possibility that the person in question may have been hospitalized previously, which may have been, personally, a bad experience.

To begin the actual assessment process, it is useful to try to learn what is healthy and positive about the person, because even acutely disturbed people have some ego strength. It is wise to try to approach the situation in a manner that inspires confidence, and to convey to the person that his or her safety and well-being are the primary concerns, and that you respect him or her as a person. Next, the therapist should try to discover what the person's reasons are for his or her behavior. Even acutely disturbed people who are behaving in a bizarre manner have some reasons for their actions, and often behavior that appears to be bizarre is quite reasonable when one grasps the logic behind it. It cannot be emphasized too strongly that acutely disturbed people—even those who may be acting in a violent or abusive way—are usually very frightened people. They are not only frightened of their own impulses but also of the imagined or real impulses of others as well. How well this process unfolds will depend largely on a therapist's ability to inspire trust in, and develop good rapport with, the disturbed person, guiding the person to a safe environment.

Disturbed people are acutely sensitive to (and perceptive of) the behavior of others, even though they may not be able or willing to behave appropriately themselves. Hence, they are often very aware of the subtleties of nonverbal communications, as well as mixed messages or deception on the part of the clinician; for example, when a therapist claims falsely that he or she is not afraid of the disturbed person, or when a therapist claims falsely to like the person. A wiser course, in such a situation, is for the therapist to admit some of his or her feelings in a neutral manner. For example, a therapist can say that the person is making him or her uncomfortable instead of saying that he or she is unafraid—which could be misunderstood as a challenge to act out more. This kind of neutral admission of discomfort is advisable because, if a disturbed person is afraid or angry and is trying to express fear or anger or keep the therapist at a distance, it lets the person know that the therapist got the message. By contrast, a denial of discomfort may inadvertently provoke more anger, because the disturbed person will be resentful that the intended message was not heard. Above all, it is a more honest answer that, in the long run, the person will appreciate.

A clinician needs to adopt a firm but reassuring manner and to control the direction and flow of this kind of conversation. Initial questions need to be uncomplicated, direct, and capable of being answered by simple one-or-two-word answers. The therapist can then slowly move on to more open-ended questions as the conversation progresses, and as the disturbed person becomes less anxious. If the person refuses to talk, a therapist can relieve some of the tension and avoid a confrontation by suggesting that the person may wish merely to nod or shake his or her head "yes" or "no." If the person still refuses to speak, the therapist may pursue a paradoxical approach by pretending to "order" the person not to talk. A therapist can say, for example, "It appears to me that you are upset and that talking may be too stressful, so I think that it would be best if you did not talk." This paradoxical approach may accomplish one of two things: if the person subsequently talks, the clinician has avoided a possible confrontation; or, if the person remains silent, he or she may have been relieved of considerable pressure to talk.

It is most important that a clinician both maintain control and behave appropriately, no matter what the disturbed person does. Acutely disturbed people may be very skillful at provoking the anger or disgust of others, and frequently they use this means to control a situation or to make others leave them alone. Such persons are often very perceptive and are able to choose just the right word or action to frustrate, disgust, or anger someone. Consequently, a therapist needs to be well aware of himself or herself in the situation, and to be sensitive to, and supportive of, fellow clinicians in these emotionally demanding moments.

In the course of an assessment interview, a therapist should convey to the person being assessed that he or she will do what is necessary to help; but, even if the person does not agree about what is the wisest course of action, the clinician will take whatever steps he or she believes to be necessary to help. In short, a therapist *will* use an external control such as hospitalization if the person cannot control himself or herself. Even though initially protesting, a disturbed person will often be relieved to learn that the clinician is willing to take full responsibility for seeing that control is restored.

Once the decision has been made to hospitalize someone, it should be undertaken in a thoroughly planned manner (when possible), and the plan should be presented to the client firmly but positively. Ideally, the arrangements themselves should have been made before the client is informed. The reason is that when someone loses control or decompensates to such an extent as to require hospitalization, the experience of entering a hospital itself can be terrifying. Even very belligerent or violent people may be frightened by their own impulses and their own expanding loss of control. It can be quite reassuring in such a situation (even if the person protests vehemently at the moment), for the hospitalization process to be conducted in a humane but well-organized manner. In fact, disorganization and lack of direction on the part of a clinician may inadvertently provoke more acting-out on the part of a disturbed person. Consequently, it is advisable, when possible, to call the hospital in advance to check available bed space and, if the therapist is not a physician, to discuss the situation with the on-call psychiatrist. Should the therapist later decide not to hospitalize, it will be a simple matter to telephone the hospital and say that the person will not be arriving.

Involuntary Hospitalization

The actual statutes may vary from state to state, but almost all states permit involuntary hospitalization because of danger to the self (being suicidal), danger to others (being homicidal), or being gravely disabled. State regulations also vary in respect to which licensed mental health professionals may sign an order for involuntary hospitalization, but, in most states, police officers also may sign these orders. Thus, if a clinician is not empowered to hospitalize the person involuntarily, the police may be of assistance. If the therapist is not a physician and the client is to be evaluated by an on-duty psychiatrist, it will help the psychiatrist to have the following kinds of information, because even very disturbed people may behave quite differently once they have arrived at the hospital.

1. Identifying information: that is, name, sex, date of birth, address, phone number, marital status, referral source.
2. General appearance.
3. A brief history.
4. Current problem.
5. Client's attitude toward the current problem, toward the clinician, and toward going to the hospital (submissive, resistant, etc.).
6. Motor behavior: for example, posture, gait, possible tremors or posturing.
7. Manner of speech.
8. Affective state(s): for example, anger, fear, elation, and whether or not appropriate.
9. Thought processes: that is, whether or not the person's thoughts are logical.
10. Thought content, including delusion(s).
11. Perception or distortion(s) of perception.
12. Intellectual functioning.
13. Orientation in terms of identity, place, and time.
14. Judgment (ability to make and carry out plans).
15. A clear description of the person's behavior during the emergency situation.

Assessing Potentially Dangerous Persons

Many people who lose control, even those who become aggressive or homicidal, can be fearful of their own impulses. In many instances, this may seem an unwarranted assumption, especially if the disturbed people are rather large, powerful, or agitated. Nonetheless, no matter how formidable the people are, they may be astonished and confused by their own actions, and unaware of how frightening they might be to others. Therefore, it will be a good idea to protect this kind of person from as many aggravating or provocative stimuli as possible. A therapist should talk with the person in a quiet but not closed-in place, because an enclosed area may cause a person to panic if he or she feels trapped. It is also wise for a therapist to give an aggressive person free access to the door, so that if a person tries to run out he or she will be less likely to attack the therapist on the way to leaving the room. In most cases, a person can be brought back by the police or a security guard if he or she runs away.

If a person does become agitated and must be restrained, the clinician should attempt to avoid a one-to-one confrontation, trying instead to muster enough assistance from others to make resistance futile. A therapist should never attempt to restrain an aggressive person in such a manner that the person feels this restraint to be a challenge. In fact, when three or four people are involved in the restraining process, the odds are good that the person will not see it as a challenge. Of course, a therapist should try to arrange for this necessary support in advance. A disturbed person may be encouraged to act out more violently if the clinician recommends hospitalization and then is not able to back up this statement because no one else is there to provide support.

The following are some guidelines for making an assessment of the potential dangerousness of a person. It should be noted that the person in question may simply not appear to be violent when being seen by a therapist. Some paranoid people are quite capable of controlling their violent tendencies for a period of time when necessary. In such a case, it may be helpful to include one or more significant others during the interview, because the disturbed person may not be able to mask his or her thoughts or actions as easily around people with whom he or she is emotionally involved. Yet no amount of clinical skill will be able to penetrate the calm demeanor of some paranoid persons.

Because not all violent people are homicidal, the following critical questions may help a clinician to differentiate between the merely angry or violent and the homicidal person:

1. What is the *meaning* of the current violent behavior? Is it the venting of nonspecific rage, or is it clearly directed toward someone in particular? (Obviously, violence that is directed toward a specific victim represents the more serious situation.)
2. Did the violent behavior invite discovery because it was so blatant, or did the client attempt to conceal his or her intentions?
3. Is the intended victim an innocent party, or did he or she do something to provoke this aggression?
4. How delusional is the disturbed person; that is, does he or she have any remaining capacity to test reality, or does the person have such a bizarre and well-formed delusional system that it could justify homicidal violence?
5. Does the person have a well-defined plan and access to some means (e.g., a weapon) to carry out this plan?

A disturbed person's personal history can help the clinician to assess potential dangerousness, because a person's past behavior is the best indicator of future behavior, for example:

1. Does the person come from a violent family background, in which he or she witnessed domestic violence?
2. Was he or she the victim of abuse or brutality in some form?
3. Has the person ever been placed out of the home (removed from the parents' care), or did the parents die or abandon the child in some way?
4. Has the person exhibited the "triad" of fire-setting, cruelty to animals, and bed-wetting?
5. Does the person have a history of violence or stalking behavior?
6. Is there a recent history of some form of domestic violence?

Finally, because driving a car can offer a symbolic outlet for aggression, a history of frequent accidents or incidents of drunken or reckless driving may suggest poorly controlled impulses and greater risk of violent behavior.

If a clinician discovers that the disturbed person is carrying a weapon, the first thing to bear in mind is the likelihood that the person is carrying it to protect himself or herself from *other* people. Although the sight of a weapon may be very frightening to a clinician, a clinician should not lose sight of the fact that people who need weapons are fundamentally frightened, insecure people. Thus, the therapist should be extremely careful not to do anything that this person would view as aggressive or frightening. It may seem paradoxical, but a person who carries a weapon is more afraid of the clinician than vice versa, because the person must carry a weapon in order to feel safe. With this concept in mind, it may be easier for a therapist to negotiate with an agitated client who is carrying a weapon, because the fear and desperation that lie behind it can be understood clearly.

It is wiser to ask *why* the person is carrying a weapon than to request that he or she surrender it. After learning why the person is carrying a weapon, a therapist can attempt to convince the person that it is not necessary, because he or she will not be harmed. A clinician may then say that he or she would be more comfortable if the person handed over the weapon or placed it on the table. Under no circumstances should the therapist try to disarm a person. If the person refuses to relinquish a weapon, the therapist should *back away* and see to it that this problem is turned over to the police or to a hospital security service.

Finally, a vital component in assessing a person's dangerousness is how well he or she responds to the offer of therapeutic assistance. A person who is receptive to help and has the support of family and friends is a better risk

than someone who is resistant to help and does not have a well-function-
ing support network.

A Case Study

We were called by a police Watch Commander at eight one evening and
asked to send someone to the police station. The Watch Commander
explained that a young man had wandered into the station and was behaving very strangely. He did not know what to do with the man, although he
obviously had a problem. When the therapist arrived, he was shown into
an office where Richard McMillan was waiting. The Watch Commander
introduced the clinician and asked Richard if he would tell his story. At
first, Richard was suspicious, complaining that he had already told his
story three times. The therapist reassured Richard that he had come to
the station for the purpose of helping him, and that this would be the last
time he would have to tell his story. After some hesitation, accompanied by
exaggerated gestures, he agreed to tell the story once more.

Richard said that a man who was impersonating his father was living in
his father's mobile home. When the therapist asked him what he thought
had happened, his answer was that he didn't know, but he knew that the
man was not his real father. Richard said that, although his father had
blue eyes, the impersonator's eyes were brown. When the therapist asked
him if the man looked like his father, Richard replied, while gesturing and
grimacing, that this impersonator was extremely clever and knew a lot, but
that his car was the wrong color. When the therapist asked if there were
friends or relatives living in the area who could identify his father, Richard
explained that all of his relatives were impostors. He said they were clever,
too, and, although they thought they knew all about him, they were really
lying. Although they were friendly to him and often invited him to visit
and have dinner, he knew they were being nice so that he would not expose
them. Richard added that these relatives would try to bring up his "past,"
but that it didn't matter. The therapist asked what those people would try
to bring up. At that, Richard became very agitated and exclaimed, "We just
won't talk about that because it has nothing to do with this."

The clinician explained that he and Richard would have to figure out a
way to obtain proof of whether or not his father or those other people were
impostors. At first, Richard objected because he felt it was not necessary
since he already had proof that they were impostors. Even so, the therapist
explained, it would be better for legal reasons to decide upon some positive
means of identification. The therapist asked Richard if he would draw up
a list of names of the relatives whom he thought were being impersonated,
and if he would supply the address, telephone number, and a description

of each of those people. Richard hesitated, initially, to give addresses and telephone numbers because he was afraid that someone would call or visit the relatives. He said that they would be very angry if anyone called them late at night. When the therapist offered to telephone only during the day-time, Richard gave him the numbers. When the therapist asked Richard if he lived nearby and if he had a job, he replied that he had been living in this area for four months and had just moved into a hotel nearby; he did not have a job, but, instead, received an income from Social Security. Richard added that he was completely alone and desperately wanted to find his "real" father.

The clinician told Richard that there probably wasn't much more they could do that night, especially because he was reluctant to permit anyone to telephone the people who were impersonating his family. The therapist decided to invite one of the (alleged) relatives to visit our office next morning, so that Richard could identify him or her. Although he was still somewhat suspicious, Richard reluctantly agreed to the meeting. The clinician's pur-pose in arranging this meeting was to gain additional information because, despite the fact that his behavior was quite bizarre and clearly delusional, Richard was not at that time so disturbed that he required hospitalization.

When the therapist asked if he had thought about finding another place in which to live than his hotel room, Richard answered that he was look-ing for a place and "for a lady to live with." He said he had thought about finding a halfway house temporarily, so that he would not be alone. We told Richard that we could possibly help him find a halfway house where he could stay until he found a job and an apartment. The therapist took the name and telephone number of Richard's hotel and said that he would call him before noon the next day. When the clinician offered to walk with him to his hotel, Richard appeared to be greatly relieved that someone was trying to help him. The therapist thought that Richard, although schizo-phrenic, was still functioning on a level at which he could be treated as an outpatient. He wanted to find a placement for Richard in a halfway house, and enroll him in a day treatment program to prevent the young man's schizophrenic episode from escalating.

As the therapist and Richard walked along toward the hotel, Richard became increasingly fearful. He stopped outside the hotel door and said, "Please, could we talk some more? I don't want to go back because I won't sleep." Richard asked if they could go to a bar around the corner, have a beer, and talk a while longer; he seemed much relieved when the therapist agreed. The therapist stayed there a while with Richard, reassuring him that he would not be deserted. When he asked Richard if he had taken some kind of medication before, Richard replied that he had but couldn't remember the names of the drugs; besides, it didn't matter because he was never going to take drugs again. He talked at length about the fact that his mother had died and how much he missed her. Although Richard was 26 years old, his speech and manner were those of a confused, 12-year-old boy. After about an hour's conversation, he said that he thought he could go back to the hotel and sleep.

The next day the clinician began trying to locate members of Richard's family and to find a halfway house for him. Eventually he located an older brother named Ralph, a married man who lived nearby, and also found a halfway house that had a vacancy. The only requirement for admission was that the client appear voluntarily for a psychological interview and a financial interview. The staff felt it important that potential clients initiate contact with the house, as a demonstration of their motivation.

The therapist then telephoned Richard and told him he had spoken with his alleged brother Ralph and that Ralph would be willing to come to our office in the afternoon of the next Saturday. He added that, in this meeting, they would be able to identify Ralph as either an impostor or as Richard's real brother. When Richard agreed to come to the meeting, the clinician told him about the halfway house placement. Richard was not particularly excited about the latter idea, reiterating that he would rather find a woman to live with, but he said that he would think about the suggestion.

By the end of that week, Richard had still resisted telephoning the halfway house, despite several attempts by the clinician to get him to do so. When Richard arrived at the office for Saturday's meeting, the therapist placed a long-distance telephone call to Richard's (alleged) father. Richard spent some time talking with the father and, when he finally asked him to meet with him and the therapist at some later time, the father agreed. Richard's only comment after the lengthy telephone conversation was, "He's a pretty good impostor." The meeting between Richard and his brother Ralph was not a successful one—the brother suddenly became extremely angry and left, saying that he was "through" with Richard and his "crazy nonsense." The therapist guessed that a show of warm acceptance and concern, suddenly being transformed into angry rejection, was a typical dynamic in the family system.

A meeting was arranged between Richard and his father, and this meeting repeated the same acceptance-rejection theme that had characterized the earlier one between him and his brother. The therapist learned that Richard's father had, some years ago, spent 10 months in a state mental hospital; he apparently felt insecure and ashamed of that illness and hospitalization. In the meeting, the father would coldly reject Richard (because he reminded him of his own schizophrenic break), and then feel guilty for rejecting him and make vaguely fatherly gestures. But, when Richard responded to his father's overtures of friendship and tried to feel closer to him, the father would reject him again. Throughout the meeting, the father's manner was brusque and businesslike, whereas Richard obviously expected that his father would indicate some concern. The father did not say it, but he made it perfectly clear that he wanted nothing to do with Richard. He stayed for about half of the scheduled 1-hour appointment and then left, claiming that he had to go to a business meeting.

Following these rejections by both his brother and his father, Richard's condition began to worsen. The clinician was reluctant to permit him to remain in an unsupervised living situation, but Richard had neither family nor friends to help or lend their support at that time. For that reason, the clinician repeatedly urged him to enter the halfway house. Richard stubbornly refused, insisting that he had to find his real father. The therapist finally decided to hospitalize Richard involuntarily because he was deteriorating rapidly, to the extent that he could no longer care for himself properly. When this decision was made, the therapist made the necessary preparations before informing Richard about them, because he was aware of Richard's intense feelings against hospitalization. The hospital had been called and the case discussed with an on-duty psychiatrist who assured the therapist that there would be an available bed in a locked ward. The therapist asked that the hospital have two strong ward attendants at the ready, should assistance be needed, because Richard was above average in size and quite athletic.

When the clinician presented this plan for hospitalization to Richard, he became quite agitated and began pacing around the office. At this point, the therapist rang for assistance; when two of our staff members arrived for help, Richard jumped up, grabbed a cup from the therapist's desk, and smashed it in defiance. But, when he saw that the staff members were determined, he agreed to go to the hospital. The therapist accompanied Richard through the entire hospitalization process. He visited regularly and had several consultations with the staff of the psychiatric ward. At first, Richard was extremely resistant to treatment, but after about a week he began to make progress. When Richard was to be transferred out of the locked facility, the therapist was consulted in the decision about where he should be sent. Richard agreed voluntarily to enter an unlocked residential facility that provides aftercare treatment for patients who had once been acutely disturbed.

Richard responded well to treatment. Even his brother Ralph commented that he could not remember when he had seen Richard "in such good shape." The brother also made some progress in establishing a better relationship with Richard. Even so, the attitude of Richard's father toward his son did not change. Richard subsequently made several telephone calls to us to express his thanks and to tell the therapist about his progress.

A Case Illustrating That Things Are Not Always What They Appear to Be

Dan Wilson was a 51-year-old chronic alcoholic who was first brought to our attention by a police officer who had become his friend about 2 years before. Unknown to any of Wilson's family or friends, he had noticed that a growth on his upper lip had become inflamed and enlarged. He went to his physician, who referred him to a surgeon. The surgeon looked at him briefly and said he thought that Wilson had a carcinoma on his lip; he would have to go into a hospital the following week for surgery. After the surgeon said that, he excused himself to see another patient. Wilson was told to talk with the secretary, who would make the necessary arrangements for his hospitalization. Because Wilson had heard of carcinoma, he thought that he had an incurable cancer, that the operation would disfigure him greatly, and that he would soon die an agonizing death.

Wilson purchased a gun after he left the surgeon's office, and later that evening he began drinking heavily. He attempted suicide by driving his car into a cement wall at high speed. The car was wrecked, but, miraculously, Wilson was not hurt. The next day his family (son and daughter-in-law) tried to get him to enter the alcoholism ward of a local Veterans Hospital, but when they took him to the hospital he became frightened and refused to commit himself. Thereupon, the family members became so angry with him that they left him at the hospital.

Wilson walked several miles to the house of a friend, who drove him home. As soon as he was home, he called his son and told him that he had a gun, and, if anyone tried to hospitalize him, he would shoot anyone who came near him and then commit suicide. The son, in turn, called Wilson's police officer friend because he thought that his father had simply gone crazy and needed to be locked up. When the officer telephoned Wilson, he repeated his threat that he planned to barricade himself in his home and commit suicide. The officer then called us for assistance, and two therapists who were on duty met him at Wilson's house. The three of them began talking with Wilson through the front door. With time, the story about the feared carcinoma came out; it became clear that Wilson was not a violent person who wanted to harm others. Instead, he was terrified about the growth on his lip causing him to be horribly disfigured and, eventually, suffering a painful, prolonged, and terminal illness. The clinicians eventually convinced Wilson that he had other options and that he should at least obtain a second medical opinion. Grudgingly, he agreed to go voluntarily to the psychiatric ward of a general hospital (by then he was completely sober).

When the two therapists visited Wilson at the hospital that evening, they found him to be an extremely pleasant man. He said that he was very sorry that he had caused everyone so much trouble, but he was obviously fighting very hard to control his terror about the cancer on his face. He recalled that the surgeon had told him that he had a carcinoma and that half of his entire upper lip would have to be removed. One of the therapists then suggested that the general hospital staff could help him find another surgeon. Wilson agreed that it would be sensible to consult another surgeon and added that, at one time, he had worked as a surgical technician. He had seen too many cancer operations that were not successful. He appeared to be somewhat relieved to be able to talk about his fears concerning the operation.

After this interview with Wilson, the therapists believed that he was still suicidal. They asked the head nurse not to release him until after a second surgeon had evaluated the growth on his face. She agreed, saying that she would find someone to accompany him to visit a surgeon's office. The next day, Wilson was examined by a highly regarded cancer specialist.

Two days later, Wilson called one of the therapists to report that he had seen the specialist, who had taken enough time to explain the problem to him. The surgeon had said that, although he could not be sure whether or not the growth was a carcinoma until he did a biopsy, he would remove the growth in his office and then conduct a biopsy. The surgeon added that Wilson would have the biopsy results by the following week; if the growth were a carcinoma, he would take a little more tissue out to be sure that all was removed.

Dan Wilson called us again on two occasions. The first time, he told us that the operation had gone well. With the second call, he reported that the biopsy had shown that he did not have a carcinoma. In this case, a suicide or barricaded situation had been prevented, an involuntary hospitalization had been avoided, and the main contributing factor to an alcoholic binge had been identified and alleviated.

CHAPTER 5

Assessing the Risk of Dangerousness

Clinicians are sometimes called on to evaluate threats and the risk of dangerousness or violent behavior in nonclinical situations such as potential workplace violence. Instances such as those of domestic violence or child abuse, which have nothing to do with deciding whether or not to hospitalize, may cast the clinician in new roles that require extraordinary approaches to intervention. Many therapists have not been specifically trained to evaluate people in situations such as these, nor to conduct the threat assessment procedures that these situations may require.

Many potentially dangerous people live and work within the "normal" spectrum and wear well-crafted façades until one or more "triggers" bring the violence to the surface. For example, his or her stalking or predatory behavior may have gone undetected for years, or might even have been rationalized away by a victim or witness to it. Furthermore, although many of these people have diagnosable conditions, those conditions may be well hidden and, unlike most clients in a clinical setting, even manipulative or angry ones, they are not looking for help in the traditional way. They may, in fact, view others as being in the wrong: they are the ones who need help—not them.

In some instances, a clinician may be asked to evaluate people such as these from afar, as, for example, from threatening letters, emails, or phone messages. It may be necessary to read reports of witnesses to the alleged threatening behavior, simply because it is impossible to meet with the possibly dangerous person.

Cultural Issues and Misinterpretations

When one assesses a threat, potential violence, or dangerousness, one should be extremely sensitive to cultural issues and intercultural differences. Cultures differ so widely in appropriate expressions of anger or frustration, that what may be a perfectly acceptable greeting in one culture may be perceived as insulting and condescending in another. The English language lacks the built-in social information that many other languages have. North Americans are very quick to use first names as a sign of friendship or familiarity. By contrast, in some cultures it would be extremely insulting if one addressed a person by his or her first name, unless they knew each other well or the speaker had been invited to do so. This is especially true if the person being greeted was older than the person speaking, and the meeting was in a public setting.

It has been our experience that many mistaken or misperceived threats are caused by cross-cultural failures of communication or misunderstanding. Nonverbal circumstances such as touching or distance from the other person hold both obvious and subtle meanings that, if misinterpreted, could lead to serious conflict or resentment.

When evaluating a crisis situation in which potential threat is involved, if one or more of the people in crisis are of different cultures than the clinician, he or she should seek out training or consultation about the differing culture—including its customs and social rules. When clinical consultants are not available, local college or university language or anthropology departments, or certified court translators, can be good resources for consultation.

Who Becomes Violent: Myths and Realities

Potentially violent people (e.g., psychopaths or sociopaths) are fortunately rare in our culture. The DSM-IV labels them as having Antisocial Personality Disorders, and estimates that approximately 3 percent of males and approximately one percent of females can be diagnosed with this label. In our experience, "normal" people become violent when, in certain situations, they feel humiliated or desperate or "cornered" by some provocation they cannot evade. There is, of course, greater potential for violence when the person is impaired by alcohol or a drug, or by stress or trauma.

Related mental illness and character disorders that may lie beneath the surface of violent people include:

- Borderline Personality Disorder
- Narcissistic Personality Disorder
- Histrionic Personality Disorder
- Paranoid Personality Disorder
- Bipolar I Disorder (Manic Phase)
- Intermittent Explosive Disorder

It is imperative that each of these conditions be also considered when making a diagnosis. Furthermore, there is often an obsessive-compulsive element in the personalities of violent or antisocial people; in such cases, the person should be considered as posing a higher risk of acting-out, because he or she may lack the ability to "let go" of a situation and see it in perspective.

Stalking

Stalking is the toxic blend of narcissism, obsessive-compulsive behavior, and a thought disorder such as paranoia. Stalkers also may exhibit symptoms such as those associated with schizotypal or borderline personality disorders. The obsessive-compulsive and narcissistic components are predominant, supplying the driving forces in this form of pathology. If a clinician determines that stalking of a client is taking place, it is vital that any form of communication between the victim and stalker cease at once. A common mistake that stalking victims make is to continue trying to communicate with stalkers, in the belief that they can convince a stalker to stop the stalking behavior voluntarily and go away. Such well-intended attempts to alleviate the situation are doomed to fail; in most instances, they make the situation much worse.

Because the stalker does not want to hear the "Go away. Leave me alone." message, he or she will twist and distort the message in a way that supports his or her delusion, such as "She does not really mean it; she just can't express how she really feels." There is also a myth to the effect that only women are erotomanic or delusional stalkers who believe that the victim is in love with them; the fact is that twice as many men as women are erotomanic stalkers. Even though male stalkers tend to be more violent than female stalkers, one should never underestimate the violence potential of women.

Stalking behavior can occur in many forms. The following behaviors should be considered to be stalking if the person engaging in the behavior persists despite requests from the victim to stop:

1. Following, investigating, spying
2. Incessant phone calls
3. Repeated e-mails, text messages, letters by mail, notes pinned on the door, and so on
4. Sending gifts or cards
5. Appearing at the person's home or workplace
6. Secretly taking photographs or videotaping
7. Entering the home and leaving signs that he or she had been there

Other forms of harassment often committed by stalkers include spreading rumors or making false accusations about the victim, or harming relatives or loved ones or pets of the victim. In some cases, stalking evolves into overt acts of aggression, such as:

- Kidnapping or imprisonment
- Physical or sexual assault
- Vandalism or arson

Our experience reveals that some of the more subtle forms of stalking, which can be absolutely terrifying to the victim, may be misunderstood by the criminal justice system and even dismissed as frivolous complaints by hysterical persons. In one instance, a judge denied the request of a victim who wanted the judge to sanction the stalker for leaving flowers and a card at her door. Rather than charge the stalker for violating a restraining order, the judge admonished her, saying, "He was just trying to be nice and apologize." This was far, far from the reality of what the stalker was attempting to do. The message that he sent was "I can enter your territory, and you can do nothing to stop me."

The Person Who Makes False Allegations of Stalking

Although it is naturally rare, we have encountered instances in which people have made false allegations of stalking. Initially, the story can be quite convincing, but, over time, the accounts become less and less plausible. A telltale sign of the fictitious allegation of stalking is an attempt to undermine or sabotage efforts to catch or stop the stalker. An example of this was when a company installed a hidden surveillance camera in a woman's office to catch the employee who was leaving violent, graphic pornography on her desk. Although she was given clear instructions about how to turn on the camera, she repeatedly forgot to do so—especially on the occasions when the pornography had appeared. There were other occasions in which, she claimed, sadomasochistic material appeared on her desk. Rather than turn the offensive objects over to Corporate Security, she threw it into the trash. Thus, no one could check it for fingerprints or try to determine its source.

People who have genuinely been stalked may make well-intended but misguided attempts to convince the stalkers to leave them alone. But, they are genuinely afraid and want protection, so they are cooperative with reasonable attempts to protect them.

Assessing Threats, Dangerousness, and Risk of Violent Behavior

There are very few indiscriminately violent people. Most people who become violent are violent in situations that involve at least one person with whom he or she has, or has had, a relationship; or, situations in which violence, fueled by fear, offers a way of escape from being hurt, caught, exposed, or exploited in some way; or, there is some political or religious target. Most violent behavior does not suddenly occur without warning (with the exception of cases of psychopathy, sociopathy, Intermittent Explosive Disorder, or terrorism). Many violent people are capable of compartmentalizing their violent sides, so that people around them think that they know them but they don't. Some create this façade deliberately, hiding behind it with grim determination. They do it by such means as being devoutly religious or immersing themselves in charitable work, so that their public persona is that of "nice guy," in that way blending in with the rest of us.

To assess the threat of violence, we have developed a system of four levels of threat intensity.

Type One: Low Risk

1 . Conscious versus Unconscious Issues

When evaluating people for violence potential, try to find out if they are aware of what circumstances stimulate them to anger. (Clinicians should be keenly aware that one may be dealing with a truly psychopathic chameleon; so, to be sure, he or she should review any collateral information before making a decision about this level of risk.); people who are at a low level of threat have logical explanations for their anger; they are consciously aware of what has made them angry; they are not driven by unconscious issues, and there is no evidence of dissociation.

2. Empathy for Others

These people understand how their behavior has affected other people and have genuine empathy for others; they have a sense of remorse or understanding that there will be consequences for their actions.

3. Not Grandiose or "Entitled"

These people do not have an inflated sense of self-worth. They realize that some of their past behavior has been inappropriate.

4. Intact Cognition

Cognitive processes not compromised by:

- Drugs
- Alcohol
- Low level of intelligence
- Thought disorder

5. No History of Violence

This must be corroborated by collateral data.

6. They are aware of the negative consequences of their violent behavior.

7. There are no cultural, social, or religious issues that support or condone violent behavior in a situation such as the one in question.

8. When a clinician analyzes the situation, their anger can be understood.

9. The person does not have access to weapons.

Type Two: Some Risk of Violence

1. Poor awareness of stressors or provoking issues; possible unconscious issues; poor recall of events suggesting that they may not always be aware of others or their actions.

2. Limited empathy for others, with some self-serving elements.

3. Sensitive to stress or provocation: these people have self-control but it has limits, and they usually blame others when things turn out badly; people may describe them as abrasive, difficult, or odd.

4. Self-important: these people are self-absorbed and are able to rationalize their behavior; their abilities to accept blame are limited.

5. Cognition may be impaired by:

- Excessive drinking
- Drug use
- Limited intelligence or insight

6. One or more past episodes of:

- Inappropriate behavior
- Aggressive behavior
- Impulsive behavior
- Inappropriate anger

7. Some, but limited awareness of the consequences of his or her behavior.
8. Possible cultural, social, or religious issues that support violent behavior in certain situations.
9. Obsessive-compulsive tendencies may be present but not to the degree of a trait or characteristic.
10. A suspicious nature.
11. Some access to or knowledge of weapons, or a history of physical altercations.

Type Three: Serious Risk for Violent Behavior

1. Not delusional, but not consciously aware of what provokes their acting-out behavior; these people are able to rationalize their violent behavior as a reasonable response; there are fairly strong obsessive-compulsive aspects to their behavior, so, they also may exhibit similarities to stalkers; they may harass by sending letters, calling incessantly, or sending e-mails to their victims or their significant others; this harassing behavior may be a step on the way to violence.
2. Little or no insight into how their behavior upsets or frightens other people.
3. An entitled or inflated sense of self-worth or importance, which enables them to rationalize their inappropriate behavior as justified.
4. Cognitive processes impaired by:
   - Excessive drinking
   - Drug use
   - Limited intelligence or insight
5. The degree of their expressed anger is inappropriate to the situation.
6. Limited awareness of the consequences for their violent behavior
7. A paranoid delusional system that is beginning to focus on specific people or groups or, in more serious cases, has actually focused on specific people or groups.
8. Cultural, social, or religious beliefs that support their violent behavior.
9. A history of aggressive, inappropriate, or violent behavior.
10. Access to and familiarity with weapons, and a history of violent or stalking behavior.

Type Four: Lethal Risk of Violent Behavior

1. These people are driven by unconscious, delusional issues, such as voices, messages from God or other "worlds;" the obsessive-compulsive aspect of their personalities has become so strong that they are not able to stop or control themselves.
2. They feel no empathy for others; their behavior is totally rationalized and justified in a manner that clearly shows no empathy or understanding of others.
3. They possess a grandiose or entitled sense of self-worth or self-importance.
4. Cognition is severely compromised by:
   • Drugs, alcohol
   • Thought disorder, that is, psychiatric thought processes
   • Organicity or limited intelligence;
5. No awareness of or concern for consequences for their behavior; in fact, they feel justified, or that they will be praised or rewarded for their actions.
6. A focused, paranoid delusional system.
7. Cultural, social, religious beliefs that justify violence and would reward their actions.
8. A history of violent or aggressive behavior.
9. Access to and an understanding of weapons.

Domestic Violence

It is tragic that, other than war, domestic violence is the most prevalent form of violence among humans. Cultural and religious differences notwithstanding, clinicians around the world struggle with the same phenomenon (see Barrett and La Violette, 1993; Chalk and King, 1998; Dutton, 1992; Hansen and Harway, 1993; Herman, 1992; McGrath, Keita,

Struckland, and Russo, 1990; Yllo, 1993; Antonopoulou, 1999; Courtois, 2004; Paul, 2004).

The Scope of the Problem

Family violence is still considered by many to be a "private affair" or an event that "doesn't happen" in nice families. It is even condoned in some cultures and by some religions. Often participants (both victim and perpetrator) will go to great lengths to conceal the violence within their family from outsiders. We have observed that persons may publicly disapprove of violent behavior that they may privately permit or excuse. Similarly, we have observed the "Jekyl and Hyde" type of husband who is at one moment friendly and affable, particularly in public, but later, in private, can suddenly become violent to his family. As a consequence of the abuser's façade, people do not believe that he is capable of abuse and do not support the victim. Jacobson and Gottman (1998) studied 200 couples in which serious domestic violence occurred. They describe two types of batterers: the "pit bull" type of person who is quick to explode into violence and is obviously a batterer; the other is the "cobra" type of person who is calculating and often is able to hide violence. The "cobra" methodically humiliates and inflicts pain on his victim, but whereas the "pit bull" may be more frightening, the "cobra" can be more dangerous if unrecognized.

Only recently have many people been willing to acknowledge the extent of domestic violence. For centuries, the family realm has been considered to be a sanctum that no one, least of all a person from outside the family, had a right to invade. When wife-beating and other forms of intrafamily violence were first brought into the open, they were often dismissed as rare occurrences, except in poor or foreign families. Or they were blamed on "provocative" women who really wanted or needed to be "put in their place" once in a while.

A major factor that has contributed to family violence internationally is the fragmentation of families. Modern industrial society has inexorably caused the large, extended family group to break down into smaller, nuclear families. We have noticed that there tends to be less violence in the large, extended family. When there is fragmentation, the support system that often serves to prevent intrafamily conflict soon disappears. Without grandparents, uncles and aunts, cousins, et al., the nuclear family is a "private place" where feelings of hurt, anger, and frustration can become acutely focused on one or two people. Because the nuclear family can become progressively more isolated from relatives, fewer and fewer people will be aware of whether or not violence is taking place within the home.

Most of us would prefer to think that violent acts such as wife-beating and child abuse take place only in "sick" or deviant families. This commonly held misconception further serves to isolate the victims of family violence, so that they tend to think that violent acts are only being done to them. And, because violence can only be happening to them, something must be wrong with them. A possible source of this commonly-held myth may have been found by Steinmetz and Strauss (1974), whose classic study surveyed the mass media (especially television and movies) to see how domestic violence was portrayed; they discovered that violence was never portrayed by a "normal" or average family. By contrast, when family violence did occur on screen, the acting-out person was portrayed as a deviant, a criminal, or a foreigner. In this respect, there has been some progress, but the myth still prevails.

Many would prefer to believe that violent families are ethnically different or, at the very least, from a different social class than theirs, but our clinical experience clearly indicates that domestic violence occurs in each class of every culture. Even homicide is intraclass and intrarace, and in a majority of cases occurs within the family constellation. Apparently, violence tends to be "closer to home" than most of us would prefer to believe. We are more vulnerable to violence in the midst of friends and relatives than with the (mythical) stranger of another race. Possible origins of the misconception being described here are complex. One may be that many practitioners have difficulty in accepting and understanding the fact that "normal" people, like themselves, in certain circumstances could be violent toward their spouses or children or close friends. It may have been this same reluctance that, in the past, caused some clinicians to relegate true accusations of incest to the realm of fantasy, because the subject of incest was too unpleasant for them to face as reality.

A further indication of our reluctance to view family violence candidly is the fact that this species of behavior was not a common topic of public concern, academic research, or even discussion by therapists until at least 1962, when Kempe, et al., published their landmark paper on battered children in the United States, or until 1974 when Pizzey published her dramatic *Scream Quietly or the Neighbors Will Hear*. Since then, several events have brought the unpleasant subject of family violence forcefully before the public eye; for example, (1) the National Commission on the Causes and Prevention of Violence was formed after the Kennedy and King assassinations, and it produced startling information on the nature and extent of violence in American life; (2) the women's movement served to raise the public's consciousness that many women were victims of violent assault in their own homes; and, (3) furthermore, it has become known, in recent years, that family violence is the reason behind a majority of calls to police departments. Perhaps it was because of the horror of the O. J. Simpson case that laws concerning domestic violence began to change.

One factor that we have found to be strongly associated with family violence is substance abuse. In fact, in the majority of our cases of intrafamily violence, alcoholism or another form of substance abuse is a contributing factor (see also Fals-Stewart, et al., 2003, 2005). That is not to say that substance abuse is, by itself, a direct cause of family violence, but alcohol or other kinds of drugs do tend to interfere with people's ability to control themselves under stressful conditions; in effect, they permit fear, anger, or jealousy, which had been controlled and hidden below the surface, to erupt into violent acting-out.

Although it should be reiterated that it is not our opinion that family violence is a product of social class or culture, it has been noted by others who are involved in the study of violence that relatively more people in working-class and lower-income families are found to experience violence in the home. The reason for this is not that these people are inherently more violent, but, rather, that working-class and lower-income families are more vulnerable to social pressures such as those caused by unemployment and financial insecurity, overcrowded housing, unplanned pregnancy, and a host of other problems. As a result of these pressures, they sometimes turn on each other and victimize each other. In addition, working-class families cannot afford the private services that middle- and upper-class families can, and thus they are more likely to take their problems to a public agency, thereby becoming a part of the record-keeping system and public statistics. It is also our opinion, and that of others, that interventions in domestic violence cases need to be culturally sensitive if they are to succeed (Valencia and Van Hoorne, 1999; Fawcett, Heise Isita–Espegel, and Pick, 1999; Antonopoulou, 1999; Kozie, 1999).

A most significant factor in the etiology of family violence, as reported in a large body of research in the United States and abroad, is that the more violence a child experiences when growing up, the greater the likelihood that the child will become a violent adult. What a sad fact it is that these, the children of violent families, will probably become the violent adults, spouses, and parents of tomorrow, unless something is done in a humane and realistic way to stop the tragic cycle.

Couples Who Fight Violently

Many disagreements between the partners of a couple result in violent fights in which one strikes or hurls an object in the direction of the other. This kind of chronic violent fighting is a quite different phenomenon from the battered wife syndrome. The present section is confined to a discussion of chronic fighting between spouses; battering is described in a later section.

Violent behavior is likely to occur when some factor (or interaction of factors) that normally prevents acting-out decreases in strength. Or the person who becomes violent may have had poor impulse control in the first place. Some factors that may cause a breakdown of control are chemical (i.e., drugs or alcohol) and some are neurophysiological (e.g., brain damage), whereas others are psychological and sociological. The following analysis focuses on the psychological, communicational, and sociological factors that lead to violence.

In describing family violence, the word "escalation" is commonly used. Unfortunately, this term has come to have more than one meaning, and it will be useful to distinguish between the two meanings and define the term precisely as it is to be used here. Watzlawick et al. (1967) used "escalation" to describe a type of pathology that occurs in "symmetrical relationships" (see Chapter 2) in which either partner in a relationship can become extremely uncomfortable if the relationship is perceived as the slightest bit "unequal." This form of competitiveness is often referred to as the "I can do anything better than you can" aspect of a symmetrical relationship. A second sense in which the term "escalation" is used refers to the exacerbation of an ordinary life difficulty into what begins to be experienced as a problem; this can occur when the way in which people choose to deal with a difficulty merely serves to intensify it. As Weakland et al. wrote, "The action meant to alleviate the behavior of the other party aggravates it; the 'cure' becomes worse than the 'disease'" (1974, p. 149). This second usage of the term "escalation" is actually closer in meaning to the term "intensification." Yet, there is a connection between how the term "escalation" was originally used (to describe the excessive competition in a symmetrical relationship) and the second usage of the term, that is, when a "commonsense" remedy turns an everyday difficulty into a major problem. The connection is that an initial, unconscious exacerbation of some minor difficulty or disagreement can bring to the awareness of the family (or couple) a major problem. This awareness having occurred, there often ensues a highly motivated struggle for control. It is in that sense—of a chain of events, sometimes intentionally and sometimes unintentionally begun, which leads to a very conscious struggle for control of the situation—that the term "escalation" will be used in the following discussion.

One way in which escalation can occur is by means of the violation of "family rules" or patterns. Such rules may be unspoken and idiosyncratic to each family, by contrast with the more commonly held family rules such as fidelity, privacy, and parental authority. Certain family rules are consciously acknowledged and others are not. Examples of some of the more subtle rules are the total avoidance of certain topics (or their avoidance in the presence of certain people), and the family myth or "shared untruth" that family members secretly agree to accept and protect. Family rules also may involve the status or power of certain family members. Violation of any one of these rules, whether of the consciously acknowledged or the unconscious variety, may instigate the process of escalation. That is especially likely when one member of the family attempts to repair the damage or restore the family status quo by a commonsense (i.e., misguided) remedy.

Usually, an escalation will proceed in differing ways depending on whether the broken rule was of the conscious or unconscious variety. Violation of a consciously acknowledged rule is more likely to lead to an immediate outburst of anger, whereas violation of an unconscious rule is more likely to result in a delayed outburst. The fact that a slower escalation should result from the violation of rules that are followed without conscious awareness is understandable, because a person who is on the "receiving end" of the rule-breaking (called here the "recipient") only becomes aware of the broken rule later on (after it has been broken); not until then do the resulting feelings of hurt or anger surface. In effect, the one who vaguely suspects that a rule has been broken may feel uneasy, wronged, or in some sense "violated," without being able to articulate to others precisely why. This recipient may retaliate with anger toward the rule-breaker and feel quite justified in doing so. Furthermore, the recipient may not be able to articulate clearly any acceptable "reason" when he or she is directly challenged on this point by the rule-breaker, because the recipient probably feels "right" in having retaliated. And, because the retaliation appeared to have no justification discernible to the rule-breaker, the rule-breaker may then retaliate in kind, because of being "attacked for no reason."

Thus do spouses or two family members often become indignant combatants, each one claiming to be the innocent victim of the other's provocation. What both fail to realize is that each is right in a sense, and each is wrong to a degree. Each person is responding to a stimulus that was provided by the other, and, naturally, each will prefer to interpret an escalation sequence in a way that can support his or her view of the reality of the situation. This kind of situation is even more complex and difficult to decode when one person holds one set of unconscious rules and the other holds a conflicting set of rules. Then, the two will continue their battle, as each excuses his or her own "responsive" behavior as justified by the "provocative" or "unjust" behavior of the other. Each person feels that he or she has been wronged by the other, but neither can clearly specify why or how it began. In this way, an interaction that begins by the breaking of an unconscious (or extremely subtle) rule can suddenly evolve into a very conscious and competitive struggle for power and control.

A salient psychological factor that we have observed as capable of provoking violent acting-out among couples is the conscious or unconscious manipulation of fear of loneliness or abandonment. People who already suspect that they are unloved or unlovable—partly because of the behavior of the loved one and partly because their early training caused them to doubt their lovability—are particularly vulnerable to real or imagined threats of abandonment. Because they are unable to face the prospect of this worst possible event (being abandoned), it is not surprising that a situation involving that kind of threat possesses a high potential for violent behavior. This is particularly true when other psychosocial factors (e.g., violent childhood role models, economic pressures, or fear of social humiliation) combine to tear down what controls the person may normally have been able to muster.

A stressful situation may be exacerbated further by the person's attempts to solve a problem by one or more of the well-intentioned, but potentially dangerous, commonsense remedies, for example: "If I hit her a couple of times, she will realize how much I love her;" "If I throw something at him he will know how much he has hurt me and stop;" or, "If I threaten to leave, it will scare him and he will change." Other commonsense myths that are sometimes believed by people who doubt their ability to be loved concern sexual matters, such as the notion that "sex is better after a fight." Notions of this kind are usually based on the feelings of one or both partners that one of them is not sexually adequate under more normal circumstances. So, the couple develops a pattern or set of rules based on the tacit agreement that intimacy will be preceded by a fight. But, if during one of these battles, staged as a prelude to intimacy, one person "strikes a nerve" by saying something truly wounding to the other, this "mock" fight can easily become quite violent and ugly.

Because anger is notoriously contagious, these pathetic commonsense measures, which are naively designed to elicit demonstrations of love and affection, can produce a paradoxical outcome. Actually, each partner, in order to respond in the desired manner, would have to know the feelings of fear and desperation that lay behind the other person's mask of angry behavior, requiring a degree of perceptiveness that is rare in these couples. In general, this sort of commonsense attempt to manipulate the other person to provide needed reassurance is doomed to fail because it requires that one angry person "read" the mind of another. The needs of the would-be manipulator are not going to be met for still another reason: many of these needs for nurturance on the part of an adult result from dependency needs that were not met as a child. Few of these needs can be adequately met by a marriage partner.

The following is an example of how a fight between two people can escalate when there are differing or conflicting perceptions of the reality of the situation. A couple in their late 20s was frequently involved in vicious fights. They had been married for 5 1/2 years, and, since the first 6 months of marriage, they had occasion to quarrel almost daily. About once every 2 months, their word fights erupted into physical confrontations that reached the threshold of actual violence. The problem, according to the wife, was that the husband ignored her and would not give her the affection she needed, so that she was forced to take extreme measures to make him pay attention to her. She periodically was reassured of his *need* for her by the outbursts of jealousy that she would consciously provoke in him when she became fearful. He, in turn, claimed that he was unable to be affectionate toward her because she constantly kept him at a distance. He said that when he was feeling most insecure and most fearful that she might be interested in another man, she would leave the house and refuse to tell him where she was going or when she would return. When he demanded to know where she was going, she would say, "Where I go and what I do are my business!" At this point, the husband would tear her away from the door and, usually, a heated struggle would follow.

Many family fights, which, on the surface, appear to involve an easily identifiable "victim" and an equally obvious "villain" (depending on which family member is asked), have their true origin in a shared, interactional context. Because family members and marital partners share considerable history, they have had plenty of opportunities to learn the behavior patterns that constitute family rules. In effect, the husband, in the case described earlier, had good reason to know that if he ignored or was not affectionate to his wife, she would become enraged—thus reassuring him that she needed his love. But, because he was not capable of providing her with the reassurance she needed, her fear and anger would continue to grow until she would make her provocative "parting speech;" to that, he would respond by trying to restrain her physically. By the time that happened, the wife would be far too enraged to see that her husband's attempts to restrain her were no more than a misguided attempt at affection. In the struggle, she would respond with still more rage and resist his restraint. The husband would retaliate by striking her to "make her realize" how much he loved her, so that she would not actually go.

The wife, also, had had plenty of opportunities to notice the pattern of her husband's jealous and violent responses to her parting speech. But, as mentioned earlier, two entirely different descriptions of the situation would be given, depending on which person was being questioned. To review, the wife's image of the situation was that of being a loving person who was ignored and emotionally starved by her cold, self-centered husband. His perception of reality was that he had tried to be affectionate to her in his way, but she had kept him at a distance by being vague and secretive.

The fact that these patterns of interaction had been going on for more than 5 years suggests that either partner could have interrupted the cycle, if either had perceived it as being too painful. The fact that neither did anything to stop the cycle of their increasingly more violent fights (at first, they were quite resistant to outside intervention, despite complaints from neighbors and several visits by the police), further suggests that some need was being satisfied by this repetitive pattern. For example, the husband may have acted so as to induce his wife to "jar" him out of his usually unexpressive, withdrawn shell of self-protection. Also, the husband's jealous rages provided the intensely dramatic, emotional display that the wife required to feel that she was loved by someone.

In order to treat such a couple successfully, a therapist should first decode the two disparate "realities." The clinician can then interpret how these two realities interact in a healthy way, as well as how they interact in a neurotic or destructive manner. Next, the therapist may explore what each person is capable of perceiving in respect to the other—considering the status of their current self-images. Because people tend to think in a more rigid manner when frightened or angry, each person's behavior will, in turn, need to be clarified, interpreted, and reframed; that is, put in terms that will fit within each person's cognitive set and will not threaten the current self-image of either. Finally, the therapist needs to encourage alternative behavior that will create new and healthier interactional patterns.

In the example of the couple described here, the therapist first focused on the transparent fact that the two partners actually cared for each other, but did not express their affection appropriately and did not request affection in terms that the other person could understand. The husband had been raised in a blue-collar family in which men were tough and not talkative; they expressed their affection by working hard and by being "good providers." Because of his background, he thought that he was being what a good husband should be, and he perceived himself as a loving husband. In addition, he thought that his wife's constant demands for attention or affection meant that she did not appreciate him.

The wife, by contrast, came from a family in which both the father and mother were alcoholics. She was forced to grow up quickly, in order to care for her younger siblings because her parents were seldom at home. She was attracted to her husband because she thought him a strong, stable, and loving man who would never abandon her as her parents had done. The clinician helped clarify that she had created an idyllic fantasy, the theme of which was that everyone outside her terrible family of origin was loving; once she left her parents' home, she thought, everything would be different. The therapist helped the husband to realize, as time went by, that it was all right—possibly even manly—to show affection. Eventually, the therapist helped this couple to communicate with each other in terms that each could understand and that would not require loss of face on the part of either person.

This case shows one typical way in which conflicting self-images may contribute to an interactional situation in which family rules can fuel the escalation of domestic violence. If the couple is especially unfortunate, these periodic eruptions of violence will satisfy enough of each person's needs so that each will allow it to continue. Occasionally, they will actively restart the cycle and resist any attempt to stop it from rolling relentlessly on.

Evaluating Risk Factors in Couples Who Fight Violently

1. How consciously aware is each person about what triggers his or her anger?
2. Are they able to establish and follow basic safety rules that the therapist will establish to stop escalation, for example, can they follow an agreed-upon signal to stop the argument for an established period, and separate long enough to calm down?
3. Can they agree that there will be times when they will disagree and that it does not have to be a win/lose situation?
4. Can the couple tolerate being able to take time out from each other, or are they too enmeshed?
5. Can the subject of jealousy be discussed in a rational way? Is a jealous partner able to realize that protracted interrogation will never resolve his or her jealousy; instead, it will inevitably make the situation worse? Can rules be established that interrogation is to be avoided?
6. Can the couple develop a safe way to vent or alleviate stress, for example, take a walk, write in a journal, hit a pillow?
7. Is there passive–aggressive, provocative behavior on the part of one or both people; if so, are they able to become aware of it, acknowledge

it as destructive, and stop it? Is each willing to listen to the other and stop it if the other points out this behavior?

Clinical and Ethical Issues

Evaluating and treating children, adolescents, or adults in families in which domestic violence or child abuse may have occurred raises many complex, clinical, ethical, and legal issues. Cases such as these often are fraught with strong emotions that affect the therapist. These cases often are extremely polarized, with each side attempting to influence or manipulate the clinician. Therapists often worry that, by reporting abuse, they may lose rapport or the client's trust. A child or adolescent may exclaim, "I'll never trust you again if you tell!" Because of this issue, the duty to report must be clearly explained in writing in the consent form, and reviewed orally before therapy begins. A clinician must always put the safety of the child (or elderly person) first, and make a report if abuse is suspected. With respect to evaluations, the fact that the clinician will be making a report and that the relationship is *not* confidential, must be stated clearly in writing; this written explanation also should clearly describe what is to be evaluated, and to whom the results or a report will be provided.

Treating clinicians should also remember to stay within their roles as therapists, not evaluators. Investigations or evaluations should be conducted by qualified experts who have a neutral role. A treating clinician who attempts to investigate or evaluate will be entering into a serious conflict of interest that may compromise his or her ability to treat. If a therapist, in the course of treatment, suspects abuse, he or she should report this to the proper authority or to an evaluator and let him or her investigate.

Evaluation of Suspected Cases of Violence

Evaluators should be sure that what is reported to them is true. To do so, one should attempt to review neutral, collateral information such as police reports, Child Protective Service reports, information from medical records, and so on. Police reports should be viewed with caution. An inexperienced clinician may believe that, if a police report or a protective service report has been made, the event described actually occurred, but this is not always true. Such reports contain basic intake data, generated only when someone has telephoned or come to a police department with a complaint. It offers no proof that any actual abuse has occurred. Only a subsequent investigation can substantiate the occurrence of abuse. An evaluation could be misled by a false accusation intended to bias the evaluation. This does not imply that clinicians should not pay attention to police or child protective reports, but they should appreciate their lack of probative value and be wary.

From another perspective, the absence of this type of report does not mean that there was no dangerous conflict in a home. If a clinician is evaluating domestic violence, he or she should attempt to obtain a record of possible police calls to the home. Often, such calls for service neither result in an actual report nor an arrest, but they may show a pattern of aggressive or problematic behavior in the home that may be very helpful to a clinician when evaluating the safety of a home.

In a study reviewing 9,000 divorce or custody cases, it was demonstrated that child sexual abuse allegations are no more prevalent in divorce and custody cases than in other types of cases. Moreover, intentionally false allegations occurred in no more than 8 percent of all such cases. The myth that abuse is commonly alleged and often falsely is still very widely held, and could lead to a serious clinical error and expose a child to harm.

Victims as Witnesses

Clinicians should be aware of the APA guidelines for "Psychologists Working With the Area of Interpersonal Violence" (2003, Section 2). As pointed out in that document, some of the people, both children and adults, with whom they work also may be witnesses in legal proceedings. As a consequence, it is essential that the clinician does not do anything clinically that could possibly contaminate, influence, or damage the person's ability to testify. This does not mean that a therapist should not talk about violent or abusive events with his or her client; but, when one does, he or she should be very careful to document what was said and who initiated the discussion. In complex or serious cases, it is wise to tape the sessions, so that no one can accuse the therapist of influencing or compromising testimony. We also have found that, if one focuses on how the person felt about the event, as opposed to the actual facts of the event, one can treat the person without affecting the testimony.

Repressed memories are a highly controversial subject, but it is the authors' experience (substantiated by APA reports from 1995, 1996a, and 1996b) that memories of this kind do exist and may be called back into one's recollection by present events. What is essential in such situations is that the clinician should proceed with great care and not assume that such memories are necessarily false or suspect. Our experience is that, in the majority of cases of repressed memory, there will be collateral information to support or deny the accuracy of the memory. It also is our experience that most people who have genuinely repressed memories are open to seeking collateral data, because they, too, want to understand what really happened.

A case illustrates this point quite clearly. A young woman was referred by her company's EAP. She had broken down at work; one of her coworkers found her huddled in the corner of the ladies' room. She was mumbling and speaking like a child. The coworker took her to her own office, and, as they walked, the young woman was obviously terrified and spoke vaguely about "Mommy" and "Daddy." When they got to the coworker's office, she insisted that the door be closed before she would speak. Her coworker called the EAP, and when a crisis counselor spoke with her by phone, she determined that the woman should be seen immediately. The coworker agreed to bring her to our office immediately.

When the woman met with the therapist, a history of events was revealed. Earlier that day, a manager in her company had sexually harassed and assaulted her. He had followed her to an isolated area and tried to molest her. She struggled to get free, but he grabbed her by the arm and pinned her against the wall. She continued to struggle. When she pulled free from him, he kept holding her arm and threw her across the room; she fell to the floor. He panicked and ran off while she stumbled to the ladies' room, where her coworker found her.

Although the situation definitely appeared to be one of sexual harassment in the present time, the young woman kept talking about "protecting Mommy" while describing the current traumatic event. As she talked, the following past trauma, which the young woman had totally repressed, began to surface. Her natural father was a very violent, abusive man whom her mother had finally left and divorced when she was about 5 years old. Until the assault at the workplace earlier that day, she had had no recollection of those early years with her father. But, that day, she began to remember. When the manager grabbed her arm and threw her across the room, it was a trigger that brought back her memories of abuse.

Her father had struck her mother and knocked her to the floor. As her mother lay on the floor, her father continued to kick her and scream at her. The girl was probably 3 or 4 years old at the time. Terrified, she rushed to help her mother and, as she did, her father grabbed her by the arm and threw her across the room. She hit the wall and was dazed and terrified. One could only imagine what it must have felt like to a child to be thrown across a room in such a violent manner. The young woman said that her mother has since married a very kind man whom she considers to be her real father, and she has had no contact with her natural father since the divorce.

Her mother lived in a nearby suburb, and the young woman said that she needed to talk to her and be close to her, because she was flooded by the memories. She asked the therapist to call her mother, and her mother confirmed that the daughter's memories were true. The mother had never talked about the domestic violence in her first marriage because she wanted to put it behind her. She also suggested that she take her daughter home where she could care for her. When the therapist suggested that both women should enter therapy, they agreed. The therapist provided referral names, but both chose to begin treatment with the therapist.

The clinician told the young woman that she should report the sexual harassment to the company, so it could be properly investigated. She was apprehensive, but agreed with the suggestion because, if she reported the abuse to the company or the police, it could be a corrective experience for her.

Confrontation in Therapy

Although the authors are Fellows of MRI and are firm believers in systemic therapy, they are also very aware that in cases in which domestic violence or child abuse has occurred, couple's therapy or family therapy may have a dangerous aspect and could actually expose vulnerable family members to intimidation or further harm. Intervention strategies that may be appropriate for many families to work through or express conflicting views may be problematic in families in which violence or child abuse has occurred. Clinicians should carefully evaluate the individual family members to be sure that such interventions are safe.

Extreme caution also should be exercised in situations in which abuse survivors wish to confront their abusers. It is our experience that such confrontations should be done with great care, if at all. There is a considerable risk that the abuser may lash out at, or further abuse, the victim, rather than admit his or her wrongdoing or apologize. We believe that empty-chair work, role-playing, or journaling can be equally effective in producing catharsis—and far safer.

A Violent Husband

We were called by a police officer who had been dispatched to a violent family disturbance. We were asked to respond immediately, because the couple (Mr. and Mrs. Campbell) were still actively combative. The officer met the therapists in front of the Campbell home with the news that the situation inside the house was still very "hot:" the husband had tried to stab his wife earlier, but a friend had stopped him. The officer added that the husband was sitting in a corner, swearing and mumbling about flowers.

When we entered the Campbell's dimly lit, lower-middle-class home, furniture had been thrown about and there were empty bottles and beer cans on the floor. Mr. Campbell was sitting in a far corner of the living room; Mrs. Campbell was in the next room with a second police officer. The police had concluded that this couple would not stay apart without supervision. At this point, it was decided that just one officer would remain on the scene with the therapists.

We decided to interview the husband first, because he was by far the angrier of the two and the one more likely to explode violently. After he had settled down a bit, one clinician asked him what he thought the principal problem was. He answered that he could not stand the sight of his wife. When asked how long he had not been able to stand the sight of his wife, Campbell replied that, for the past 3 years, she would not let him "live down" his drinking. He said that he was currently unemployed, but that he was looking for work. The clinicians talked for a while with Campbell, but it was obvious that he was too intoxicated to be interviewed effectively that night. A therapist then decided that Campbell should, if possible, go to an alcoholism facility for detoxification immediately, as he had been drinking heavily for a long interval. When the idea was proposed to him, Campbell reluctantly agreed to go to the inpatient facility.

Next, a therapist talked with Mrs. Campbell in order to learn her view of the problem. She said that, when Campbell got drunk, he became irrational and violent. She said that he was too proud and too "blind" to see the impact of his drinking on his family and his work. She said that he had been laid off from a foreman's job, which he had held for 11 years, because of his drinking. She added that she was fed up with him and had threatened him with divorce. When the clinician presented the idea of hospitalizing Mr. Campbell, Mrs. Campbell agreed that it would be a good idea, considering the extent of her husband's recent drinking.

We called a local detoxification facility to reserve a bed and asked the workers at the facility to send a car to fetch Mr. Campbell. He was quite cooperative at first, but when the car arrived, he refused to leave and became belligerent again. Finally, the police officer had to intervene, informing Campbell that, if he did not go, he would be hospitalized involuntarily, because of his earlier attempted assault on his wife with a knife. After Campbell had been taken to the facility, a therapist stayed to talk with Mrs. Campbell, the teenage children, and the friend of Campbell's who had taken the knife away from him. The friend said that he, himself, was an ex-alcoholic who had been "dry" for 6 years. He said that Campbell suffered from the "nice-guy" syndrome, because he was nice to his enemies and strangers but was nasty to his friends and family. The friend said that Campbell had bullied his wife and children mercilessly. He added that Campbell picked on the children incessantly, but bragged about their accomplishments when they weren't around.

After some summary discussion, the clinician made a follow-up office appointment with Mrs. Campbell for 2 days later. He also suggested that she call her lawyer the next day about a restraining order and her wish to begin divorce proceedings. The therapist also offered to talk with the lawyer about writing a restraining order. He also reminded Mrs. Campbell that the police believed she should change the locks on her doors, in case her husband decided to come back for revenge.

At the first follow-up visit, Mrs. Campbell said that, during his first day in the detoxification facility, her husband had called her and had been talking in a suicidal manner. He asked her how much life insurance he had and whether or not the policy would be paid if he committed suicide. The therapist advised her not to respond to the suicidal threat, because it could provoke more acting-out. She also said that her husband was being transferred that same afternoon to a private residential clinic for alcoholics. She added that the clinic operated an intensive, 3-month program.

The therapist asked Mrs. Campbell how long Campbell had had a drinking problem, and if she knew of anything in particular that could be associated with the onset of his alcoholism. She answered that her husband had been drinking for 12 years, and that four things had happened at about the same time he started drinking heavily: (1) their son was born; (2) Mr. Campbell's mother died; (3) they bought a house; and (4) she (the wife) had started a new job. She said that Campbell was deeply remorseful at not having shown more affection to his mother before her death. She added that her husband was fearful of growing old and that he dyed his hair; but, he wouldn't allow himself to "let go" or be playful. After some hesitation, Mrs. Campbell told the clinician that she had had an abortion 2 years before and that her husband strongly resented her for that. She also said that Campbell frequently referred to her as a "bastard," because he had formed the belief that she had been an illegitimate child.

As the therapist continued to talk with Mrs. Campbell, it became clear that her husband was a man who felt he had lost control of several aspects of his life—in particular, his wife, his family, and his job. Because of her anger at her husband, Mrs. Campbell was unconsciously doing things that intensified his feelings of helplessness. During the next session, although she was still quite angry about her marriage, she began to deal with some of the problems that had led up to the current crisis. She was able to see that both she and Campbell had contributed to these problems. The therapist explained to her that she had repeatedly enabled her husband's drinking by rescuing and forgiving him and, by doing so, had hindered him in some respects, from stopping his drinking habit. When Campbell was drinking, she had more control in the family and played a sacrificing role of the martyr in the eyes of outsiders.

At the next visit, Mrs. Campbell told the therapist that she wanted to try to save her marriage. She said that her husband was making amazing progress, and that his progress was forcing her to look at herself. Now, she had to learn how to relate to a man who was not completely dependent on her, as well as a man who was not always making empty promises. She said that Campbell finally realized how childish he had been, and that he had become more understanding of their children.

A therapist who had made the original emergency home visit continued to see Mrs. Campbell for about 4 months and, on two occasions, the children. A few times, Mr. Campbell came in for individual sessions while he was still a resident of the alcoholism program. When Campbell was released from the program, he returned to his family, attended AA meetings regularly, as well as family therapy sessions with an ETC therapist. Subsequently, the Campbells have had few difficulties. On one occasion, Mr. Campbell became angry at his eldest son for disobeying him, became fearful of his impulses, and called the police. When they arrived, Campbell explained what had happened, and the police officer told the boy that his father had a right to discipline his children, so long as he was not cruel or abusive which, on that occasion, he had not been. Except for this minor incident, the Campbells have become a successfully integrated family, there have been no subsequent calls to the police, and Campbell has remained sober.

A Case of Murder Reconsidered

Madilyn Leggett called the police one rainy evening in November, because she was fearful of being alone. A week earlier, this woman in her 50s had been the victim of attempted rape by a man who had broken into her home, and what she was afraid of was that the rapist would come back and attack her again. Her daughter and son-in-law had been staying with her since the attack, but on that evening they were preparing to leave and return to their own home. Because the responding policeman was unable to calm her fears and had to return to his patrol duty, he called our number for assistance.

When two therapists arrived and were briefed on the details of the case, the officer left and Madilyn Leggett gave her account of the attempted rape and her present insecurities. As she talked, she seemed to become gradually more calm and poised, and, for some reason, decided to give us a tour of her small house. She took special pleasure in showing the library, which contained an enormous collection of books on the occult, esoteric religions, and so on.

While Madilyn showed the therapists around, the shadowy figures of a man and a woman were observed passing by from time to time. The man and woman did not seem to be getting along well with each other. They were avoiding each other, and, when Madilyn invited them into the living room, there was obvious tension between them. We learned that these were Madilyn's son-in-law and daughter, and that they had been experiencing a problem in their marriage. When we asked them if they were interested in marriage counseling, they said they were, and we made an appointment for them to see a therapist in the office on the following day. When we felt that Madilyn Leggett was sufficiently reassured by persuading the daughter and her husband to stay on for at least another night, we took our leave.

The next day, the therapist met with Mrs. Leggett's daughter and son-in-law. Anthony Rivera, 31, a machinist by trade, and his wife Gabrielle, 32, had been married for 10 years. Gabrielle had a daughter by a previous marriage who was 13, and she and Tony had a 9-year-old daughter, Maria-Teresa. Over a period of 3 weeks, they were seen several times by the therapist, both together and separately, in the course of which the following personality dynamics emerged. Gabrielle Leggett Rivera was convinced that she possessed two identities: (1) that of an angel or equivalent of the Virgin Mary; and (2) that of a whore or agent of the devil. In her angelic state, she was a dutiful wife and mother, and in her devilish state she indulged herself with a lover. The lover, Buddy Baker, was a 25-year-old whose sole ambition in life was to be accepted into the Hell's Angels motorcycle club. For a while, the therapy with Gabrielle focused on her relationship with her mother, who was said to have read thousands of books on the occult. In this context, the therapist asked whether or not the Leggetts had a "family secret" or "myth," and Gabrielle responded by saying that, in fact, she was the victim of a family curse, which she explained as follows. She had discovered, in a family album, a newspaper article from 20 years before, which was about her grandmother. The grandmother (whose middle name was Gabrielle) had murdered her husband in collaboration with a lover. The lover had been executed and the grandmother had been sentenced to 20 years in jail. This was a curse that, to Gabrielle, represented her own certain destiny. She added that Tony had once taken a wild rifle shot at Buddy Baker when Buddy had been discovered at their home.

For his part, Tony Rivera admitted that he was a murderously jealous person concerning his wife. He said that Buddy Baker had once been a friend of his, and he acknowledged having fired a shot at him in a fit of rage. Once, in fact, he and Buddy had engaged in a furious chase around town in their cars, bumping into each other in a mad version of the game of tag. When asked what weapons he kept in the house, Tony replied that he had six guns in all. When asked whether or not he was planning to take a shot at Buddy Baker again, he replied that the answer would depend on what Buddy did in the future. The therapist asked Tony if he would promise to telephone first if, at some time in the future, he had an urge to shoot someone. To the clinician's surprise, Tony agreed.

Two weeks later, precisely at midnight, Tony (whose voice the therapist recognized at once) called to announce, "Tonight's the night." The therapist asked, "How soon can you meet me at my office?," and Tony's answer was, "In fifteen minutes and I'll have my gun with me." The therapist took a deep breath and said, "I can meet you in fifteen minutes, but please leave the gun in your car." When Tony agreed to this condition, the therapist asked if it would be all right if he invited two of his colleagues to join them at the meeting, and Tony acquiesced.

At the appointed time, Tony appeared at the bottom of a stairway leading to the therapist's office. When asked, "Have you left your gun in the car?" his reply was, "Yes, but I brought the barrel inside with me, because some kid might break into the car and get hurt." During the long session that followed, Tony kept the gun barrel tucked under his jacket. From time to time, it was visible, and the three therapists soon realized that it was part of a sawed-off shotgun.

In their work with Tony that night, the clinicians began with the premise that Tony was a neurotic young man whose jealous rage had reached the breaking point. He was not psychotic nor likely to become so, but his potential for violent acting-out was acute. Even so, because he had clearly designated the target of his rage, the therapists felt assured that he would not harm any of them.

As the hours dragged on, Tony was tearful and angry by turns. He alternated between berating himself for his murderous thoughts and summoning up courage for what he knew he must do: "I got to do it. I know I'm crazy, because I got to do it." The therapists let him know that they did not think he was crazy, and that what he was feeling was understandable because of what his wife had put him through. But, with the passage of time, the clinicians felt that they were not weakening Tony's resolve to kill Buddy Baker, and, because they knew that he had been a frequent drug user, they surmised that he had taken some kind of "upper" that night, because his energy level and stamina were formidable.

At one point, Tony related, with some pride, the story of an incident that had taken place the previous day and which demonstrated the desperate lengths to which he was willing to go to "settle things." He wanted the therapists to know that he had given Buddy Baker fair warning that he was going to kill him: only yesterday, he had taken Buddy with him to the local police station and had insisted that the officer put him (Tony) in jail, saying, "Arrest me because I'm going to kill this guy." The policeman had remained unconvinced and had asked both men to leave the station.

At about 3:00 in the morning, when the intervention was becoming totally unproductive, one of the clinicians asked Tony if there was one person in the world whom he truly loved. When he replied, "My daughter," the therapist said, "Lean back and close your eyes and imagine this scene: You are in prison because you have killed Buddy; you are pleased with yourself and you are basking in the glow of your accomplishment; now, Maria-Teresa comes to visit you in jail and you ask her, 'How are you, honey?' and she says, 'Okay, Daddy,' and you say, 'Tell me what's wrong, honey,' and she says, 'The kids at school sing a song like this [Here, the therapist began to sing softly and, in a few seconds, his colleagues joined in]: "Your daddy is a murderer. Your daddy is a murderer. Your daddy is a murderer."' They sang in unison for about 10 seconds, while Tony slumped in his chair, obviously shaken. He sighed and, after a silence, took a deep breath. After another long silence came the nearly whispered words "All right, I won't do it." Later on, at about 4:00 in the morning, the therapists let Tony leave, convinced that he would keep his promise—especially because, by then, he was extremely tired and emotionally spent.

The next day, when the therapists conferred about the events of that night, they had some second thoughts about the propriety of what they had done. On the one hand, they wished to preserve the confidentiality of their meeting with Tony, but they also were mindful of the requirements of the Tarasoff decision, which mandates the duty of a therapist to warn the intended victim about a dangerous client. In addition, they agreed that something should be done about Tony's sawed-off shotgun, the mere possession of which is a felony in every state.

After seeking the advice of an attorney, a therapist telephoned the chief of police in the town where Tony lived. The therapist explained the situation without giving Tony's name, and the chief decided that the best thing would be for us to try to get this man to give up his guns. If we could deliver the guns, the police would store them for an indefinite period and, more important, would take the sawed-off shotgun into custody without charging its owner with illegal possession.

For the purpose of providing a timely warning to the possible victims, the therapist who had been seeing the Riveras most recently asked Gabrielle to come in that same day and bring Buddy Baker along. When they arrived, it soon became obvious that the Tarasoff warning would not likely be heeded. Buddy, in fact, greeted the news with belligerent disdain: he said that he was willing to confront Tony at any time and that he had no intention of breaking off his affair with Gabrielle. For her part, Tony's wife did not seem alarmed and showed no inclination to change her behavior.

The therapist then telephoned Tony, asking him to visit the office at about nine that same night for the purpose of persuading him to give up his guns. The message was as follows: because Tony had agreed the previous night not to kill Buddy, what was the purpose of keeping the guns, especially as they were a source of temptation to do what he had promised not to do? It took a while before Tony gave his permission for the guns to be turned over to the police temporarily, and it took even longer to convince him to let the therapist follow him home in order to confiscate the guns that very night.

It was quite late when the two men arrived at Tony's house. The six guns, fully loaded, were lying on a table and on the top of a cabinet. Slowly and with care, Tony unloaded each while the therapist compiled a list of the type of gun, its caliber and serial number, and listed the 450 rounds of ammunition by type and quantity of each type. Naturally, the list did not contain the owner's name, but the therapist gave Tony a signed receipt for his guns and ammunition. Then a solemn Tony helped the therapist to carry his arsenal to the car. After driving at an extremely slow rate of speed to the police station, the therapist asked to see the Watch Commander and said, "Please come out to my car. I have something to give you."

The delivery of guns and ammunition to a police station marks the beginning of the last chapter in this story of murder reconsidered. The next day, Tony appeared at the station and asked to have his guns back, but the police refused to give them to him. The therapist continued seeing Tony on a regular basis for a while. Once, Gabrielle came to the office for a visit, and the therapist reminded her that her life script called for a murder to take place and warned her to break off the relationship either with Buddy or with Tony; again, Gabrielle was adamant that she would not leave either man.

In therapy with Tony, the clinician was able to reframe the situation so that Tony could see that the stronger (or more "masculine") resolution of his problems would be to get a divorce from Gabrielle. Subsequently, after a period of indecision, Tony filed for divorce and continued to visit his therapist during the 6-month waiting period. He again asked to retrieve his guns, but the therapist refused on the grounds that Tony was too agitated at that time. Later on, when he was more calm, Tony asked again and the therapist got the guns (except for the sawed-off shotgun) from the police and returned them to Tony.

About 5 years later, Tony asked to see the therapist once more. He was then divorced and had obtained custody of both his daughter and step-daughter. The stepdaughter, now 18, had been experiencing "growing pains," and Tony was seeking advice about how to be a better father.

Thus ended our involvement with Tony, Gabrielle, Buddy Baker, and Madilyn Leggett. A case that had begun with a grandmother's experience of attempted rape had ended with her grand-daughter's adolescent crisis. This case is relevant to the emergency therapist because it demonstrates that:

1. Help for one kind of problem may not only serve to solve that problem but permit another quite different, and much more serious problem, to emerge and be given attention.
2. Successful therapy can be reached by many routes, often by taking the opposite direction from that usually taken; for example, thinking processes can be influenced by means of changing behavior instead of the other way around—the more customary direction of therapy.
3. In respect to providing protection for the community, it may be that mental health professionals, instead of the police, will be called upon to play a major role more often in the future; when clinicians are prepared and willing to take on the task, they can be successful in this role of deterring violence.
4. A gun is a gun; this and any other potentially dangerous weapon cannot be ignored, even by the clinician; indeed, if a therapist's client does possess a potentially dangerous weapon, this fact should not be ignored in therapy; when in doubt, a therapist should make the assumption that the client is capable of using it against someone (or as a means to suicide); the alleged or identified client may not always be the person in the family constellation who most needs help.

In sum, there will be times—often very inopportune times—when a therapist cannot not act, when a clinician must commit his or her total energy to a life-or-death intervention. Finally, remember that people are capable of changing, and some of them can become as opposite to their former selves as day to night.

Battered Spouses

Battering is the most severe form of domestic violence. One spouse strikes the other, with full force and intent to harm—sometimes as the final act in a fight, and sometimes in cold blood. This section separates spousal battering from the situation of couples whose fights periodically erupt into incidents of violence such as pushing, shoving, throwing small objects, or slapping. The authors believe it is useful to distinguish between these two major types of violence for the sake of clarity. It is necessary to show how markedly different kinds of family systems function, and how the couple that fights violently may later evolve into a couple in which battering occurs. This distinction does not mean that the authors do not consider any situation in which one human being strikes another as being an extremely serious matter—we do.

Incidence and Prevalence of Battering[1]

Conservative studies indicate that two million women per year are assaulted by their partners, but experts believe that the true *incidence* of partner violence is probably closer to four million cases per year.

- Nearly one quarter of women in the United States—more than 12 million—will be abused by a current or former partner some time during their lives.
- 47 percent of husbands who beat their wives do so three or more times a year.
- According to FBI statistics, 30 percent of women who were murdered in 1990 were killed by husbands or boyfriends. It is estimated that 52 percent of female murder victims were killed by a current or former partner.
- 14 percent of ever-married women report being raped by their current or former husbands, and rape is a significant or major form of abuse in 54 percent of violent marriages.

Clinical studies underscore the *prevalence* of domestic violence and its relationship to continued or repeated trauma and consequent medical and psychiatric problems. More than half of all nonfatal assaults result in injury, and 10 percent of the victims require hospitalization or emergency medical treatment. Seventy-five percent of battered women first identified in a medical setting will go on to suffer repeated abuse. According to various studies, battered women may account for:

- 22 percent to 35 percent of women seeking care for any reason in emergency departments, the majority of whom are seen by medical or other nontrauma services

- 19 percent to 30 percent of injured women seen in emergency departments
- 25 percent of women who attempt suicide
- 25 percent of women utilizing a psychiatric emergency service
- 45 percent to 59 percent of mothers of abused children

Most research has focused on women who have been battered by male partners and, in fact, women are more likely than men to be seriously injured by their partners. However, the terms spouse-abuse and partner-abuse reflect an awareness that men also can be abused in intimate relationships.

Forms of Abuse[2]

Physical abuse is usually recurrent and escalates in both frequency and severity. It may include the following:

- Pushing, shoving, slapping, punching, kicking, choking
- Assault with a weapon
- Holding, tying down, or restraining her
- Leaving her in a dangerous place
- Refusing to help when she is sick or injured

Emotional or psychological abuse may precede or accompany physical violence as a means of controlling through fear and degradation. It may include the following:

- Threats of harm
- Physical and social isolation
- Extreme jealousy and possessiveness
- Deprivation
- Intimidation
- Degradation and humiliation
- Calling her names and constantly criticizing, insulting, and belittling her
- False accusations, blaming her for everything
- Ignoring, dismissing, or ridiculing her needs
- Lying, breaking promises, destroying trust
- Driving fast and recklessly to frighten and intimidate her

Sexual abuse in violent relationships is often the most difficult aspect of abuse for women to discuss. It may include any form of forced sex or sexual degradation, such as:

- Trying to make her perform sexual acts against her will
- Pursuing sexual activity when she is not fully conscious or is not asked or is afraid to say no
- Hurting her physically during sex or assaulting her genitals, including use of objects or weapons intravaginally, orally, or anally
- Coercing her to have sex without protection against pregnancy or sexually transmissible diseases
- Criticizing her and calling her sexually degrading names

It should be noted that many battering husbands love their mates; on occasion they feel tremendous remorse, and some even make great demonstrations of affection after an attack. Certain of these men rationalize their behavior by explaining that the woman caused the beating to occur. Others argue that they did it because she "needed" it. In some subcultures, a beating is actually interpreted as a demonstration of love. After a time, a battered women's thinking becomes distorted in a way similar to that of the victims of brainwashing, in that she begins to accept whatever the abusive spouse tells her. Also, considering that many adults who remain in abusive relationships had parents who were themselves abusive, it is not surprising that some people associate loving interaction with abuse. Their thinking becomes so distorted that they make statements such as, "He beat me because he loves me." Or, they may look on abuse as "a part of life," because they believe that they have no other choice.

Some spouses are battered because they are too dominant or competent and pose a threat to the submissive or "inferior" partner; thus, they provoke the battering by their very being. Others are battered because they, themselves, are too submissive or "inferior;" this frustrates the dominant member of the system, who in turn does the battering. A woman may be battered, in essence, for the role that she plays in a complementary system that has gone out of control.

In one all-too-familiar scenario, the husband will originally have been attracted to the spouse because she was so gentle and naïve; but, this same naïveté and passivity has led to frustration with her because she cannot cope with domestic responsibilities. This, in turn, leads to the battering. For her part, she attempts to placate and please him by being even more submissive, which leads to his greater frustration, and further beatings ensue. What the wife has done in an attempt to make the situation better has in fact made it worse. Because each spouse is unaware of what the other is thinking and feeling, each becomes more and more bound to this escalating, cyclical pattern. As the pattern progresses, both partners appear to develop an almost fanatical fear of breaking free from the system, while at the same time the system oscillates further and further beyond control.

A differing form of complementary system may exist when the abusive husband has chosen his spouse because of his own dependency needs and because she was so strong and capable. It is that spouse's competence which eventually will threaten him and provide a stimulus to the assaults. On one level, he wants her to be competent and to take care of him, but at the same time he hates her for her competence. His threshold of frustration is, at the best of times, very low; alcohol may disinhibit him, and when his anger and resentment rise beyond the level of tolerance, a beating is the result. The woman, in turn, tries to placate and please him by doing what she thinks he wants, and this ultimately activates the cycle of battering again. Once more, what each spouse thinks can make things better will in reality make the situation worse and has unwittingly provoked violence. At the core of this situation is a (pathological) complementary relationship to which both partners are obsessively attached. Each goes to extraordinary lengths to preserve this unhealthy pattern of interaction and, with time, each develops the overwhelming delusion that neither could survive without the other. This irrational fear that one could not survive without the other is a critical component of the system, as evidenced by the lengths to which each will go to preserve the system as long as possible.

Initial Assessment of a Battered Woman

1. How impaired is the woman's cognition by the batterer's psychological manipulation while she was in a physically traumatized, vulnerable state of mind?
   - Does she blame herself for the violence?
   - Is she ashamed?
   - How damaged is her self-esteem?
2. Have the children been brainwashed by the batterer; have they formed an "identification with the aggressor;" do they believe the batterer's rationalizations for the abuse, or do they support the mother?
3. How serious are her injuries, and is she aware of the seriousness?
4. How long has she endured the abuse?
5. Does she have a realistic escape plan, or any escape plan?
6. What resources are available to her for
   - Emotional support?
   - Physical safety?
   - Financial support?

- Emergency shelter?
- Legal support?

7. What is the seriousness of her emotional condition; is she
   - Severely depressed?
   - Severely anxious
   - Acutely traumatized?
   - In shock or denial?
   - Alcoholic or chemically-dependent?
8. How strong is the victim's pathological attachment to the batterer?
   - Does she still feel the need to be with him?
   - How anxious is she about being apart from him?
   - Does she recognize that the relationship is toxic and that she must leave?
9. How aware is she of the batterer's dangerousness (her level of awareness or denial of the real danger in remaining in the relationship can predict whether or not she will be able to leave)?

The clinician should be aware that a batterer may only need to hit a woman once, but a threat or a gesture by him may be all that is needed to terrify her from then on.

Clinical and Ethical Issues

The American Psychological Association's "Guidelines on Ethical and Legal Issues Concerning Interpersonal Violence, Maltreatment, and Related Trauma," (1996, Section 3) state that a therapist should not treat those cases without specialized training in the subject. The rationale is that treatment techniques that are used in the field of general psychotherapy may validate future abuse or provoke more violent behavior toward family members or even toward the therapist. We do not recommend accepting cases in which spouses or children have been battered, unless the perpetrator is:

1. In or under some formal supervision by the criminal justice system
2. In a certified program for batterers
3. In a certified program for anger management

The clinician should not underestimate how powerful the batterer's influence on the family system is, even when the person appears sorrowful or contrite. The batterer's intention is to reconstruct the homeostasis of the family system in order to regain control. Spouses and children are seldom strong enough to stop this without outside structure and support. If a therapist (even in group therapy) attempts to change the balance of power in the family, he or she or the clinic or agency may well become the target of the batterer's wrath.

As noted earlier, it is much safer and easier to lessen, gradually, structure imposed on abusive people as they act in more healthy, responsible ways, than to reimpose control after the situation escalates and someone is reabused.

A Battered Wife

This case is not a typical one from a socioeconomic standpoint, because the majority of battered wives are working class or poor; but it is a typical case from a psychological standpoint. It is presented to clarify several misconceptions that are commonly held about battered women and to demonstrate that the dynamics of *battered spouse syndrome* cross all socioeconomic boundaries. It is not unknown for women to return home from their professional jobs and face battering by their husbands.

Joyce was 35 years old when she consulted a therapist because of chronic headaches and depression; her physician had suggested that hypnosis or relaxation training might be of help. She had been married for 10 years and had two children, a boy of 8 and a girl of 6. Joyce was quite anxious and rather vague when describing the frequency and symptoms of her headaches. She was also evasive about her current family situation. The clinician had a sense that there was a more serious, hidden problem in Joyce's life, but if pushed into disclosing more than she was prepared to tell, she would not return.

Joyce did give consent for the therapist to consult the physician who had referred her, in order to obtain information about medical aspects of the chronic headaches. Joyce also revealed that she was an attorney with a local law firm and that she specialized in civil litigation. Her husband, Steve, was an architect. She subtly indicated that even though both their professional lives were quite successful, their married life was at times turbulent and unstable. She made an appointment to return the following week.

When the therapist called Joyce's physician to obtain more information about her headaches, the doctor was most cordial and said he was glad that Joyce had followed through with the recommendation to see a psychotherapist. He explained that while he was concerned about Joyce's headaches, he was also very much concerned about her situation at home. She had required medical treatment for several unexplained falls and other odd accidents during the past few years. Although the physician was genuinely worried about Joyce, he didn't know what he could do to help.

He described Joyce's husband, Steve, as a self-assured, obviously success-ful man who was difficult to approach on a personal level, and added that Joyce had been extremely secretive about her marriage. This conversation with her physician served to confirm the therapist's suspicion that Joyce was hiding a family secret.

During the next few weeks of treatment, Joyce's story slowly came out. Her headaches were caused by beatings which had begun about a year after her marriage to Steve—a history of 9 years of abuse. In telling this, Joyce tried to be protective of her husband and went to great lengths to give reasons why he periodically beat her. She described Steve's childhood as having been traumatic and tragic. His parents were alcoholics and he had been on his own at an early age, refusing any help from the parents. Joyce had met him when they were in college, and she had admired his determi-nation. She described Steve as someone who was energetic and hard-work-ing, but was really very shy and awkward in showing his feelings. Joyce went on to say she had "mothered" Steve and tried to make up for the lack of love in his childhood. Because of this mothering, he had come to need her very much.

Joyce described her own family as having been completely opposite from that of her husband. Her family was solidly middle class and entirely stable. Even though she had two siblings, she had clearly been her father's favorite. Joyce said that she felt almost guilty for the happiness and stabil-ity of her own childhood, by contrast with Steve's. They had been married shortly after she graduated from law school, and as long as they had to struggle to make ends meet, they had been happy together.

A few months after she passed the bar exam and had taken her first job, Joyce came home about an hour late from work and found her hus-band in a rage. He accused her of having an affair with one of the men at the law firm where she worked. The more she tried to explain why she was late and to insist that she had no interest in any of the men where she worked because she loved and needed him, the more violent Steve became. He struck her several times, knocking her to the floor. The next morning he said he was deeply sorry for what he had done, adding that the only rea-son it happened was that he loved her so much; if she would forgive him, it would never happen again. It didn't happen again for about a year, and by this time Steve was rapidly becoming successful in his own business and Joyce had given birth to their first child. The next beating took place shortly after the birth of the baby, and resulted from Steve's feeling that Joyce was paying too much attention to a business acquaintance of his dur-ing a dinner party at their home. Steve, who had too much to drink, had burst into a jealous rage. This beating resulted in a black eye and cracked rib that caused Joyce to stay home from work for a period of time, during which Steve was extremely solicitous and remorseful. As before, he swore it would never happen again and she forgave him because she felt so deeply sorry for him.

More than a year passed before another beating occurred, shortly after the birth of their second child. It was presumably provoked by the threat of another child taking more of Joyce's attention and love away from Steve. This time Steve, in a drunken rage, threw her down the stairs and broke her arm. As Joyce explained to the therapist, it was as if the more successful he was in his work, the more fearful and easily provoked he became. Joyce said that she had a deep sense of tragedy in her thoughts of this man who had worked so hard for his success in life, only to find himself unable to enjoy it when it came. She did not seem aware that the births of their children had been threatening to Steve because of his feeling that the children would take some of her nurturance away from him.

Joyce described her life as "living with a time bomb" that might "explode" at any moment. She said that every minute of her time had to be accounted for to Steve, and thus she could only meet with the therapist during the noon hour (she frequently missed appointments). Joyce added that her husband completely controlled the family finances and that she did not know in which banks the family had accounts. She gave Steve her paychecks and he would give her an allowance, plus additional cash if she needed anything more. Joyce had accepted this situation and tried to rationalize Steve's need to control the finances as a result of his childhood poverty. She saw it in terms of Steve always wanting to make sure that the family had enough money, rather than as his need to control her.

In its initial stages, therapy was somewhat ineffectual because of Joyce's fearfulness and resistance, as well as to her failure to keep regular appointments. She was terrified that Steve would discover that she was seeing a therapist and flatly refused to discuss the possibility of his entering treatment with her. Despite Joyce's resistance, the therapist believed that if she were given time to develop trust, she would eventually be able to face the need to make some changes in her situation. The therapist was well aware that many battered spouses are reluctant clients and that it is difficult to persuade them to enter a therapeutic relationship which can truly facilitate change. These women require a combination of patience, deep understanding of their situation, and firmness. The woman must be led to face the fact that eventually she will have to take steps to end the violence, either by leaving her home or insisting that the husband receive treatment as a condition of her remaining in the home. But this takes time in many cases, as rarely is the battered spouse capable enough or ready to accept or carry through these necessary prerequisites for a change in the system. A clinician needs to be aware that many battered women are not emotionally prepared for separation from their spouses, nor from the violence-producing, complementary system in which they are trapped. They usually need to make several attempts before eventually breaking the cycle. Too often, therapists become discouraged with these women and prematurely dismiss them as being unmotivated, at the instant when they are making their first tentative attempts toward separation.

It is possible to interrupt a cycle of battering on the first try, but our experience suggests that this would be an exceptional outcome. A battered woman usually makes between three and nine attempts to leave home before she is capable of staying completely away or is able to insist upon the spouse's receiving treatment as a prerequisite to her return. It will be helpful for the clinician to view these early attempts to end the batterings as a learning process that, in the long run, will have a cumulative effect to assist the woman in making her final break. Battered women need to learn gradually to counter the psychological effects of their battering; these effects are similar to those of brainwashing in that they distort the victims' views of reality and debilitate them emotionally. Changing a woman's previously distorted view of reality requires that she experience a different reality. For example, she needs to know that there is a place of refuge for her, such as a woman's shelter where professionals and volunteers will try to assist her.

Even though Joyce was herself an attorney and knew her rights on an intellectual level, getting her to stand up for them proved difficult. Over the years (even though she was in a sense the strong, nurturing woman whom Steve depended on) she had become, psychologically, totally dependent on her husband. It was as though Joyce were two people: the working woman who was competent, successful, and had developed a reputation as a person who tolerated no nonsense; and the woman at home who, in her wifely role, was a fearful spouse who nourished and protected the husband's every whim and desire. To a certain extent, Joyce thought of Steve as a child who, in his fashion, had become hopelessly dependent on her.

Joyce made several attempts to leave her husband. The first came one night when Steve arrived home in a drunken state. After he went to sleep, she ran away with the children to a friend's house. At about 4:00 in the morning, the clinician received a telephone call from a hysterical Joyce. Steve was on his way to the friend's house to get her and the children, and she didn't know what to do. The therapist agreed to come to the friend's house and try to talk with both Steve and her. At the very moment when the therapist arrived, Steve was forcefully escorting a sobbing Joyce and her two children to his car, and in a controlled but angry voice he warned that the clinician should "stay away from [his] wife."

Joyce did not call the clinician for about 6 weeks after that incident, and when she did she was apologetic and afraid that the therapist would be angry with her and refuse to see her again. The therapist reassured her that this was not so and made an appointment for them to meet again. During this renewed course of treatment, the therapist made several attempts to bring Steve into treatment, but each attempt was unsuccessful. Subsequently, Joyce made two other unsuccessful attempts to leave her husband. The final separation came after a beating in which Joyce's jaw and cheekbone were broken and she had to be hospitalized. A major reason for her making the decision to leave was that her 6-year-old daughter had been injured by Steve in the course of the latest incident of battering. In an attempt to reach Joyce, he had grabbed the girl and dislocated her arm as he pulled her away from her mother.

This injury to one of her children was more than Joyce could tolerate. When the clinician met her at the hospital next morning, Joyce was barely able to talk. The therapist helped her plan where she would go after her release from the hospital. The therapist also convinced Joyce that she should contact a new attorney and have a restraining order issued against Steve, to prevent him from harassing or harming her or the children. At first she was reluctant to do so, but she finally agreed to have the restraining order prepared. The therapist then made arrangements to visit Joyce's children, who were staying with a friend.

This time, Joyce stayed away from her husband. Even though she eventually resolved to end the relationship entirely because Steve still adamantly refused any from of treatment, the entire process of separation, divorce, and rebuilding a life was not easy for her. Joyce remained in treatment for about a year, during which time much therapy was devoted to working through how she could have permitted the battering to happen to her for so long, and how she could have been one kind of person at work and another kind at home. One reason was that Joyce had come from a traditional but loving family in which the father was unquestionably the dominant figure. In addition, because she was her father's "pet," she came to believe that male authority figures were mostly benevolent; thus, if they became angry, it must be because someone had done something wrong. When Joyce saw that she did not make similarly naïve assumptions in her professional life, she felt quite free to assert herself for a change.

It is worth reiterating that the present one is not typical of the majority of battered spouse cases, but shows that the dynamics of battering transcend socioeconomic boundaries. The reality of a typical battered spouse is that she does not have a career nor does she have any prospects for one. Most have major responsibility for the care of one or more children. Without resources, either financial or emotional, the woman feels as if she is isolated in every sense from the help and concern of others, and thinks herself totally trapped in a battering situation, which, to her, is unique and seems without possible remedy.

CHAPTER 7

Physical Abuse and Neglect of Children

In 1992, 2,936,000 American children were abused or neglected (National Victim Center, 1993; in van der Kolk, et al. 1996). Before recommending treatment strategies for use with families in which child abuse or neglect may be occurring, it will be useful to introduce the topic by means of a clear and concise definition of what "abuse" is in this context. It will then be possible to present a description of the kinds of people who abuse their children, as well as the psychological dynamics within a family system that can set these pathological events in motion. In general terms, parental abuse of children is not a sex-linked phenomenon. It has been said that more mothers abuse their children than do fathers, but it is also said that abuse by fathers is far more brutal and devastating to the child. The dynamics referred to here, as well as recommended strategies of therapy, are assumed to apply equally to abuse by fathers. And even when the actual abuse is carried out by only one of two parents, the other bears a considerable measure of responsibility for acquiescence in the assault.

What Is Child Abuse?

Child abuse is neither strict punishment, nor spanking, nor rough handling. Corporal punishment is permitted in our culture, and corporal punishment, in and of itself, is not child abuse—no matter what someone's personal views on the subject of corporal punishment may be. Child abuse has occurred when corporal punishment has caused bruises or other injury to the child, or when the child has been injured in such a severe manner that medical attention is required.

Federal legislation provides a foundation for States by identifying a minimum set of acts or behaviors that define child abuse and neglect. The Federal Child Abuse Prevention and Treatment Act (CAPTA) (42 U.S.C.A. §5106g), as amended by the Keeping Children and Families Safe Act of 2003, defines child abuse and neglect as, at a minimum:

1. Any recent act or failure to act on the part of a parent or caretaker that results in death, serious physical or emotional harm, sexual abuse or exploitation; or,
2. An act or failure to act which presents an imminent risk of serious harm.

Within the minimum standards set by CAPTA, each state is responsible for providing its own definitions of child abuse and neglect. Most states recognize four major types of maltreatment: neglect, physical abuse, sexual abuse, and emotional abuse. Although any of the forms of child maltreatment may be found separately, they often occur in combination.

The examples provided here are for general informational purposes only. Not all states' definitions will include all of the examples listed here, and individual states' definitions may cover additional situations not mentioned here.

Neglect is failure to provide for a child's basic needs. Neglect may be:

1. Physical (e.g., failure to provide necessary food or shelter, or lack of appropriate supervision); or,
2. Medical (e.g., failure to provide necessary medical or mental health treatment); or,
3. Educational (e.g., failure to educate a child or attend to special education needs); or,

4. Emotional (e.g., inattention to a child's emotional needs, failure to provide psychological care, or permitting the child to use alcohol or other drugs).

These situations do not always mean that a child is neglected. Sometimes cultural values, the standards of care in the community, and poverty may be contributing factors, indicating that the family is in need of information or assistance. When a family fails to use information and resources, and the child's health or safety is at risk, child welfare intervention may be required.

Physical Abuse is physical injury (ranging from minor bruises to severe fractures or death) as a result of punching, beating, kicking, biting, shaking, throwing, stabbing, choking, hitting (with a hand, stick, strap, or other object), burning, or otherwise harming a child. Such injury is considered abuse, regardless of whether or not the caretaker intended to hurt the child.

Sexual Abuse includes activities by a parent or caretaker such as fondling a child's genitals, penetration, incest, rape, sodomy, indecent exposure, and exploitation through prostitution or the production of pornographic materials.

Emotional Abuse is a pattern of behavior that impairs a child's emotional development or sense of self-worth. This may include constant criticism, threats, or rejection, as well as withholding love, support, or guidance. Emotional abuse is often difficult to prove and, therefore, child protective services may not be able to intervene without evidence of harm to the child. Emotional abuse is almost always present when other forms are identified.

It is evident that injuries such as those described here go far beyond what would be considered the result of normal punishment for a child's misbehavior. Just about every adult has had the urge or impulse to strike a difficult or unruly child at one time or another. Child abuse, by contrast, transcends this acute but temporary arousal of angry feelings that most adults are capable of keeping under control.

What kind of adult is not able to control himself or herself? What species of adult anger, hurt, or confusion can spill over onto children, and can eventually lead to their abuse or neglect? In many cases, this abusive behavior has had its genesis in the parent's own childhood. There is considerable evidence that a majority of abusive parents were once abused or rejected children themselves, or came from homes in which domestic violence occurred. Many of these abusive parents possess an exceptionally low sense of self-esteem, having the tendency to feel that they are failures as people; also, they are persons who tend to be frequently depressed.

The following vignette indicates how a person's low self-esteem and deep-seated feelings of inadequacy can contribute to abusive behavior. The sad scenario begins in this way: a young person feels a terrible sense of inadequacy when growing up. She feels rejected by one or both parents, and may have been abused by one or both. She marries early and has a child, perhaps trying to fulfil an acutely felt need for affection and love. By conceiving a child, carried to full term and healthy at birth, the person achieves a sense of "doing it right" that was lacking in childhood. On the baby are projected the sources of love and affection that were lacking in youth, and an expectation is placed on the child that at least one person will love him or her without restraint or qualification.

When the baby is taken home, this parent may inadvertently hold the baby awkwardly or tentatively, and the child may respond by feeling uncomfortable and squirming or crying. Instead of viewing the squirming or crying as a natural result of its feeling uncomfortable, the parent may believe the behavior to be directed at her, or as an attempt to escape. The parent may experience the fantasy that the child is placing blame, and that may lead to obsessional thinking, such as: "I have failed; while I may have thought for a moment that I succeeded, instead I have failed."

Parents of this kind have such great needs within themselves and such hope that their children will make up for all they have lacked as children themselves, that they are unable to see or understand the needs of their own children. As parents who have frustrated dependency needs themselves, they displace their anger at their own parents for lack of nurturance and love onto their children, as a further episode in this unhappy chronicle of abuse.

Many abusive parents have a marked lack of understanding of (or empathy for) their children's moods and behavior. They often project adult motives onto a child's actions, when, in fact, the child may be upset because he or she feels sad or wet or hungry. This naïveté may account for the fact that there is a considerably higher risk of child abuse in young couples than in older couples. In fact, younger, less experienced parents often have a lack of knowledge of a child's capabilities. That is, they are largely unaware of what is reasonable and appropriate behavior for children at the various age levels. Because they are so lacking in understanding, they have acute gaps in the most basic parenting skills. They often make unrealistic demands of their children in terms of obedience or skill or intellectual ability.

Many abusive parents are isolated people, having few or no support systems to back them up or assist them when they are experiencing stress or are caught up in crises. Many such parents have serious marital problems that may not be obvious upon first meeting. Some of them put forth the pseudo-appearance of having a very tightly knit, loving, "us against the world" kind of family. This, on closer inspection, is revealed as a family in which there is great fear of intimacy and closeness. Some mothers who abuse their children are themselves being battered by their husbands. Other abusive parents will "scapegoat" a child as the cause of problems in the marriage relationship. For example, the abused child may be seen as a competitor, by a dependent and jealous parent, for the spouse's attention.

There appear to be fewer instances of child abuse in large or extended families, and several good reasons can be found for this. First, in a large or extended family there is a ready-made social network to assist in child care when a mother is experiencing stress or having some difficulty: for example, when there are sisters or aunts or nieces who can assist in child care or relieve the mother for a period of time from the duties of parenting. Second, in a large or extended family children have more experience in caring for other children so that, by the time they themselves are adults and married, they have had considerable practice in caring for a child. Also, these children can form a good understanding of what is normal and appropriate behavior for a child at the differing developmental stages. We have noticed, in many child abuse cases, that an abusive parent's first experience of caring for a child has occurred when the first offspring arrives. In other cases, the abusive parent has had few opportunities, because of the social isolation and deprivation of his or her own childhood, even to be in the company of small children. These circumstances can lead to vastly unrealistic expectations of a child's capabilities and needs.

Another factor that has found to play a role in child abuse is that many abusive mothers had given birth prematurely or had had much difficulty in giving birth. Because of the complications of a premature or difficult birth, children often are isolated from the mother shortly after birth, and thus the child and the mother are not together for a critical period during which "bonding" between mother and child normally takes place. Perhaps as a result of this lack of infant–mother bonding, child abuse may occur. It is no coincidence that in the first year of life, the risk of infant mortality by abuse is greater than any other period (Zeanah and Scheeringa, 1997).

The image of a pathetic, isolated, lonely, and fearful parent emerges as a portrait of those who abuse their children. Most are people who themselves were once victims of neglect or abuse. Many lack friends or family members who live nearby and can provide actual help, support, or useful information during stressful times. Because of their isolation, loneliness, and low self-esteem, when they are under stress they have considerable difficulty in asking for the help that they so desperately need. This inability to ask for help is often carried over into their daily lives, in that they have great difficulty in asking for assistance with everyday problems. For example, going to a neighbor and asking to borrow something that they need for the house (a cup of sugar, some coffee, or advice) is a relatively simple matter for most people; but for the abusive parent—because of lack of self-esteem and fearfulness—this relatively simple request becomes an overwhelming task. These are people who fear closeness and intimacy, probably because they have not experienced it themselves as children. Or, when they did experience intimacy, it was often interrupted by episodes of violence.

Many abusive parents are idealistic and upwardly motivated people. They desperately want to succeed but, at the same time, perceive themselves to be failures in life and see their task as parents to be virtually impossible. They tend to be impulsive people who have great difficulty in controlling themselves when they are hurt, frightened, or frustrated. And although the reader may find it a difficult leap of faith, it is helpful to be aware that these people who lash out at or injure children are not sadists; that is, they are not people who take pleasure in hurting their own children. Quite the opposite is true of abusive parents. Most are people who love their children very much, but who are so troubled and are experiencing so much psychological pain that they cannot control themselves in even mildly stressful situations. They often use the defense mechanism of denial to protect themselves from facing what they have done (or are doing) to their children. They will claim not to remember when or how the actual injuries to the child were sustained.

Alcohol or substance abuse by the parents also may be a contributing factor to child abuse (Widom and Hiller-Sturmhöfel, 2001; Ammenmann et al., 1999). When doing an evaluation for child abuse, a therapist should always be careful to assess the potential of alcohol or drug abuse on the part of one or both parents.

Child abuse also is a phenomenon that is blind to social class or economics. Indeed, our experience has been that many upwardly mobile couples who appear socially connected on the surface may, in fact, be very socially isolated, driven people who are haunted by profound feelings of fear or self-doubt.

Culture and Corporal Punishment

Although many cultures condone corporal punishment, none condone child abuse. Of course, cultures may vary greatly in child-rearing practices. People may become very defensive and feel demeaned if someone not from their culture informs them that a time-honored child-rearing practice such as corporal punishment is considered child abuse in *this* country.

Instead, therapists should be acutely sensitive to cultural issues in family crises that involve possible child abuse. One should not make assumptions based on one's own social or cultural experience. Training or consultation on cultural issues can be essential aids in such cases. If the clinician has to tell a family that a practice such as extreme corporal punishment is against the law, it may be wiser to have someone from the family's culture explain this. By doing so, the family may be less apt to feel criticized or demeaned by an outsider.

General Diagnostic Indications

This section reviews some of the indicators that may assist a therapist or counselor in determining whether or not child abuse is taking place. Here are condensed some of the salient diagnostic signs. If, when involved with an emergency situation, a clinician encounters a family in which there is evidence of two or three of these indicators, there is probably a case of child abuse that should be investigated more thoroughly[1].

1. An unexplained or unexplainable injury: if a parent is reluctant to explain the cause of the injury and makes statements such as "We just found him like that;" or if the family is unwilling to discuss details of how the child was injured. Most parents are very concerned when their child is injured, and go to considerable lengths to find out how and why the injury occurred.
2. A discrepancy between the descriptions, on the part of each parent, of how the child was injured, when the parents have been questioned separately; or a difference between the explanation given by one or both parents and an explanation given by the child when questioned separately.
3. A discrepancy between the type of injury or wound of the child and the reported "accident:" for example, when the parents say that the child tripped over a chair and fell down, but the child is covered with severe bruises over several areas of his or her body, or with long narrow welts which indicate that he or she has been beaten with a belt or ruler.
4. Suspicious injuries that are said to have been self-inflicted. Children who are not emotionally disturbed rarely injure themselves intentionally, and the child may have injuries that could not have been self-inflicted; for example, if the parents claim that a baby rolled over and broke his or her arm while asleep, or imply that the child is masochistic or has hurt himself or herself in a temper tantrum.

5. Injuries inflicted by a third party, as when parents blame someone such as a baby-sitter, friend, or neighbor. These accusations should be investigated thoroughly. Other suspicious third-party injuries are those said to have been inflicted by rough siblings or playmates; if, after making such an accusation, the parents are unwilling or unable to produce the name of the third party who injured their child, the accusation should be regarded with suspicion. Few parents will permit their children to continue to play with or be cared for by persons who injure them.

6. A delay in obtaining medical care for the child's injury. Most parents seek medical treatment immediately when they discover that their child has been injured; if a parent waits 12 to 24 hours before obtaining treatment for a child's injury, this fact by itself may strongly suggest that the injury was inflicted by one of the parents.

7. A history of repeated suspicious injuries: if the child has suffered unexplained injuries on more than one occasion or if a sibling exhibits similar injuries. Many children such as these are referred to by the parents as "accident-prone," "clumsy," or "rough."[1]

Physical Indications

Wounds that are considered diagnostic of child abuse include bruises, welts, lacerations, and scars, for example:

1. Bruises and other injuries that are predominantly located on the buttocks and lower back are usually the result of punishment, that is, of spanking; numerous bruises on the cheek and pinpoint bruises on an earlobe are usually the result of being slapped or cuffed; similarly, most wounds on the inner thigh and genital area have been inflicted by another person; while accidental falls rarely cause bruises in the soft tissue, they usually result in bruises or scrapes that involve bony prominences such as the forehead, the cheekbone, or the hip; in addition, if fresh bruises are accompanied by fading or yellowish other bruises, abuse should be strongly suspected; handmarks and pressure bruises resembling fingertips or an entire hand, often found along the arm or the leg of a child, or pinch marks which appear as two small crescent-shaped bruises facing each other are also injuries that are diagnostic of child abuse; human bite marks also take the form of paired, crescent-shaped bruises; this type of injury should be carefully examined, as parents usually claim it was inflicted by a sibling or playmate; strap marks are often rectangular-shaped bruises of varying lengths; bruises that appear on several

different bodily planes are usually inflicted wounds, unless there is clear evidence of a tumbling accident; tumbling accidents often do cause minor bruises and abrasions, but they will appear predominantly on elbows, knees, or shoulders.

2. Approximately 10 percent of physical abuse cases involve burns: the most common burn is that inflicted by a cigarette; these generally consist of more than one circular, pinched-out burn; when a child accidentally bumps into a cigarette, it will normally make only one circular burn mark unless a cinder catches the clothing on fire; smaller but similar burns can have been inflicted by a hot match tip. Another form of burn that is very suspicious is one that has been caused by immersion in hot water; such a burn will leave marks above the ankle or wrist but no splash marks; children do not put their limbs into hot water and keep them there voluntarily.

3. Eye damage, in respect to the abuse syndrome, can include acute hyphema, dislocated lenses, or detached retinae; retinal hemorrhage is a clue to subdural hematoma in children who may have unusual central nervous system symptoms. Retinal hemorrhaging in children (absent clinically important intercranial hemorrhage) also can result from sudden compression of the chest.

4. The worst possible injury, in terms of potential lethality, is subdural hematoma: victims often have convulsions and may enter a coma; the typical subdural hematoma is associated with a skull fracture resulting from a direct blow by hand, or from being hit against a wall or door; external bruises related to the same blow are usually present; intra-abdominal injuries are the second most common cause of death in battered children; children who have been beaten in this way tend to have recurrent vomiting or abdominal distension, among other symptoms; a most common finding is a ruptured liver or spleen.

5. "Failure to thrive" manifests itself in an underweight, malnourished child; these children usually have prominent ribs, wasted buttocks, and spindly limbs; failure to thrive usually occurs in the first 2 years of life, because this is normally a time of rapid growth and dependence on adults for feeding; this syndrome has been detected in babies even before they have reached the age of 8 months; the causes of failure to thrive are estimated as being organic in 30 percent of the cases, underfeeding as a result of understandable error in 20 percent of the cases, and deprivation resulting from maternal neglect in as many as half of the cases.

6. If a child is extremely passive or seems catatonic, this also may be an indication of neglect or abuse; in fact, abused children may exhibit a wide range of abnormal psychological symptoms; some appear "flat" emotionally, with depressed mood; they seem to lack the color and energy of normal children; by contrast, some abused children can behave in an impulsive or aggressive manner; but, one fairly consistent element in the behavior of abused children is that they do not easily trust people and are acutely distrustful of strangers.[2]

Assessing the Safety of a Home

In some cases, it will be necessary for a clinician to determine whether or not it is safe for a child to remain in his or her home. In other cases, if, for example, a child has been temporarily removed from the home, it may be necessary for the clinician to decide whether or not the child should return. Some risk factors that may affect this often difficult decision are addressed here.

1. The first factor to take into consideration is whether one or both of the parents fits the description of abusive parents. Were they themselves abused or neglected as children? Are they isolated and lonely people or are they, in general, fairly well-adjusted socially? Are the demands that they, as parents, place on their child appropriate or inappropriate? Do these people have reasonable parenting skills? Are they able to discipline their child effectively? Are they able to differentiate their own needs and feelings from those of their child? If there are any indications of underlying pathology, a psychological evaluation and testing should be considered.

2. Another key factor to consider is the age of the child. Most research on the subject of child abuse suggests that children are extremely vulnerable between the ages of 3 months and 3 years; this is the period in a child's life when he or she is most demanding, most helpless, and places relatively more demands on the parents; also, during this period of life a child is virtually unable to get away from an abusing parent to ask for help, whereas an older child would be more capable of seeking help or assistance should a crisis occur; these considerations suggest that it is wise to take a more conservative stance in deciding whether or not to allow a child to remain in the home when the child is under the age of 3, because the risk is so much greater for a child of that age (Zeanah and Scheeringa, 1997).

3. It is necessary to consider if this child is described as "difficult" or sickly. Does the child, because of some limitations or handicap, put unusual demands on his or her parent(s); or does a parent perceive this child as being "strange" in some way, or capable of making extreme demands; have there been prior incidents of abuse in the family; has this or another child of the family ever been removed from the home in the past? If that has happened, considerable caution is in order unless there is evidence that the parent or family has made significant changes.

4. Eventually, it will be necessary to assess the psychological adjustment level of the parents; if one parent is a chronic or borderline schizophrenic, that fact plus evidence of abuse may definitely indicate that the child should be removed from the home; even so, being schizophrenic should not by itself disqualify a person from parenthood; a more important factor is the severity and duration of proven abuse; if a parent loses control and strikes his or her child once, is remorseful and does not strike the child again, the situation is different from one in which the parent injures the child repeatedly for a long time; the essential difference is between a moment's loss of control, under extreme pressure, and serious psychopathology.

5. Finally, a vital factor in assessing the resources of a family to decide whether or not an abused child should remain there is: does this family have a support network of relatives, friends, or professional advisors to whom it can turn in time of stress; or, are the parents isolated and reluctant to seek help?

When a majority of these factors is present in a family in which an incident of child abuse has occurred, the indication is strong that at least a temporary separation of abusive parent and child will be appropriate until a further, more thorough assessment of the family can be conducted.

Treatment

Discovery of child abuse in the course of an emergency intervention can be a brutal, shocking relevation. It is extremely important for a therapist, in such a situation, to be able to monitor his or her own feelings of anger and disgust and keep these emotions under control. If they are not contained, a clinician's feelings may only serve to isolate (further) and wound the abusive parents who may have been abused children themselves. It is also necessary to accept the difficult awareness that these people are not horrible monsters. Instead, they are persons in need of compassion and understanding, who, in their own pathetic way, are crying out for help and need protection from themselves.

Initially, most will deny the abuse, and the clinician should avoid being drawn into their anger and rage but remain, instead, detached from the pathological system. A therapist should be prepared to find that the family members will not like him or her and will likely blame the therapist for causing the problem. An abusive family will fear and resent any outsider—including the therapist—for invading and disrupting the family system, and this resentment is likely to persist for quite a while. Although it may be tempting for a therapist to agree not to report abuse in an effort to gain the trust of a parent or as the result of angry threats, failing to do so is a serious error of judgment that will not help the child victim in any way.

A therapist should keep clearly focused on the fact that treatment is available that is problem-focused (i.e., strategic) and utilizes cognitive/behavioral techniques. This approach to therapy can improve parent-child communications, parenting skills, and develop parental empathy (Lieberman and Van Horn, 1998). Nevertheless, a recent study suggests that parents will have to participate in such a program of treatment for at least 1 year (Skowron and Reinemann, 2005). Furthermore, the therapist should not be deterred by the claim of abusive parents that the report by a clinician of child abuse will "destroy the family." Remember that these parents are frightened people who have lived in highly dysfunctional family systems; they know no other way to behave and are terrified of change. In this situation, try to avoid a power struggle with the parents by reminding them that you had no choice but to report the abuse, because it is the law. Even so, the therapist will do his or her best to help the parents find the support that they need to be more effective parents.

Often, a clinician will be called into the suspected abusive situation by a third party. Sometimes, a member of the immediate family calls for help, but we have found this to be quite the unusual occurrence in true child abuse syndrome families. One way in which a therapist or other professional often discovers an abusive family is by means of treating a family member for another problem, in the course of which child abuse is suspected or revealed. The main thing to realize, at the beginning of an intervention, is that many abusive families do not seek or want help, will be defensive or secretive, and will try to conceal the abuse. The clinician should try not to appear outwardly suspicious in such a way that a parent will become even more guarded about admitting possibly abusive behavior.

During the initial encounter with a parent who is suspected of child abuse, it is wise for a therapist to avoid acting impulsively or emotionally, no matter how worried he or she may be about the child in question. One reason is that a need may arise to prepare the foundation of a legal case. But if the parents are inadvertently warned of the therapist's suspicions in advance, they may attempt to cover the evidence or try to prevent the therapist from seeing their child a second time. In many cases, it will be necessary to visit with the child more than once in order to confirm suspected abuse. Another vital issue is that of gaining the trust of the child—that is, children who have been abused not only are fearful of strangers but may distrust adults in general, for very good reasons. Moreover, most abused children "love" their parents, and thus any outsider who threatens the family will be perceived as an enemy. Also, if the family comes from another country, an intervention by public authorities may lead family members to fear dire consequences, because of past social injustices or maltreatment.

Above all, before taking action, it is important to consider what may happen to the child if this attempt to help fails. What if the professional person rushes into a situation too quickly, and the family is able to conceal the abuse or escape detection by moving to a different address? What if a child finally learns to trust an adult—the clinician—but the help so desperately needed is not forthcoming? What will the child be left with then?

The first encounter with a family in which there is suspected abuse should be as nonconfrontational and nonthreatening as possible. If necessary, this position can be changed to a more assertive one later. The clinician should try to learn as much as possible about each of the family members and their backgrounds. Using the profile of the abusive parent, it is wise to examine how closely these parents fit the profile. Next, the clinician should weigh the seriousness of any apparent injury and reflect on the age of the child. When a child needs to be removed from his or her family, it may be best to arrange this during a natural separation time, such as when the child is at a day-care center or school. If possible, the therapist should try to avoid the dramatic scene of separating a child forcibly from his or her parents. In many cases, children who are suspected of being abused can be more easily taken out of a school setting (and brought to a pediatrician for an examination) than by confronting the parents directly, with the child present.

The following is an example of a first intervention with two abused little sisters who will be called Annie (7 years old) and Carolyn (8 1/2 years old). This case study also serves to illustrate types of behavior which are characteristic of abused children. We were called by a teacher who was concerned about these two little girls: According to the teacher, their clothes were always dirty, they had not been sent to school with complete lunches for at least 6 months, and there were bruises and scratches on their arms and legs. A clinician went to the school to meet the girls, both of whom were very reluctant to speak to her. From their teacher, the therapist learned that each girl had had serious behavioral problems at school. Annie was very withdrawn and would intentionally hurt herself, commenting, "See, it didn't hurt." One day she even stabbed herself with a pair of scissors. Carolyn, by contrast, was an extremely aggressive and destructive child; she would be quiet at one moment and then act out explosively. Carolyn had attacked other children on several occasions, and had once destroyed a classroom display in an outburst of rage.

The clinician met with each girl separately, and, during the second meeting with Annie, asked her how her parents punished her if she did something wrong. She replied, in a very matter-of-fact manner, that they would strap her, and if she was "real bad," she would have to sleep outside of the house (on the ground) all night. When the therapist met with both girls toward the end of this session and repeated what Annie had disclosed earlier, Carolyn suddenly jumped up and attacked her sister, screaming "I hate you, you liar."

By the end of this second meeting with the little girls, the therapist had decided that there was sufficient reason to send both of them to a pediatrician and to report the suspicion of child abuse. The police were called, and the therapist and the Juvenile Officer took the children to be examined at the local county hospital. The pediatric examination revealed that each child had, in fact, been beaten. Annie's nose had been broken previously, but she had received no medical treatment for the injury. Both children were suffering from malnutrition and each had bruises, welts, and scratches that could not have been self-inflicted.

After learning of this finding, two staff members had a meeting with the parents, who were quite young: The mother was 24 and the father 25. As a couple, they were both struggling to "make ends meet;" he worked at a garage and she worked as a waitress at a fast food restaurant. At the beginning of the meeting with them, they became furious and threatened to sue us. One of the clinicians explained that, because of the results of the pediatric examination, they had no choice but to report the abuse and to arrange for both children to be placed in a children's shelter until a thorough family evaluation could be done. That visit with the parents lasted approximately 3 hours, most of which consisted in reassuring them that we wished to help the family members live together in a healthy, supportive way. Even though the parents continued to be angry with us for some time, we were able to persuade them to continue in therapy. They were referred to an intensive, 12-week program for abusive, high-risk parents. Two follow-up visits were made with the parents as well as with the children, who were temporarily placed with relatives. Later, the children were returned to the home and, presumably, there has been no recurrence of abuse in the family.

Early in therapy with abusive families, it is essential to state clear ground-rules for behavior during treatment. Because many of these families are receiving treatment involuntarily, the parents may have exaggerated or distorted fantasies about what therapy is and is not. Hence, it is advisable to clarify what the role of the therapist will be, and what the family can and cannot expect from a therapist. The following is a combination of some of the basic therapeutic ground rules that we have found helpful.

An incident of child abuse that occurs in the course of treatment does not necessarily mean that therapy must terminate, that the parents must be jailed, or that the child must be removed from the home. But, although such an incident should be confronted clinically, the highest priority must be given to child protection. The clearest message that needs to be given to the parents, from the start, is that a clinician will not help them cover up their abusive behavior. From now on, they will have to learn nonviolent ways of coping with life stress and raising their children. These parents must learn to admit their problems and difficulties and to accept help. Lending force to these requirements, we have found it necessary to have the support of the local criminal justice system or the child protective service of the local welfare department, in order to ensure that these families remain in therapy during the critical early stages of treatment.

Because abusive parents have a chronic inability to control their aggressive impulses, it is vital to establish the rule that not only this but also any subsequent incident of abuse will be reported. The rule will apply to each person who is involved in the therapeutic situation, and there can be no reprisals between or among members of the family. Furthermore, if the parents quit therapy before a therapist feels that they are ready to do so, that fact will be reported—which may result in the child's being removed from the home. Our policy is to recommend to the court that a therapy requirement include these provisions: not only should a minimum duration of time be established for therapy but also a minimum number of sessions should be specified; if the family members fail to attend this number of sessions, they must make them up. By building therapy on a firm foundation in this way, we seek to overcome the parents' lack of motivation for change.

Every attempt should be made to coordinate the therapist's efforts with schools and other agencies that will be working with an abused child, for several reasons. For example, many abusive parents cannot deal with any type of stress, and possibly a teacher or agency worker could inadvertently provoke a new child abuse incident by sending home a note complaining of the child's poor performance or poor behavior. When feasible, a clinician should ask that messages such as this be channeled through him or her and thus be dealt with as a part of therapy.

We have found the following arrangement of therapy appointments to be the most advantageous for abusive families: weekly group sessions with other parents and weekly sessions for the parents as a couple. If the abused child is old enough to participate in therapy, either family therapy or a multifamily group (with other abusive families) is recommended in addition. We also have found that it is best if at least two clinicians are involved with each family or multifamily group, because treating an abusive family can be very stressful for a therapist. Two or three therapists who coordinate their work can support and relieve each other during some of the more demanding phases of treatment. In most cases, individual play therapy sessions for the abused child will be necessary and, for this to be feasible, a team of several therapists will be required. Multifamily groups have proven to be a promising modality for treating abusive families because they serve more than one therapeutic function: the arrangement helps to break each family's isolation and prevent the family members from feeling that theirs is the only family to which this tragedy has happened; it also helps to dispel the belief that the parents' abusive behavior is a result of some peculiarity that is unique to them.

When we treat abusive parents, we let them know that someone from our team will be available to them at any time of the day or night, should an emergency occur or an overwhelming problem arise. This often can be of considerable importance because, by beginning in this fashion, a clinician can establish the combined role of "good parent," helper, and teacher. These parents need to have someone whom they can call on when they find themselves to be overstressed and are fearful that they may act out once more against their child. The therapist should be aware that events that most people would consider to represent minor difficulties may be catastrophic to abusive parents; in general, they need someone to turn to for advice.

In general, treatment of abusive families proceeds as follows. At first, there is a stage during which the parents are frightened and angry and will deny the abuse as best they can. It is best not to fight this, but allow it to run its course. A clinician should try to avoid asking why the parents did what they did, how or when or where it was done, or any question that may imply an accusation of blame during this initial phase. The primary aim is to "ride out" the anger and be as supportive as possible, in an attempt to gain some trust. Although the parents' anger will appear to be capable of going on forever, usually within 2 to 4 weeks this anger will turn (in many cases quite suddenly) into dependency. During this stage of dependency, it is important for the therapist or cotherapists to be readily available to these parents. It is a period when the family can be thought of as most vulnerable to stress. For the first time, the parents have allowed someone to enter their hermetic family system, and thus it is important for a therapist to "be there" at those significant moments when they permit themselves to ask for help.

Some initial requests for assistance may appear on the surface to be trivial. For example, a parent may want to find out the name of a good medicine for colds, or perhaps one of the children has asked a question and the parent wants advice about how to respond. The point is that many events that most people can take in stride are exaggerated in the case of those who are as deeply psychologically impoverished as abusive parents are. Finding them overwhelmed by these momentary crises, perplexed and unable to cope, the therapist soon realizes that they, themselves, are needy children who require reparenting to become healthy adults. This stage of dependency in therapy will be a time when the abusive parents, having passed through phases of anger and denial, will feel much relieved, and the clinician will very likely be able to make substantial therapeutic gains. But, the therapist must be aware that this course of treatment will proceed slowly and will very likely be time consuming to complete. It is during this phase that true cognitive/behavioral work can be done to change behavior patterns.

Our work with abusive families consists in playing three essential roles: the first is that of therapist, the second that of reparenter, and the third that of teacher. As teacher, a clinician endeavors to explain appropriate and realistic expectations of children, because abusive parents know so little about normal child development. In order to help abusive parents improve their parenting skills, we focus much attention on the concepts of punishment and praise. Abuse often begins with a parent's simple attempt to stop undesired behavior by punishing the child for something he or she has done. What the parent lacks is knowledge of a means of punishment that does not require violence. For example, the parent should know about alternatives such as "time out," that is, putting the child in his or her room for a period of time as a form of punishment. Another alternative is to establish a point system by which the child may win or lose points for good or bad behavior. These approaches to behavioral control can serve to make violent punishment unnecessary.

For many of these parents, it is useful to provide "empathy training," a method intended to teach people to recognize, understand, and experience the feelings of others. We have observed that abusive parents are so consumed by their feelings of personal inadequacy that they are unable to recognize feelings of sadness or pain in others. In order to learn empathy, the person is asked to recall incidents in which he or she was hurt by someone, as well as incidents in which he or she was made to feel joy or happiness. The object is to focus attention on the interaction (positive or negative), thus showing how one person's behavior affects and influences the behavior of another.

Finally, working with abusive parents requires teaching them new ways to respond when they feel anger. The goal is to persuade them to restrain their impulsive and volatile reactions to challenge or stress. One way to do this is to use "guided imagery." In guided imagery, a person is encouraged to recall moments in life that were the most gratifying. It is not surprising to find that many abusive parents have considerable difficulty in recalling periods of time in their lives that were happy, considering their own histories of deprivation and abuse. Later, the parents are asked to remember incidents in their lives when they knew they weren't supposed to do something and, in fact, did not do it because it was "wrong." Then, we suggest that they recall how good it felt to be able to control themselves in this manner. A final step is to persuade the parents to connect these positive feelings from the past to events and situations that are occurring in the present. This approach can be extended even further by asking the clients, in the course of treatment, to report moments in their present lives when they have delayed in acting-out their frustrations or anger. Moreover, asking parents to keep a diary or journal can be useful as a device to get them to record anger-producing incidents. Part of the problem is that many such parents are largely unaware of the kinds of events that cause them to act-out in an aggressive manner; some respond so rapidly that they lose track of the chain of events that led to their violent behavior. Once parents are more aware of their triggers, they can be taught to connect pausing in their actions for a moment to think about being in control, with what behavior would make them feel good when in control.

In this stage of treatment, our aim is to teach the parents to follow a more problem-solving approach to coping with angry feelings, instead of permitting a provocative stimulus to trigger anger time after time. We encourage them to believe that, when experiencing pressure or stress, they are capable of discovering the cause of the problem and of making a more rational decision about what will be accomplished by their behavior. Finally, they can choose what is the most appropriate action to take.

CHAPTER 8

The Incestuous Family

Incestuous impulses and fantasies have been experienced by nearly every person, and yet our society reserves its most powerful taboos and its most severe condemnation for incestuous acts. If impulses such as these cannot be kept in check appropriately by a parent because of poor impulse control, they may come crashing into the world of reality with more damaging effects than either parent or child could have imagined. Because incest fantasies are such a deep and significant part of normal sexual development, there is a temptation to think of actual incest as potentially beneficial. Although this phenomenon may be exotic in the realm of dreams, it is not so in reality. For example, the French film *Murmur of the Heart* was a highly romanticized story of incest between a mother and son, but rarely does incest have anything like an ideal outcome. In reality, the story is more likely that of a son and mother who are both very disturbed, often psychotic people. At best, the story is that of a young man who feels deeply betrayed and confused and who will have trouble in relating to women sexually—let alone trusting or being able to express love for a woman. In each of the rare cases of mother-son incest that the authors have encountered, the result was far from romantic. The theme of this chapter is that incest represents a tremendous breach in the basic trust relationships that together form the foundation of family life. Thus, the primary issue that a clinician must address in the treatment of incest is not sexuality, but, rather, this basic trust relationship between parent and child around which future love and trust relationships will be built.[1]

The incest taboo, which is almost universal to cultures, has a purpose. It serves to protect the family structure and it assists in the healthy development of the human species. Although there are some exceptions to the incest taboo, closer examination of these exceptions reveals that, in most cases, specific limitations are placed on what incestuous behavior is, in fact, permitted (Meiselman, 1978, p. 3). Socially accepted incestuous behavior is usually restricted to a special social class, for example, royalty, or limited to specific religious rituals. The few cultures that do permit incest do not condone promiscuity among the privileged group, nor do they permit incestuous behavior outside of rigidly prescribed circumstances. Moreover, a majority of these cultures only sanction incestuous relationships between brothers and sisters, while prohibiting incest between parents and children. To exemplify how all-pervasive the incest taboo is, Murdock (1949) surveyed 250 primitive societies and found that each of those societies had strict sanctions against incest within the nuclear family.

Many theories have been put forth concerning the origin and purpose of the incest taboo. Despite Freud's explanation of the role played by incestuous fantasies in the development of the psyche, many critics believe that he failed to formulate a plausible theory of the origin of the taboo (e.g., Meiselman, 1978). One attempted formulation was the allegorical tale in *Totem and Taboo* (1913), in which Freud described a "primal herd" ruled by a cruel and tyrannical father who would not permit his sons to have access to women; because of this, the sons united in revolt against their father. When the sons had defeated the tyrannical father, they devoured him in a cannibalistic ritual. But, afterward, they were overcome with grief and guilt because they also had loved their father and realized that they would now be in competition among themselves for the women. Out of this conflict the sons "created" the incest taboo and agreed to practice exogamy. This theory has never enjoyed wide acceptance, and Freud himself was not pleased with it as a rationale for the taboo (Meiselman, 1978).

The anthropologist Malinowski (1927) advanced a theory that held that incest, if practiced, would destroy the structure of the family system by confusing family roles and generational boundaries. The intense emotional feelings that are produced by sexuality between parent and child would cause the balance of power within each family to collapse, such that the family could not function any longer as a social or economic system. More recently, the sociologist Parsons (1954) pointed out that incestuous *fantasies,* on the part of the child, can be a positive motivating force in personality development. His thesis is that the erotic attachment between a parent and a child serves as a mechanism to draw the child through the sometimes difficult and painful stages of normal development.

There is very likely a biological basis for the incest taboo as well. Meiselman (1978) summarized the biological research that had been done on nuclear family incest, and although research on this subject is very difficult to carry out, two of the studies bear consideration here. Adams and Neel (1967) studied 18 children who were born as a result of nuclear family incest, by contrast with a matched control group. Each group was examined twice, at birth and at 6 months. At 6 months, only 7 of the 13 surviving children of incest victims were considered to be normal and adoptable. (The children of five of these victims had been stillborn or had died very early in infancy.) In the control group, 15 children were considered to be normal at 6 months.

Another significant study was that of Seemanova in Czechoslovakia (1971): 161 children of nuclear family incest victims were studied over an 8-year period; these children of incest were contrasted with a control group of their half-siblings who were not the result of an incestuous union. Moderate-to-severe retardation was found in 25 percent of the children of incest, by contrast with no cases of retardation in the control group. In addition, 20 percent of the children of incest were found to have congenital malformations or at least one serious physical abnormality. Eighty-nine percent of the control group were considered to be normal children, by contrast with 41 percent of the children of nuclear family incest.

In review, the all-pervasive incest taboo likely has its roots in many essentially separate but intertwined human needs. The taboo serves a vital function in that it protects the structure and integrity of the family as the foundation stone of a social system. The taboo plays an important role in the process of psychosexual development and serves a biological function by advancing the healthy evolution of the species.

Case Finding

Before beginning the treatment of parent-child incest, it will be necessary to define the problem clearly. All too often, an unsubstantiated or questionable claim of incest is simply dismissed as a "story" that has been fabricated by a "bad" or manipulative child, or a child who has been coached by a vindictive parent. There is a growing body of evidence that suggests that most reports of child molestation or incest are true. In this respect, it is tragic that some clinicians look upon children as capable of lying unless proven innocent. A more kindly approach would be to assume that a report of incest is true unless proven false. It is better to err on the side of believing the report than to shut off what may be a cry for help.

If a child makes either a veiled hint of incest or a direct accusation of incest, each by itself is a serious matter. If the story turns out to be untrue, the child may be exhibiting hysterical symptoms or suffering from child-hood schizophrenia. In another context, the false report might be a form of emotional blackmail. The following imaginary situation gives an example of this. A single-parent mother who has a teenage daughter remarries, hoping to bring authority and stability to the home. If the teenage daughter wants to get rid of this newcomer who is an intruder to her world, gives orders, and poses an emotional threat to her, one thing she can do is falsely accuse her new stepfather of incest, or behave in a sexually provocative manner toward him in front of her mother or other people. Thus, in beginning an intervention, the therapist must weigh the relative contributions of reality and fantasy.

The Child Sexual Abuse Accommodation Syndrome, identified by Summit (1983), by which a child is believed to conceal the fact of intrafamiliar sexual abuse because of fear and a need to accommodate an authority figure, has been seriously challenged by subsequent research, as summarized by London et al. (2005). Another tenet of Summit's theory, namely that accommodation can lead to delayed disclosure of incest is supported by research findings .

As a general rule, we have found that the younger the child, the more credence can be given to the child's report of some kind of sexual advance toward him or her on the part of a parent. A small child is the more credible because he or she has probably had no prior opportunity to learn about adult sexuality. For example, when a child of 5 accurately describes an erection or ejaculation, the story may well be true because a child of this age would very likely have had to see something in order to give an accurate description. With an older child, the report should not be rejected out of hand, but more careful investigation will be needed because many other reasons may lie behind an accusation, or even a suggestion of incest.

Everyone knows that children are sensitive and have an uncanny ability to know when something unusual is happening or something has gone wrong. Because they may not know the right words, what they say about what they have sensed may sound as though an incestuous advance is being reported when, in fact, it is not. What the child may be feeling could be some sort of misdirected threat or tension in the family, and what the child describes (something that is half real, half fantasy) may be only a premonition. A classic example of a child's "knowledge" of a problem on the feeling level is the case in which parents say, "Yes, we are getting ready to separate and get divorced. We haven't told the children; they don't know anything about it." At the same time, the therapist may have observed that the children have been acting-out and are showing other, deeply felt signs of anxiety. Children are quite often aware, on a feeling level, of basic family dynamics that the parents wish to avoid. A child may *feel* that there is something wrong or about to happen, but what that intuition means may be unknown to the child and beyond his or her ability to express in any way.

Another hidden reason for a child to accuse a parent of incest is that the child may be asking for protection from that parent because he or she senses either an impending sexual threat or a shifting of roles within the family. It has been found that many incestuous situations begin with the uninvolved parent as the *failed protector* (Weinberg, 1955; Howard, 1993). Usually, the sexually involved parent is made out to be the monster/villain, whereas the other parent is seen as an unknowing bystander. But, in fact, the uninvolved parent may play as important a role in the incestuous family system as does the sexually involved parent (Meiselman, 1978; Howard, 1993; Levang, 1988; Gordon, 1986). Too frequently, therapy is focused on getting the ("perverted") sexually involved parent to change, or getting a ("perverted") brother to stop his assaultive behavior, and does not take into account the complicity of other members of a family system who may be helping to maintain this problem.

Sometimes sheltering an incestuous relationship can serve to protect the uninvolved parent from adult sexual demands that he or she cannot accept. A sad example of this was the case of a 13-year-old who was a good student and a "nice" girl. When making an emergency visit to her home, a therapist found that she had taken an overdose of pills. The therapist called an ambulance to take her to the hospital and was there with her when she began to regain consciousness. In a semiconscious state, the girl described 5 years of sadomasochistic sex that had been inflicted on her by her father. The Sex Investigation Officer of the local police department was notified, and the officer soon verified that her story was true. The father was out of town but was due to return in a few days, and because of what her father's return meant to her, the girl had attempted suicide. During a subsequent meeting with the mother, the girl's mother became enraged. Her parting words were, "How could she say that about him? He gave her a stereo last Christmas." Generally, in a case in which that kind of massive denial persists, we have found it prudent to recommend removal of the child from the home. The mother's response was typical of the signs that reveal that it may be impossible to work therapeutically with a family, because there are not enough strengths or resources within the family system to protect the child or children. The mother in this case was presumably enmeshed in a deeply pathological relationship with the father, and had become so dependent on him that she could not sustain a protective role on behalf of her children. In the experience of the authors, the ability of the mother to assume, competently, an empowered, maternal role in the family will be one of the most important factors that will determine whether or not the family can be successfully treated.

It is worth noting that the subject of incest introduces much more tension into a conversation than the concept of child abuse does. At the mere mention of the word "incest," many people become nervous or hostile. This is probably one reason why so many people preferred, for so many years, to ascribe an accusation of incest to the realm of fantasy. The phrase "child abuse" occupies a certain common ground of understanding, perhaps because nearly everyone can admit to having felt an impulse to strike an unruly child. And, although many people have had incestuous impulses, it is far less socially acceptable to admit them to another person.

Evaluation

Incest does not mean that it is always necessary or advisable to break up a family situation. An incestuous family may have a good chance to reconstruct itself if provided with essential treatment structure and a variety of support services. The prognosis, in cases of those incestuous families who are appropriate for treatment, can be positive. In order to decide whether or not a particular family is appropriate for treatment—and, if so, what type of therapy should be provided—a thorough diagnostic evaluation will be required. This evaluation is important because one of the causal factors that might go undetected in an incest case is borderline psychosis or a personality disorder on the part of the sexually involved parent. Careful diagnosis is especially relevant when the offending parent is fully adult and the victim is a quite young child (11 years or younger). If the sexually involved parent is schizophrenic, he or she may well be of the paranoid type. Or, the parent may be borderline antisocial, or narcissistic and appear, superficially, to be normal; but, when he or she is intoxicated or under psychological stress, the serious pathology may emerge. A clinician should determine whether or not the parent who has committed the incest is utilizing hysterical defense mechanisms such as repression or denial, to protect himself or herself from facing the harm that he or she has inflicted on the child. If such defenses are employed, the risk of the child's being reabused is far greater.

Once a thorough pretreatment evaluation has been done, more pointed and realistic plans for treatment can be made. Another clinical issue that needs to be taken into account, when deciding on a treatment plan, is the possibility of alcoholism as a confounding factor. In general, there is a strong possibility that one (or more) family member(s) is a chronic alcoholic (Gebhard et al., 1965; de Chenay et al., 1988; Liles and Childs, 1986). The sexually involved parent may be the sort of person who appears to be fine until he or she takes a drink. For such persons, the saying, "the superego is soluble in alcohol," may be relevant; and, if so, serious pathology may lie beneath the surface.

The pathology (whether or not it includes alcoholism) in an incestuous family may be difficult to find, because one way in which an incestuous family system survives and protects itself is by unspoken family myths and rules of conduct. These methods of defense ensure privacy from an outside world that is sometimes perceived as hostile to (or wishing to destroy) the family. Because of this fear of outsiders and because of the potential for hidden pathology, a therapist will be wise to begin treatment with an incestuous family in a slow and systematic manner. Also, one should be aware of the fact that, although the abuse to the child may be extreme, many parents who commit incest *appear* to be within the normal population, inasmuch as they are employed, sometimes successfully, and have no mental health or criminal histories. As Meiselman wrote:

> The key to understanding the family's behavior is to realize that its members perceive themselves as being on the brink of disaster in the form of separation, public shame, loss of financial support, and possibly severe punishment for the perpetrator of incest. With occasional exceptions, the "collusive" family members have not demonstrated that incest is their preferred way of life by their uncooperativeness—they have only demonstrated that they are fearful of the alternatives to the status quo. (1978, p. 338)

Moreover, many incest victims believe that they are protecting the family or their siblings, so they sacrifice themselves.

The following types of cases differ markedly in many respects: incest between a 40-year-old father and a 3-year-old child; and between a 35-year-old stepfather and his 16-year-old stepdaughter in which the incest took place one drunken night. Yet, according to law they are the same. A therapist will, of course, be required to report the suspicion (or evidence) of incest in both cases (and, for those who work primarily with children and adolescents, this need to make a report of incest will sooner or later occur). Incest is one of the most underreported crimes in the United States; for each reported incest case, three or more are not reported. It is vitally important that clinicians who work in emergency services establish a good working relationship with the local juvenile probation department and with the Juvenile Officer(s) and Sex Investigation Officer(s) of the local police department. Once these relationships have been established and the therapist has become known and trusted, he or she will have more available options if incest is suspected in a family. For example, if recent or past incest has been discovered in the course of family therapy, and if one is known and trusted by the police or the juvenile probation department, one of those agencies may be willing to receive the report and, in turn, possibly decide not to take further legal action if the prognosis for successful treatment is good. But, if the family drops out of treatment or renewed incidents of sexual assault occur, the original report can be reactivated at once. Even though a convicted parent or sibling must go through the criminal justice system, if a clinician is known to that system, the chances for the person's being ordered by a court to receive psychotherapy (with probation instead of incarceration) will be much greater. Finally, when a family comes in for treatment and the therapist feels that the accused parent or sibling should be removed from the home or prosecuted, he or she will be better able to assist remaining family members through the painful criminal-legal process, as a result of being acquainted with people in the justice system.

The discovery of incest in a family may mean that a great deal of pressure will be placed upon a therapist, by family members, not to report it to the authorities. It is not uncommon for a victim to recant his or her story and try to convince the therapist to drop the entire subject. Often there exists a kind of myth, in an incestuous family, the theme of which is that if incest were revealed the family would be destroyed; that is, their "world" would dissolve and it would be the therapist's fault. This kind of myth-making was ably described by Watzlawick et al., who wrote, "There can be no doubt that a large part of the process of socialization in any society consists in teaching the young that which they must *not* see, *not* hear, *not* think, feel or say" (1974, p. 42).

There follows a suggested protocol for interviewing a child or adolescent who may have been the victim of incest, as well as the uninvolved parent.

Guidelines for Interviewing Children and Adolescents Who May Have Been Sexually Abused

- Be sure the environment feels safe and neutral to the young person

- Give him or her plenty of space
- Be sure that the child or adolescent has had enough to eat and, if possible, is not overly tired
- If he or she is extremely nervous, you may wish to engage him or her in a neutral activity, such as drawing or playing a well-known game
- Unless you are part of a law enforcement agency or an *official* investigative government agency, your role is to document accurately and report the abuse
- It is a serious role- and boundary-violation if a therapist engages in an independent investigation; this could lead to legal and ethical consequences, unless the therapist is court-appointed to conduct such an evaluation or investigation
- Try to learn how the child or adolescent defines the sexual abuse and his or her relationship to the abuser. This may take some time, because the child may not define it as abuse and may view the relationship as one of friendship or love; your own values or definitions may frighten or silence the child; try to remain or appear to remain neutral
- Be careful not to ask leading questions, instead giving open-ended instructions such as, "Please tell me what happened."

During the interview, ask the child or adolescent:

1. To describe the abuser in positive and negative terms.
2. How he or she gets along with the suspected abuser.
3. How the parent disciplines him or her.
4. Does his or her nonabusing parent know about what happened?
5. Did he or she tell the nonabusing parent about what happened? How long ago? What did the parent do about it?
6. Did the parent believe the child or adolescent? Did the parent help the child or adolescent?
7. Does the child or adolescent believe that the parent will believe him or her? Will the parent help him or her?
8. Will the parent keep the abuser out of the home (as CPS will ask him or her to do)?
9. Will the parent protect him or her from the abuser?
10. How does the nonabusive parent get along with the abuser and with other family members?
11. What is the best thing about the nonabusive parent? the worst?

Also include, in the assessment of the child, the following:

1. Is the child protective of the abuser (is there a role reversal)?
2. Is the child talking spontaneously or is he or she concealing information or acting fearful?
3. How anxious is the child to be with his or her parent?
4. Is the child saying that he or she cannot go home and must have somewhere else to stay?

Ask the uninvolved parent during the initial interview:

1. Does the parent believe that the child is telling the truth or that there is at least a possibility that the abuse has occurred?
2. Now that the child has disclosed this and, looking back, did the parent notice that there were indicators that the abuse was occurring?
3. What does the parent believe that the child might be feeling now?
4. Ask the parent to describe to you what the child is normally like. Is this description appropriate for a child or adolescent of this age?
5. Ask the parent to tell you what his or her relationship is like with the child or adolescent; how does he/she solve problems, set limits, discipline, etc.?
6. Where does the parent want the child to be, pending the completion of the investigation?
7. Will the parent cooperate with having the abuser leave the home; or, enforce no contact between the child and the abuser so that the child can remain at home?
8. Will the parent agree to seek treatment for the child and himself or herself?
9. How does the parent feel about the child's talking with the police and prosecuting attorney about what the offender has done?

Also include in the assessment of the uninvolved parent:

1. Is the parent angry at the child or the abuser?
2. How upset or hostile is the parent about the disclosure?
3. How does the parent react to the therapist and to the prospect of further involvement with other professionals?
4. How much empathy is the parent showing for the child or adolescent?
5. Is the parent calm enough to do any planning with the therapist for the child and himself or herself?

6. Is the parent able to suggest the names of supportive people whom he or she and the child can use during this crisis?
7. Are his or her basic concerns for the child or for himself or herself and the abuser?
8. How does he or she compare this child to siblings?

Family Dynamics

Both incestuous and abusive families are notorious for trying to avoid treatment. They tend to fear change, and they fear facing the insidious problems that they have kept so well hidden. Because of this tendency, it may be necessary to take advantage of the court's jurisdiction over the case in order to induce them to stay in treatment beyond the initial, frightening stages. There is considerable evidence to suggest that incest will not stop, even after it is reported, unless the family receives some form of treatment and legal supervision.

Other important questions will have to be answered as the therapist continues to evaluate the situation and decides what action to take. Were there many incestuous incidents or only a single occurrence? If the child has reported just one (and only one) incestuous act to an adult or the uninvolved parent and the parent protected the child, a therapist could assume that there is less serious pathology in that family than if it had been going on for years. But is it possible that intercourse between one parent and his or her child could have occurred repeatedly for 2 or 3 years without the other parent suspecting something? It would not seem likely, but such a situation *did* actually take place, according to the mother of the family described in the following case.

The police were called to a home where incest had been reported. A clinician arrived shortly after the police had left, and one of the first things that the therapist noticed was that there were only three doors in the entire house—the front door, the back door, and the bathroom door; the other interior doors had been removed. Incest had been a part of this family's way of life for many years, as we learned later. The father was no longer with the family because he had been discovered to have been having sex regularly with his oldest daughter (now 17 years old) for about 3 years. Soon after this was revealed, the wife filed for divorce, and the divorce had just become final.

Now it was discovered that the 16-year-old son had been sodomizing his sister, aged 13; in addition, he had forced her to have oral sex with him when she was 6 years old, and had done so regularly through the ensuing 7 years. The mother claimed that she had known nothing about it until the 13-year-old girl had written her a note, reporting it, that morning. She also claimed that she had known nothing about the husband's incestuous behavior with the older daughter until the daughter had reported it to a school teacher. One of this mother's comments may add force to the assertion that great denial characterizes the uninvolved parent in these families: she told the clinician, with great relief in her voice, that she was grateful to God that it was only sodomy because her daughter was still a virgin.

In a case such as this, when incest has been occurring for a long time and should have been detected and reported years earlier, much psychological energy has probably been expended by more than one member of the family in order to keep the incestuous system going. In effect, when incest has been reported to a parent who denies the problem, who refuses to listen or to investigate whether or not the accusation was true, that "uninvolved" parent has become an *integral* part of the problem.

Father-daughter incest can be conceptualized as an event (or series of events) that has the effect of radically revising generational boundary lines, that is, the role of the father changes in relation to one or more of the children (Figure 8.1).

In many incestuous families, the mother is very immature and does not want to accept an adult sexual role. As a consequence, she gradually tends to push her child into adopting a simulated "adult" role. One predisposing factor in the development of an incestuous situation may be initiated when

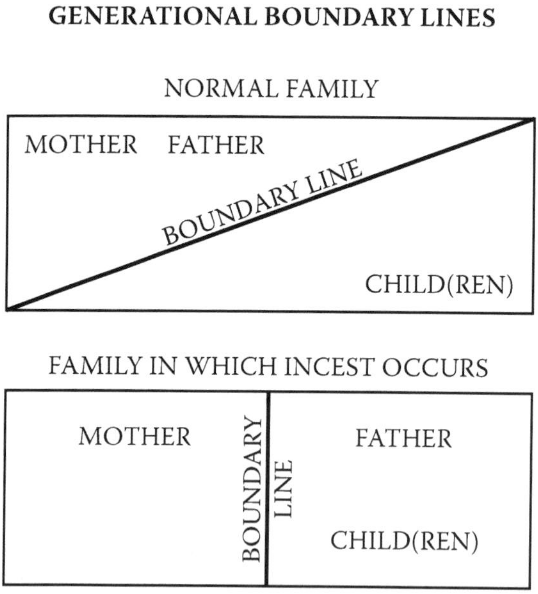

GENERATIONAL BOUNDARY LINES

Figure 8.1

a mother tries to cajole her daughter out of the child's normal role in the family, because she herself wants to regress to being a child.

This type of mother's life script may read as follows. She is probably fearful of sex or is extremely inhibited sexually. She may have had highly romanticized fantasies about what "being married" meant. She may have thought she married someone who was "safe" in the way that a fairy-tale father/husband would be safe, but she may have found that the realities of an adult relationship are distasteful to her. In many cases, sexual relations have completely ceased between the parents in an incestuous family (Lustig et al., 1966; Maisch, 1972; Weiner, 1962; Carson et al., 1990; Lanktree, 1991). Because of the wife's unrealistic expectations, the marriage has become a disappointment to her or, at best, it has become a "truce" relationship. The dirty dishes and diapers and responsibilities have dashed her unfulfilled wishes and dreams. Many of these women use denial as their primary defense mechanism (Machotka et al., 1967). Denial is very important to the internal system of this kind of family and is often very difficult to break through, probably because denial is such a primitive defense mechanism. Moreover, instances in which a mother of this sort proves to be supportive of her daughter-victim are in the minority.

The incestuous father, as noted earlier, may be an alcoholic or drug abuser or may be suffering from a form of paranoid personality disorder. Many are openly obsessed with sexual concerns (Gebhard et al., 1965; de Chenay et al., 1988; Liles and Childs, 1986). This father is very likely neither sexually adept nor a sensitive person. Through reflection on how these kinds of marriage partners are likely to interact sexually, there unfolds a probable blueprint of how the incestuous family system is established. The husband's reaction to his wife's childishness and sexual inadequacy is, usually, hostility and increased ineptitude or insensitivity. He may not be able to recognize or to admit his anger toward his wife. This interpretation may seem confusing, because, outwardly, incestuous families can be those in which much mutual respect is professed and in which protecting the "home" is given great importance. However, although both the parents and the siblings will stress concern for family pride and security, beneath this façade can be tremendous anger and mistrust that the family takes great pains to deny. But when a father commits incest with his daughter, he has chosen the one sexual partner most calculated to punish and humiliate his wife. Thus, even though much family loyalty may be displayed superficially, under the surface lies tremendous resentment, rage, and shame.

Another product of this emphasis on loyalty to the family is that a heavy burden of guilt may be placed on the child victim if she should permit the shared secret to escape the family setting. A case in point is that of a woman of 34 years of age who had been involved in an incestuous relationship with her father from when she was seven until she was 13. As an adult, she still felt tremendous guilt, because she believed that she had destroyed her parents' marriage. She sincerely felt that, at 7 years of age, she had done something to seduce her father and that it was her fault because she was a bad, promiscuous child. She was convinced that if it had not been for her the parents would still be happily married, even though she knew that her father at that time had been, and continued to be, a hopeless alcoholic. This weight of guilt is carried on into adulthood in too many cases and must not be ignored in therapy.

It is true that children are sexual. Even though they are not sexual in an adult-genital way, they have some sexual feelings and they seek affection. In turn, adult responsibility requires a measure of self-control, so that the child's need for affection will not be exploited. It is realistic to estimate, from our experience, that many childhood suicide attempts or psychotic episodes, particularly those incorporating bizarre sexual fantasies, had their origin in situations involving either incest or child molestation that were not discovered or reported. We have encountered several cases of children who were severely psychotic, even though quite young, and who suffered from wild sexual delusions. After they had been hospitalized and were feeling safer, these children were able to reveal that they had been assaulted sexually. One boy had been molested by a stepfather; in his case, experiencing a psychotic break for a period of time was, in a certain sense, a healthy response, and probably the only chance that the child had to work through what had happened to him.

Risk Factors

How do incest cases first come to light? What are some of the "presenting problems" that may eventually reveal an incest situation? Incest may first surface with the case of a runaway adolescent, the suicide attempt of a child or adolescent, or an episode of sudden promiscuity by the child or adolescent. Alternatively, incest may be revealed when an adolescent girl first shows interest in boys and the father blatantly overreacts or behaves like a jealous lover. The child may have confided in an adult outside the family although, in our experience, that is extremely rare. Here is a list of potential risk factors, that include our experiences as well as those of other researchers (i.e., Browning and Boatman, 1977; Meiselman, 1978, p. 334):

1. Alcoholic or chemically dependent father
2. Father who is unusually suspicious and puritanical
3. Violent or authoritarian father

4. Mother who is very passive, absent, or incapable of being a protective force in the family

5. Daughter who plays the role of mother, assuming many of the mother's household functions

6. Parents whose sexual relationship is troubled or nonexistent

7. Situation in which the father often must be alone with the daughter

8. Factors that may limit the self-control of the father, such as drug or alcohol dependency, psychopathy, or limited intelligence

9. Sudden onset of promiscuity on the part of a young girl

10. A child who does not allow people to be close friends with her

11. Parents who are reluctant (or refuse) to allow a clinician to talk with their child alone

12. Hostile or paranoid attitude toward outsiders on the part of one or both parents, especially the father

13. Previous incidents of incest in the nuclear family (families) of one or both parents

14. Parents who had deprived childhoods in which there were inadequate role models

15. Extreme jealousy displayed by the father in a case in which the daughter has recently reached puberty

These warning signs of an incestuous situation are offered as guidelines for looking more closely for incestuous behavior within a family. For example, a therapist may be working with a family when, suddenly, the therapist observes a change in the father-daughter relationship. Perhaps the daughter was once "daddy's little girl," but recently, now that boys have started looking at her, the father has become jealous in a way that is reminiscent of a lover. Soon excessive rules and restrictions are arbitrarily being placed on the girl by her father. (In response to one emergency call, our staff members found the father marching about the house and yelling at his daughter, more like an angry boyfriend than a father.) That kind of clearly reactive behavior on the part of the father can be a cause for concern.

Other warning signs may possibly be observed in the context of an initial crisis visit. For example, during such a visit, the clinician often may make a point of talking briefly in private with each member of the family present, in turn. Whenever dad or mom says, "No, we can deal with this as a family," or when there is a reluctance to let us have a few minutes alone with each member of the family, we often become suspicious that some family secret lies buried. A case-in-point was referred to parenthetically in the previous paragraph. The father in that case was a rigidly controlled man and his very beautiful, 15-year-old daughter was quite socially mature for her age.

The family was referred because the daughter was supposedly beyond parental control. What we discovered was an angry, troubled (but to all intents and purposes normal) adolescent who was behaving with defiance toward her father. When she would defy him, he would become enraged and throw her against a wall or slap her repeatedly. It appeared that the father was placing limits on her that were more appropriate for an 11-year-old child: for example, she could only go out on one night each weekend, and she always had to be home by 9:00 p.m., never later; after she had gone out once, she could not leave the home again that same weekend. After talking with the whole family awhile, a clinician asked to talk with each family member alone. When each had agreed, the therapist talked with the two parents in turn. But when it was time to talk with the daughter alone, the father refused to leave. Smiling, he said, "We are a family and can work everything out together. Besides, it is important for me, as her father, to understand what is troubling my daughter." There was no way that he would permit the therapist to speak in private with the girl. When the therapist talked with the girl, she appeared angry but also seemed to be extraordinarily fearful of her father. Later, in family sessions, the therapist attempted to focus on family communication and the establishment of more realistic rules for the daughter, as well as helping the father accept the fact that teenage girls do have dates with boys.

As time went on, we became increasingly concerned that some form of incest might be taking place in this home. For one thing, the girl simply could not form close relationships with anyone. She would keep friends for just a short time and then drop them, or have fights with them and use the fight as an excuse to end the friendship. The clinician discovered from the mother that the daughter had suddenly become extremely promiscuous, and the mother also confided that she simply could not understand her daughter's behavior. Whenever the daughter became hurt or angry, she would simply "pick up" the first boy that she could find. In fact, she would often choose boys who were rough with her and would abuse her physically. Finally, one night the daughter ran away from home and called the therapist. She was drunk, had taken some pills, and was very, very frightened. The therapist found her and brought her to our office where, drinking coffee, they talked for several hours. The girl told a story of sexual abuse that began when the father first had intercourse with her when she was 6; it continued until she was 13, when he began insisting that she perform oral sex. She begged the therapist not to make her go back home. The therapist reassured her that she would not have to return home and made arrangements for her to stay in the county's children's shelter. Later investigation proved that the girl's story was agonizingly true in every detail. Both parents then denounced her as a "tramp" who had betrayed and destroyed the family. The girl is currently living in a foster home and, following a period of "testing limits," is adjusting quite well. Her parents suddenly moved away to another state and broke off all contact with their daughter. It is worth noting that incestuous intercourse between father and daughter may stop when the daughter becomes old enough to conceive a child. In many cases, sexual activity then shifts to oral or anal copulation or to masturbation. Alternatively, the father may select a younger daughter.

Another tragic outcome of incest occurs when a child or adolescent confuses sexuality with anger, as when having sex and being hurt are confounded. By contrast, the more normal line of reasoning is as follows: "Sex and affection and 'being close' feel good, but when I am hurt or angry, I feel bad and I don't want to be close." Yet, in many incestuous situations, the reasoning becomes: "I was close to my parent and he [or she] used me sexually; I feel impossibly confused and uncontrollably angry." As a result of this confusion, many of the children of incest have acted-out promiscuously—in our experience—especially when they felt wounded or perplexed.

Much of the foundation supporting family life is the basic bond of trust between parent and child, that is, "My parents will protect me," which provides the elementary lesson plan by which normal person-to-person attachment is taught. But the incestuous kind of family interaction implies a profound betrayal of that fundamental parent-child bond of trust. When basic trust is destroyed in a sexual way (quite often in a physically painful way), it is not hard to imagine the terrible perplexity that the child experiences. It is our observation that many children of incest cannot keep close friends. In many cases, when something bad happens, or when they are hurt or unhappy, many will sleep with anyone who comes along. These adolescents tend to describe their behavior in terms epitomized by this young girl's statement: "Yeah, I don't know what it is, but something bad happens to me. I'm hurt and I go out and I want to get messed up. I want to party and I want to get it on with any guy. I just don't care—anybody."

One little girl, who had "gone through" 10 foster homes and also was a victim of incest, would immediately approach—in a very sexual way—any adult male in her current foster family, as a means of getting what she perceived as the inevitable sex "over with." It was as though she was saying: "Let's get it over with now because I'm not going to attach to you and then have you do the same thing to me that my father did." As soon as she moved to a foster home, she would express this totally inappropriate means of defense by sitting on the foster father's lap in a very provocative way, thereby infuriating the foster mother. For about a week she would seductively cater to her new foster father's every whim. Then, when the foster mother discovered her acting-out sexually with boys in the neighborhood, that would be the "last straw" and the foster parents would ask to have her removed from their home. This behavior had been repeated many times before anyone became aware of what the problem was. Hence, a clinician who observes this type of promiscuousness would be well advised to investigate its origins. A clinician should be equally curious about an inability to "attach" or to let people get close without being seductive toward them.

Another example of this fear of attachment can be found in the case of a pleasant young woman who was being seen for individual psychotherapy. When a teenager, she had been sexually abused by her father for a period of about 3 years. By the time she began therapy, she had had five or six fiancés. Each time she prepared to marry, she would unconsciously reflect that her future husband would possibly become a father, and she would suddenly find an excuse to end the relationship. Having a husband who would eventually be the father of her children was just too terrifying a thought for her. In this case, the memory of an incestuous experience had been deeply repressed, with extremely self-punitive results.

If a clinician suspects that incest is occurring with a 2- or 3-year-old child, the intervention should be quite thorough and aggressive, because serious psychopathology can be expected on the part of the sexually involved parent—with the attendant risk that this parent will lose control. A child of this age is desperately in need of protection. By contrast, when the suspected victim is a teenager, a therapist should intervene more cautiously, with a view to developing a trust relationship in which the therapist is seen as a person in whom the adolescent can confide. The therapist will want to establish at least the kind of relationship in which an adolescent will seek out the clinician in a moment of crisis or when he or she is in danger. It is not a good idea to "push" young people who may have been involved in incest unless it is absolutely necessary, because issues of trust are so essential in doing therapy with them. We have discovered that there are an amazing number of family emergencies in which incest (or incestuous impulses being confronted inappropriately) represents an important element of the family's problem.

Treatment

A wise approach in therapy is to view incest as a whole-family problem, in which sexual roles, sources of power, and boundaries have become distorted. In this context, a clinician should strive to do everything possible to reassure the child that it was not his or her fault. Often, the sexually involved parent attempts to place blame on a "seductive" or malevolent child, but in therapy it is vital to restore responsibility for self-control to the parents. Treatment that is focused on a single victim and a single villain fails to acknowledge that each family can be viewed as a system. Even so, the parents must assume responsibility for what has happened.

When incest has been reported by a child to an uninvolved parent who has, in turn, ignored the accusation or dismissed the child as a liar or "bad child" without further investigation and action to protect the child, one usually finds that this parent is also an integral part of the incestuous situation. Imagine a child of yours telling you that your spouse had had sexual relations with him or her; reflect on what your reaction would be. Think how desperately weak and terrified a parent would have to be to ignore such an accusation. Too often, an uninvolved parent will condone or even try to protect, this extremely pathological, symbiotic relationship between the incestuous parent and the child.

When treating an incestuous family, it is useful to structure the therapy sessions according to the way in which the therapist would like to see the family change. For example, it is advisable to offer sessions for the entire family as well as sessions for the parents as a couple. Of course, individual sessions for the child victim are a vital component of treatment. During these individual sessions, the child may be encouraged to ventilate his or her private feelings, whereas in the family sessions the subjects discussed should be whole-family issues. Problems of the parents as adults, such as their sexual relationship, should be subjects of the couple's sessions. In both the family and couple sessions, it may be useful to include a cotherapist of the opposite sex, because working with families can be emotionally exhausting and the support of another therapist will help, especially during the initial, emergency phase. It is also important for a therapist to be aware of his or her own limits and to guard against the intense feelings that incest arouses in every one of us.

It is generally recommended that the child victim be treated by a therapist of the same sex. Because in many cases the incestuous trauma has been a child's first sexual experience, much of therapy involves encouraging the boy or girl to describe his or her feelings, as well as providing appropriate information on sexual subjects. Moreover, a clinician should not be surprised or suspicious if the child's emotional reaction to incest appears, at first, to be emotionally bland. This reaction will pass when the child begins to feel safe with the therapist. Later on in treatment, it may be appropriate for the child to be seen by a therapist of the opposite sex. At first, a young girl may simply be unable to talk with a man, but after 6 months to a year of treatment it may be a good idea to refer her to a male therapist.

When working with the children of incest, it is vital to take into account how much they can or cannot accept. In many cases, the first thing a therapist will want to do is reach out and reassure the child, but most children will be fearful and lacking in trust. Their trust has already been betrayed by an untrustworthy adult. This issue is a primary one, for in the process of establishing a relationship, a child may "test the limits" of the therapist for a long time. Adolescents will break appointments or simply forget them and will find many ways to ask their most pressing question, "Do you really care about me?" With some clients, a clinician does not permit evasive behavior; but with a victim of incest, a clinician should expect considerable resistance or even provocation and be prepared to take action to ensure that the child remains in treatment.

How does a therapist bring up the subject of incest, or ask a child if it has occurred? If the child is 10 or 11 or older, the therapist may say something like this:

> "As you know, relationships between fathers and daughters [or mothers and sons] can be very close. In some ways, they can be difficult. I had feelings of love toward my own father [mother]. Everyone does. But some of the things that you told me gave me the feeling—and you can stop me if I am wrong because I am not always right—that something might have happened between you and your dad [mom] that hurt you or frightened you."

At a deeper level of inquiry, the therapist may say:

> "What you told me is understandable. A lot of people think it is terrible, but even though it can be very frightening, it happens in a lot of families, and it is not the end of the world. Just because it happened in the past doesn't mean it has to happen again, and I shall do everything I can to prevent it in the future. But I think it is important that I know the truth. Some things you said to me made me a little concerned that, maybe, one time your father [mother] put his [her] hands on you and frightened you, or maybe tried to have sex with you."

It is vital, at this moment, to be alert and watch the child's nonverbal behavior very closely, looking for sudden movement or averting of the eyes or rubbing the nose (when a person rubs his or her nose, it usually indicates that the other person has referred to something that has made him or her angry or uncomfortable). Also, it is useful to watch the child's feet—most people can control the nonverbal behavior of their facial musculature when they try to do so, but the feet may "leak" information about feelings (cf. Ekman and Friesen, 1969). When a foot is bobbed up and down suddenly, as though by reflex, the therapist can make a calculated guess that the inward emotion may not be matched by what is being said. By observing these indicators of stress through nonverbal behavior, the clinician may not have to pursue the subject of incest further with the child at this time. Instead, the therapist can merely note that the subject has proven to be a sensitive or painful one, at the same time letting the child know that no matter what he or she says it will be accepted, and that he or she is not the only person in the world to whom this may have happened.

When the proper moment arrives, a therapist can establish a situation in which the child will feel at ease about telling his or her story. Having done the initial framing, the clinician can say something like this:

> "I have worked with a lot of families before who have had this problem in which there has been a relationship between a father and a daughter [a mother and a son], and there are certain patterns and certain things that happen in these families. There seems to be a similarity between your family and that kind of family. Now I could be wrong, but . . . "

Here, the child can be given an opportunity to get out of the situation, for example,

> "I could be wrong, and please tell me if I am, but I have about an eighty percent hunch that this is happening in your family. I am not one hundred percent sure . . . "

Then the therapist can proceed in this way: "Now it might not have been actual intercourse or sex, but. . . " At each step, the therapist gives the child a chance to move toward the subject and a chance to test the therapist's reactions as well. "Maybe there was some petting" is another means of approach. By this procedure, a child will be permitted to describe a little bit about the event but is given the option to withdraw from the conversation if necessary.

In summary, incest is the culmination of a complex and pathological series of events which arise within the context of an entire family system. When a clinician first intervenes in a case of actual or suspected incest (by definition an emergency situation), there are several key issues to investigate fully. Was the incest a one-time event or did it occur repeatedly over a long period of time? Repetitive incest is rarely the result of only one family member's psychopathology, and is naturally more difficult to treat. Because the family has conspired to tolerate this problem for a long time, it may have depleted its internal strengths and may lack the necessary energy to accomplish changes in the system. Although repetitive incest very likely involves the whole family, participation by some family members may take the form of "selective inattention," passive acceptance, or denial. Another important issue is the age difference between the sexually involved parent and the child victim. In most cases, the greater the age difference or the younger the child, the greater the likelihood of serious pathology on the part of the incestuous parent. Finally, a vital issue is whether or not a child has been able to tell someone about the incestuous events. If he or she did not tell the uninvolved parent, but instead went outside the family system for help, it may indicate that this family presently contains few sources of support or protection for the victimized child.

Preventing Suicide

Suicide is the most unnatural human act. It defies the most fundamental power that governs living creatures—the instinct for survival. No other animal takes its own life.[1] There is a terrible irony in the fact that, among the world's creatures, human beings know better than others that they are mortal; we even have a realistic sense of how long we might live. To take the matter into our own hands seems both absurd and contemptuous of life itself.

Mental health professionals have an implied obligation to help their clients solve their problems and guide them toward healthy ways to resolve conflicts and cope with life's stresses and disappointments. They have an unspoken but undeniable duty to keep their clients alive; it follows that preventing a suicide may be the finest contribution that a therapist can make toward the welfare of another person. In short, reducing the suicide rate is the acid test of our art.

In America in most years, approximately 30,000 persons kill themselves; the rate varies little, and it has not risen significantly in relation to the population rate.[2] There is no epidemic of suicidal deaths in our country, which means that it is not commonly a public health problem. Huge publicity campaigns advising people to do this or that as an alternative to thinking suicidal thoughts are not likely to appear and, even if they did, not much would be accomplished. No, the impulse to suicide is a personal matter, and each instance of suicidal intent must be dealt with on an individual basis. That's why therapists play a vitally important role in prevention.

Who kill themselves? It may seem that there is no definable type of suicidal person, especially when we reflect that each death of this kind seems to baffle those who were close to the person; their anguish after the fact is best expressed by something like "We never knew." There are two categories of suicidal people, the first consisting of those who have been diagnosed as terminally ill and fear suffering, those who have recently lost a cherished mate and seek to join the other in the afterlife, those who face the death penalty or a life sentence, war combatants who wish to be remembered as heroes, or religious fanatics who seek martyrdom. People in this category are best described as *involuntary* suicides, because they are in the grasp of forces beyond their control. Giving in to those forces seems the only way to resolve their crisis and, to escape, they are convinced that they *need* to die.

A second type of suicidal person wants to send a message to those who will survive his or her untimely death. This is the *voluntary* suicide. These people use their deaths to accomplish a diabolical purpose: the symbolic "death" of another person. The act itself is immeasurably cruel, as will be shown in the pages to follow. It ranks with mayhem and murder in its sheer inhumanity toward one's fellow man. This act is not the product of accident or weakness or diminished capacity of any kind, nor is it a manifestation of mental illness strictly defined. It is willful harm motivated by evil intent.

Dynamics of Suicide

The first step toward understanding the suicidal impulse is perhaps the hardest for clinicians, because it contradicts conventional wisdom: disconnecting suicide from depression. A form of mental illness that affects millions of people, especially in Western nations, depression can be a severely debilitating disorder; many a life has been ruined by it and, in its chronic form, its torment can last a lifetime. Even so, it is not responsible for suicide. The founder of the discipline of Suicidology, Edwin Shneidman, has written, "Depression *never* causes suicide" (A sobering message for those who believe that only antidepressant medication can dispel suicidal thoughts.). Certainly, it is true that there is a correlation between depression and suicidal ideation, but a correlation is not a causal connection. Suicide may be preceded by a depressive episode, but the episode itself is not a *sufficient* cause of the suicidal act; if it were, the incidence of suicide among those millions who are depressed would be a staggering figure indeed. Furthermore, people kill themselves who have never been diagnosed as having been depressed; that is, depression is not a *necessary* cause of suicide. These elements of causal connection, the necessary and the sufficient, must be found elsewhere. Everything that we know about depression, its onset, course, treatment, and resolution will not help us here, because being depressed and being suicidal are *qualitatively* different states.

How can we learn about suicide when the subject of our inquiry ends in horror and silence? The suicidal person has foiled our efforts to understand what might have happened to him or her to produce this result. Of course, some leave notes, but many of these are couched in such cryptic language that they provide no certain clues (some suicide notes are suppressed by family members or the police, and are never made public). The only research procedure that can claim some validity is the "psychological autopsy," by which interviews are conducted with those who knew the suicidal person, usually after a considerable interval in deference to their feelings about the death. This approach depends heavily on the truthfulness of the interview subjects, some of whom may have reason to let bias influence their accounts, as will be shown later.

Newspaper stories about people who kill themselves often describe the person as having been "despondent" or "troubled" or "in despair," because lay opinion equates the idea of suicide with the symptoms of depression or, at the very least, some form of mental disorder. It is true that suicide and depression are like two buildings erected side by side on the same foundation. The key to explaining both rests on a thorough understanding of that foundation.

The primary motivating force in the depressive condition is anger that can find no outward expression. Or, in a more cynical view offered on the Internet, depression is "anger without enthusiasm." Animosity leads to hostility and, in turn, hatred, rage, or fury, but none of these emotions can be released, nor can they reach the object for which they are intended.[3] When a confrontation with the hated object is impossible, the repressed negative energy remains trapped within, festers, and is turned toward the self. In the most extreme cases, such as those of people who are "warehoused" in the back wards of mental hospitals, this self-hatred is given voice in desperate cries like "I'm no good" or "Just take me out and shoot me."

Seldom are depressed people aware of the hateful thoughts that are kept buried at a subconscious level. Many such people are the products of pathogenic childhoods in which they were intimidated and browbeaten by an abusive parent or a tyrannical church or school environment. They know that they were abused and who was responsible, but they also have been programmed to forgive their tormentors or "turn the other cheek;" even worse, they may have been brainwashed into believing that they *deserved* their punishment. The latter are the most impervious to any kind of psychotherapy and can only be "maintained" by antidepressant medication, some for the rest of their lives. Depressed people need to confront the object or objects of their anger and expiate their negative feelings, in much the same way that the body must purge itself of poisons.[4] Many people dream about this sort of confrontation for years, planning what would occur and rehearsing it in their minds. Sadly, many never achieve this in real terms, fearing retaliation which would make matters worse. The fact remains that, until the anger is vented or diffused, depression will persist.

The qualitative difference between depression and suicidal ideation is subtle but profound. Suicidal people are angry to be sure and, as noted earlier, some are clinically depressed. But, with time, they no longer turn their anger onto themselves; they no longer blame themselves for their troubles, and stop feeling that they are worthless. Subconsciously, they see that they can, by ending their lives, achieve a goal they could not reach by continuing to live. Without being aware of it, they take a different path from the one that leads to depression. They make of their death a *weapon*. This process is shown graphically by Figure 9.1.

Suicidal people are trapped in a malignant relationship of some kind with another person or persons; usually, one person in particular is the source of the pathology. The suicidal death is intended to *punish* the other person, who must live on and bear the guilt that follows from the death. This person who is being punished can be called the "target" of the suicide. To the extent that friends and relatives knew these two antagonists, they

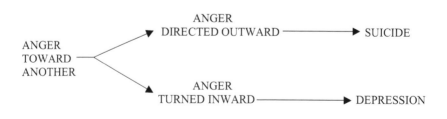

Figure 9.1

will help to administer this guilt, but the target will be his or her own primary accuser, judge, and tormentor.

After a suicidal death, we often speculate that it might have been, in reality, accidental, or in some way a product of poor impulse control. This quite natural response, based on the wish to excuse what has happened, has the effect of trivializing the act and underestimating its cruel intent. Voluntary suicide is a willed assault on its target, a brutal effort to ruin the life of another person, an act of spite. It cannot be justified or excused.

The Threat

Righteous indignation alone will not suffice to reduce the suicide rate. Clinicians will, but only if they can intervene early, soon after depression "lifts" and suicide is contemplated. If a client makes a threat of suicide in the course of therapy, therapy must change; a crisis has occurred and must be dealt with; therapy becomes focused on suicide prevention. In some cases, the threat is ambiguous and the only sign of distress is a burst of tearfulness or bitter aside such as "It's too much" or "I can't take it anymore." Then it is vitally important to acknowledge what has been said, as by asking "Were you thinking of doing something to hurt yourself?" If the answer is even vaguely "yes," a thorough evaluation of suicide potential must begin. This may or may not mean trying to elicit a "no-suicide contract," but making the contract is no guarantee that a life has been saved. The determination of a truly suicidal person to break every convention, even a promise to a therapist, is like hardened steel.

On the way to a suicidal act, people experience waves of rumination and arrive at a series of choice-points in the process of making up their minds about what to do. Some of these stages are skipped, or the sequence may be altered, but they serve as signposts for the therapist to assess the seriousness of the threat. Below is a sketch of this process.

- I have a problem.
- The problem is unsolvable.
- I am willing to pay any price.
- I shall die anyway.
- My life belongs to me.
- A person uses what he or she has available.
- My death can be a weapon.
- To cause death is a moral crime.
- The punishment for causing a death is lifelong.
- The problem will be solved when I place the *blame* for causing my death on the right person.

Note that these are not the ravings of a psychotic person, but, rather, one whose logic is coldly calculating.

If ever a cry for help was to be heard in therapy, a threat of suicide ranks as the loudest and clearest. It signifies that therapy has not been working. It also implies that, if the therapist does not do everything possible to cope with the threat, he or she may share in the eventual guilt created by a suicidal death. In short, try not to become a target yourself.

Finding the Target

Suicidal ideation emerges in the context of a relationship gone awry. For that reason, therapy to prevent suicide must come to terms with the present status of the damaged relationship, and find a means of repairing it. The preferred approach, of course, is to involve the other person of the dyad in therapy, but the intended target of a suicidal threat may be unwilling to get involved in repairing a relationship that he or she feels is beyond repair. Even so, it is entirely possible to treat a relationship with only one person in attendance, as long as the content of therapy is focused on relationship issues. The same is true when, for example, a therapist will find that more than one in a network of interlocking relationships is in need of repair, such as occurs in internecine family warfare; the threatening client may say, "They'll be sorry." Family therapy may be of help when feasible; but, if not, therapy should concentrate on the most volatile of client-family interactions, in keeping with the premise outlined in the next section.

When he or she receives a credible threat of suicide, the therapist is drawn into a situation much like that of a detective in a murder mystery. The threatener has decided, however seriously, to carry out the symbolic murder of another person by means of his or her own death. The therapist's task is to learn the identity of this person. Naturally, a therapist may know very well who the intended target is, but when in doubt the "Who?" question must be asked, in some form such as "Whom do you hate?" or "Who is your worst enemy?" or, straightforwardly, "Who would be blamed for your death?" Identifying this person is the touchstone to solving the mystery. Moreover, it is the key to changing, through intervention, the crucial relationship so that the symbolic murder doesn't occur.

The likely target of a suicide will be found among people who are close to the threatener, such as a:

- Spouse or life partner
- Boyfriend or girlfriend
- Friend
- Son or daughter

- Relative
- Boss
- Coworker
- Neighbor
- Ex-spouse
- Sworn enemy

These 10 possible antagonists are listed in descending order of the likelihood that they might have been involved with the threatener in a pathological relationship. It would be a tragic irony if the person in question were unaware that he or she was in danger of being blamed for another person's death.

It may be that a formerly malignant relationship no longer exists, such as when the threatener has been terrorized by a tyrannical father who has long since died. The purpose, then, of the suicidal act would be to destroy the relationship retroactively by discrediting the father in the memories of those who knew him. A case in point was that of the poetess Sylvia Plath, who killed herself in 1963 at the age of 30. Her father had died when she was 8 years old, but her relationship with him was undoubtedly of the love-hate variety, and haunted her all her life. Her poem, "Daddy," is a corrosive indictment of her father, whom she likened to a Nazi, and there is evidence in other poems that she never forgave him for his treatment of her. A second target was her very-much-alive former husband, Ted Hughes, who abandoned her and their children to live nearby with another woman. Plath, in "Daddy," drew a comparison between Hughes and her father, linking them as twin targets of her rage. Even though he lived with the shame and guilt of Sylvia's suicide, Hughes rose to become Poet Laureate of England. But, more than 30 years after her death, he published a book of poems that he wrote about her and for her, paying tribute to her memory, and within a year succumbed to illness and died. A Greek tragedy had reached its predestined resolution.[5]

Intervention

A client who threatens suicide presents the therapist with a dilemma and then slyly waits to see what steps the therapist will take to solve it. The first step is, again, to identify the intended victim of punishment, living or dead. Next, some estimate of lethality of the threat will be made, relying on the usual markers of plan, means to carry out the plan, and so on. This assessment, if the information is believable, will tell the therapist how much time is available for intervention. Critical behaviors that signify the presence of a plan and at least some degree of resolve to carry it out are listed here. If a majority of these have already occurred or are imminent, the threatener has decided on a means to commit the act, and will, after certain affairs are put to rest, look for an opportunity.[6]

It is a sign of danger if the person:

- Is involved in a mutually destructive relationship, or cannot let go of a damaging relationship from the past
- Speaks in absolute terms about the other person, as in "She never did understand me" or "It's finished with us" or "I'll never escape from that man"
- Expresses frustration with people in general, describing them in cynical terms such as "People don't change" or "You can't trust anyone"
- Is frequently nostalgic, reminiscing about significant events in his or her life, or returning to significant places as if to say goodbye
- Starts giving people advice about what direction their lives should take, as though he or she wouldn't be around to advise them later on
- Insists on concluding pending business matters, such as finalizing a sale or transferring titles or setting up a trust fund for a child; and, of course, makes a will when in perfect health
- Begins to sort out short-term and long-term projects, keeping the ones that are "doable" and discarding ones that might take a while to complete
- Calls an old friend with whom he or she has lost touch, or visits a grandmother for the first time in years
- Becomes inexplicably generous, giving away possessions to people, much to their surprise
- Expresses newfound religious convictions, or heatedly denounces religion as "worthless"
- Becomes, if vain, supervain; or, if normally unconcerned about appearance, downright slovenly
- Seeks to persuade people that the crisis in his or her life has passed, and that there is no further need for worry
- Suddenly becomes silent when asked what he or she is feeling, changing the subject by "shutting-out" or becoming distant

Finally, the therapist conducts an examination or reexamination of the status of the relationship between client and target.

One person has formed the idea that dying would be preferable to continuing in the relationship with the other person. The rage and resentment that your client feels toward the other has reached a point beyond containment. Homicide is one option, but your client has chosen another solution.

The target can be punished a thousand times over by the guilt that will fall on him or her if the client dies by suicide.

When a client makes a credible threat of suicide and therapy, of necessity, takes on a new form, emphasis should be placed on two major themes: (1) how the client deals with angry feelings and (2) reconciliation with the antagonist. Naturally, one expects to find that the client deals poorly with anger, especially since it is this emotion that fuels the suicidal impulse. By contrast with the depressed person, who seethes with self-loathing, the truly suicidal person plots and schemes over the logistics of revenge. To the observer, he or she displays only a sullen resentment, the better to conceal a guilty secret.

The therapist, having found out who is the designated target, should explore every possible reason for the client's hatred toward that person—every complaint, every grievance, every damning incident of slight or humiliation or scorn. This narrative, punctuated by outbursts of righteous indignation and thunderclaps of rage, may last longer than you would like, but it is an absolutely vital catharsis that may require more than one session. You need to hear a complete account of the "crimes" that have been committed against your client, the entire docket of charges, the full indictment. A therapist must show some empathy for a client's feeling of having been wronged, as well as some understanding of the desire for vengeance.

When the lamentation is over and emotions have cooled, it will be time to ask some trenchant questions like "That's why you hate him [her], isn't it?" Sooner or later, one can ask: "Do you believe that he [she] will be punished by your death?" this is a rhetorical question that reveals your knowledge of the threatener's motivation. No matter what answer is given, a milestone will have been reached in this therapeutic journey. A conclusion to this phase of treatment can be reached only if the client has:

1. Acknowledged the identity of the target
2. Acknowledged the anger felt toward that person
3. Agreed to attempt some sort of positive change in his or her relationship with the antagonist

If there is going to be a confrontation between these adversaries, it preferably would take place in the therapist's office so that the conflict can be mediated. If the client wants to choose another time and place, the therapist can only advise that some neutral person be present to witness the encounter.

Having vented to you, the client should be content to keep his or her emotions under control during this meeting, and in fact should be advised to do so. The goal of the meeting is to give the prospective target of suicide a chance to make a heartfelt apology for past hurtful behavior toward your client. If this does not appear likely, the meeting should be ended and a postponement offered. If the apology is forthcoming, the recipient should be given an opportunity to reflect on it and judge its genuineness.

If the suicidal client feels that the apology was genuine, it should be accepted at face value, in a way that conveys to the other that it will serve as recompense in full for the harm that has been done. If the suicidal person cannot accept it, the therapist or impartial observer should take him or her aside and ask, "For that, you would give up your life? Is it worth it?" It may be that one encounter between these adversaries is not enough or may have occurred too soon for them to make peace, and more meetings will have to be arranged.

No matter when it happens, acceptance of an apology must be followed by forgiveness on the part of the injured person, the threatener. Even if "I forgive you" cannot be articulated at the time of the apology, it has to be said eventually in another face-to-face encounter. If the apology was made face-to-face, forgiveness must be offered face-to-face. The final step in this process is for the antagonist to promise, in person, not to hurt your client again. Figure 9.2 shows the ideal sequence of events that is essential in healing this fractured but not yet severed relationship. If any event in this process is missing, the injured relationship will not be mended, there will be no closure for either person, and the battle will be joined once more.

If the antagonist proves to be evasive or simply refuses to cooperate with these efforts at mediation, work with the client will resume in earnest. Anger must find some other release than plotting to punish the antagonist. Some therapists recommend that an angry person sublimate through sports, preferably ones that involve violent contact under controlled conditions. Therapists have been known to suggest that a client beat on a pillow or, in extreme cases of repression, buy a professional punching-bag, hang it in the garage, and batter it with bare fists. As with most emotions, anger is a primitive force that, taken to an extreme, will give way to fatigue and eventual relief. Role-playing, with the therapist as the antagonist, can help

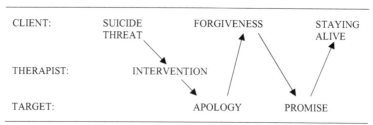

Adapted from Everstine, L. The Meaning of Life, p.89.

Figure 9.2

to expiate anger expressed orally, but should be done with care lest the therapist become the displaced target of the client's rage.

The difficulty in defusing suicidal thoughts if the intended target refuses to cooperate comes when this question arises: "Can you forgive him [her] for what he [she] did to you?" Two crucial events, an apology and acceptance of the apology, have not occurred and may never occur. Faced with this dilemma, the therapist's task is to discredit the antagonist in every possible way: " If you kill yourself, he [she] will escape punishment;" "He [she] will call you a coward;" "He [she] will invite your enemies to a party to celebrate your death;" "He [she] will steal your wife [husband];" "A person so despicable as that is unworthy of your death." "Your enemy grows older, and every day is closer to being judged for his [her] actions;" "The best revenge is living well."

To change the way in which your client perceives the object of his or her murderous rage can be an epiphany even more powerful than extracting the enemy's apology. This new assessment of the toxic relationship means that the client can walk away from the relationship without self-blame, with pride intact. In this scenario, no forgiveness is called-for because no apology was given. When the client can say, with conviction, "That person is worth nothing to me," the crisis will have passed.

A similar theme underlies the process of resolving conflict with a person who is no longer in your client's life. As in the case of Sylvia Plath, when a person has unfinished business with a dead antagonist, no apology will occur and forgiveness has no object. The person who was injured long ago lives with emotional wounds that cannot heal, and is haunted by a ghost that can never be dispelled. A true example is that of a man whose father made a decision not to speak to him and maintained his silence for 20 years. When the son came home for visits, the father would leave the room or look away when his son was present, humiliating him in the eyes of the rest of the family. There was no resolving this bitterly failed relationship, and the son eventually threw himself from a bridge into the path of an oncoming train.

If a client has unfinished business with a lost relationship, therapy consists in a review of the history of the relationship, with the purpose of interpreting what happened by shining a bright light on minute details, reflected in the wisdom of clinical hindsight; for example, the abusive parent was an alcoholic who lashed out when drunk; the neglectful mother needed to work at several jobs because she had been raised in poverty. This new perspective on what happened in the past relies on the belief that the parents were cruel or unfeeling because of diminished capacity. Or, if the father died because of liver cancer or the mother lost her husband to divorce because she neglected him as well, one can take as consolation that the antagonists got their just desserts. Through this kind of "reframing" of the past, wrongs can be understood if not righted, and a sense of retribution achieved. In short, you are helping the client to create a *new* history.

Nature's Prevention

There are far too many suicides in the world, but the reason there aren't more is that Nature exerts its own deterrent force. The instinct for survival was cited above as one vector of this force, but there is notably one other. Nearly every therapist has known a client who alluded to suicidal thoughts, some more adamantly than others, but there is a magical phrase that will convince the therapist that the threat is not serious, namely this answer to the question "What has kept you from doing something to hurt yourself?" " . . . my children [child, son, daughter]."

People stay alive because their lives are *needed* by people who depend upon them. It isn't always a child, but it is always a close relationship. The irony here is that suicide is caused by a relationship gone wrong, and survival rests on a relationship that must be preserved because it is right.

CHAPTER **10**

Introduction to Trauma

The term "trauma" means many things to many people. Its denotation has been stretched beyond reasonable limits, with the result that it has passed into ordinary parlance to describe an unpleasant surprise or a startling experience. The *Diagnostic and Statistical Manual* of the American Psychiatric Association (DSM-IV, 1994), defines "Post-traumatic Stress Disorder" in this way: " . . . characteristic symptoms following exposure to an extreme traumatic stressor."

The *Manual* is more specific in listing causal factors that can lead to trauma:

1. Direct personal experience that involves actual or threatened death or serious injury, or other threat to one's personal integrity
2. Witnessing an event that involves death, injury, or a threat to the physical integrity of another person

3. Learning about unexpected or violent death, serious harm, or threat of death or injury experienced by a family member or other close associate (DSM-IV, p. 424)

These criteria permit nearly any extraordinary event to qualify as traumatic. Even so, the emphasis on death or physical injury may be overly restrictive. In fact, few of life's most frightening events involve actual bodily harm, and very seldom do we find ourselves in a situation that is truly life-threatening. Conversely, common sense tells us that to witness an event that affects someone else is not the same as being the person affected, nor is merely learning about such an event. In this regard, the *Manual* definition of "PTSD" is incomprehensibly broad.

In our view, an event is traumatic when its occurrence is *life-changing*. The person's experience today will affect days to come. It will not be forgotten, but will rest undisturbed in the mind; unlike a benign childhood memory, it will be relived. This wound can be healed, as will be shown later in Part Two, but it can profoundly alter the person's outlook on life. That the outcome can be beneficial in the fullness of time has been established by the work of Bonanno (2004), Henry et al. (2004), and Knowlton (2004).

This concept of a psychological wound or injury is the fundamental principle of our approach to trauma. We see trauma as having parallels to a sprained ankle or a broken arm, or even a broken back. These injuries to the body are analogous to the psychological injuries represented by trauma. This view contrasts sharply with the DSM-IV model of trauma as a form of illness or "disorder," that is, pathology. Based on error and superstition, the disease model of trauma can be traced to a time when people who exhibited the symptoms of trauma were thought to be neurotic in some way—even crazy. Many who survived the battlefields of World War I, only to suffer the condition called "shellshock," returned to friends, family members, and physicians who saw their distress as cowardice or a deficit of will power. We do not consider traumatic reactions to be signs of either weakness or pathology. They occur because a person was in the wrong place at the wrong time and suffered emotional injury.

Victims and Survivors

In the chronology of trauma, there are two distinct phrases that should be distinguished by different terms. The traumatic event or events occur and come to a conclusion, after which the state of trauma begins. Initially, *in the event*, the person is properly described as a victim (e.g., of an assault, of child abuse, of a terrorist attack, of a natural disaster or war). But, during and after the period of traumatization, the victim is best thought of as a survivor. For clinicians and public agencies to continue calling them victims creates a false impression that can engender a sense of passive acceptance, by contrast with a sense of pride that he or she has stayed alive and can, starting now, rebuild his or her life. There has already been, in the process of becoming a victim, full measure of fear and paradoxical guilt (see later), not to mention helplessness and shame. The healing process of survival can be reframed into a prideful experience. The work of the psychiatrist Milton Erickson has helped us to understand that subtle shades of meaning in the labels that are applied to us can change our frame of reference and open the way to positive life changes.

How Trauma Is Viewed by Others

People have fears concerning their own vulnerability that can engender insensitivity toward those who are grieving—as from the loss of a loved one. They may set up unrealistic expectations of the survivors of a traumatic event, or stigmatize them out of their own insecurity. For example, there is the popular myth that there is a "normal" period, often thought to be 1 year, during which a person should grieve the loss of a loved one. Something is wrong if the person does not "get over" the loss in a year, and their grieving may be seen as pathological. The research of Wortman (1993) et al., has shown this product of folklore to be patently false; in many instances, unalloyed grief can last much longer, with permanent traces.

Fear, based on feelings of vulnerability, is the core emotion in the tendency to pathologize other people's trauma. Because a traumatic event occurs without warning, without reason, it perplexes and frightens those who observe and must try to help the victim. The thought that the same thing could happen to them creates a feeling of helplessness. In its wake may come the impulse, in others, to "blame the victim," or to ascribe the trauma symptoms to some underlying defect or weakness. The sentiment "There, but for the grace of God, go I" implies empathy but also hints that the victim has in some way fallen out of favor with God. By finding fault, ascribing blame to the traumatized person, or avoiding being in his or her presence, people indulge in the superstition that they can avoid the same fate.

Certainly there are traumatic situations that are a consequence of some degree of diminished capacity. The person may have behaved carelessly or recklessly or have been generally prone to risk-taking. Root causes of tendencies such as these could include youth, stress, distraction, poor self-esteem, past abuse, or chemical dependency. Nevertheless, the traumatized person could not have foreseen what random fate held in store, and must be held blameless. In therapy, these issues should be dealt with squarely and early on, and the process repeated when necessary. Many trauma survivors are deeply mired in feelings of guilt or shame, and often are acutely sensitive to the reactions of others that may support their paradoxical feelings of having contributed to their traumatic event.

An often-puzzling phenomenon is the fact that trauma symptoms vary widely, in type and intensity, from one victim to another. One way to view this is by analogy with the cleavage point of a diamond. The human psyche is constructed of strong "stuff," much like that of a diamond; but, when a diamond is struck forcefully at its cleavage point, it can be damaged or even shattered. So, too, with normally intact and resilient people, to whom a traumatic event can be devastating. In fact, those who have suffered traumas in the past and are now confronted by a new traumatic event, can be severely affected (Foa et al., 1999; Faust and Katchen, 2004; Courtois, 2004; Hembree et al., 2004). By contrast, there are those who have experienced more than one traumatic event who, through their resilient natures, have coped well and even grown emotionally in the wake of the experience (Bonanno, 2004; Rodgers, 2004).

Paradoxical Guilt

"Paradoxical guilt" is a phenomenon seen in many survivors of traumatic events, including those of any age. The term refers to a feeling of guilt or shame on the part of victims. The paradox is that, even if the victim was an innocent child, a person asleep in bed, or simply someone who was in the wrong place at the wrong time, many feel guilty for having been victimized.

There are many reasons for this unfortunate paradox. One of these is the widely held belief that, if we conduct our lives rightly, fate will treat us with kindness. So, when a traumatic event occurs, one's first thought is, "What have I done wrong?" or, "What have I done to deserve this?" Moreover, those around the victim may contribute to this false logic, because they, too, hold similar beliefs. Or, as noted earlier, they may attempt to protect themselves from the "random hand of fate" by attempting to discover why the victim was somehow to blame, and, by doing so, protect themselves from their own sense of vulnerability. They feel that they would never make such an error as the victim made, and thus are immune to such experiences.

Many traumatic events occur as a result of lapses in judgment, a moment of inattention, or naiveté. Afterward, the victim feels a sense of intense regret, helplessness, and failure. Considered rationally, the resulting traumatic reaction is by no means deserved for such a mistake. Also, those who attack or traumatize others in some way are often quick to blame the victim for their actions. The victim then is doubly wounded, having been traumatized and feeling guilty for the trauma. Many traumatic events such as rape, incest, and domestic violence carry stigma. People proudly wore T-shirts saying "I survived 9-11," but no one wears a T-shirt that says "I survived rape" or "I survived incest." The irony of this phenomenon has been observed by Lehman and Hemphill (1990).

Children also experience paradoxical guilt, and this is more likely to occur the younger is the child. Very young children are governed by self-referential thinking, viewing themselves as the center of the universe. Relying on their concrete, linear forms of logic, they have trouble in conceptualizing events in the abstract. Furthermore, they lack the adult defense mechanisms of rationalization and intellectualization. As a result, it is easy for them to believe that they have somehow caused a traumatic event to occur. Perpetrators of abuse often take advantage of their victim's naïveté, by claiming "She came on to me" or "He made me do it" or "I had to put her in her place." Small wonder that a young child is often led to believe that a terrible event was his or her own fault.

We have found that those who have experienced natural disasters (e.g., an earthquake) or noncombatant war survivors may *not* exhibit paradoxical guilt, with the obvious exception of situations in which friends or loved ones did not survive. The reason for this lack of paradoxical guilt is that the event was a nonstigmatized, shared experience. Because the experience was shared, there was open discussion and normalization of symptoms. After a natural disaster or at the site of a terrorist strike, people pull together, form support networks, and talk, which helps them to work through the experience. As a consequence of these more public and positive experiences, paradoxical guilt is less often present in survivors of these kinds of events, because they may be perceived as fortunate, "tough," lucky, or blessed in some way, and thus immune to blame.

The Neurobiology of Trauma

The response to a traumatic event is not solely psychological in nature. The pioneering work of Bessel Van der Kolk (1987, 1988) has revealed that trauma is represented in every human system, from the molecular to the emotional. The research of Van der Kolk, using a procedure called Single Positron Emission Computerized Tomography (SPECT), has shown that traumatic experiences are represented differently in the brain than are nontraumatic ones.

Under normal circumstances, when a situation is *nontraumatic*, the brain has time to process and organize information from sight, hearing, touch, and smell, and so on, and store it as a coherent memory. When the memory is later retrieved, although it may be painful or unpleasant, it is not an overwhelming re-experiencing of the event. By contrast, with *traumatic* situations, the opposite is true—as, for example, in the experience of a flashback. When something reminds the person of the traumatic event, it is like a "trigger" that draws the entire stored memory into consciousness. The flashback unusually calls forth the very worst moment of the event. (One exception occurs in cases of extreme physical pain, in which the person will recall the experience without feelings of pain.)

Trauma triggers are stored as a neurobiological trace in each of the senses that was stimulated during the experience. The nature of the experience determines which trace is strongest; for example, a person who was stabbed will be extremely sensitive to certain forms of touch. A trauma therapist should attempt to find out what the triggers are and help the survivor to cope with them.

A role that the clinician can play is educating the client that trauma symptoms such as flashbacks and heightened startle responses are neurologically mediated and not subject to conscious control. Clients can be taught relaxation techniques and breathing exercises, to lessen specific symptoms, that will help them feel more in control. Furthermore, they can learn how to avoid situations that may lead to responses of this kind. The clinician also can recruit significant others to help them understand the survivor's reactions such as these. They, too, should realize that these symptoms are not "made up," but, rather, are *involuntary*.

The trauma experience is primarily processed in the *amygdala,* a region of the brain that deals with primitive survival instincts and raw emotions. This structure processes, primarily, the emotional content of to-be-remembered memories. By contrast, another region, the *hippocampus,* serves rational and logical functions. This region is virtually nonfunctional in traumatic situations, meaning that factual information does not get processed into memory storage. Therefore, traumatized people exist in a primitive, "concrete" mode in which they are incapable of abstract, higher reasoning. The net result of these neurological phenomena is that concrete, and largely negative emotional, memories preoccupy the traumatized person to the relative exclusion of factual memories.

A consequence of this state of diminished cognitive processing capacity may be that people, while in this concrete mode, will accept as truth, erroneous or deceptive information that may be perceived by them during the event.[2] What factual information he or she does remember may have been intentionally distorted by, for example, the person(s) responsible for the traumatic event, or by his or her own misinterpretation of what happened.

A critical element of treatment will be the therapist's careful reflection on these memories. One should be sure that one learns exactly how the survivor perceived the experience and the actions of any others involved, before beginning any form of clinical intervention.

CHAPTER 11

Trauma Assessment

Trauma varies from the catastrophic—as a result of natural disasters or terrorist attacks—to the intensely personal—as from a human hand. There are complex, long-lasting traumatic ordeals such as those of domestic violence or child abuse, or instantaneous assaults such as an auto accident that might have been life-threatening. These multidimensional phenomena of trauma call for many and varied palliative types of intervention.

An intervention for trauma must strategically aim toward the particular injury or injuries that were inflicted by the traumatic event. Clinical work needs to be focused and precisely directed at the symptoms expressed by the resulting trauma experience. The psychic injury caused by the event and its impact on the survivor's normal life patterns and his or her worldview must be accounted for in the treatment plan. Survivors of a terrorist bombing, for example, see their world and the strangers in it differently after the fact. Are they paranoid? Certainly not, but they cannot put out of mind their thoughts about what people are capable of. They may flinch at sounds in an exaggerated way, or to people who approach without warning. Do they have an anxiety disorder? No, they have a startle response that is normal after a traumatic injury.

There is much that we need to know about a person's actual traumatic experience, as well as the event that caused it. And because some of this information lies at the heart of the person's feelings of loss and confusion, these subjects must be broached cautiously. Some clients can be asked about facts of this kind on the first meeting, but with others the questions will have to be interspersed through later sessions. We have found that some severely traumatized people do better with checklists or questionnaires, because, by not having to talk about the experience, they don't have to relive it. The purpose of collecting objective data is to form a strategic treatment plan. The following describes what data are needed.

Bodily Injury or Penetration

The degree to which a victim's body was injured or penetrated has a significant role in determining how severely the person was traumatized emotionally. One also should consider whether or not the person believes himself or herself to have been disfigured or permanently damaged, physically, by the traumatic event. Psychologically, to the extent that a person believes that he or she has suffered physical damage, the person *is* damaged.

Agency or Intention

Traumatic events of human agency or intention are among the most difficult to recover from, because they can raise extremely complicated social-psychological issues. Traumatic events caused by known and trusted persons or institutions can be far more harmful than those inflicted by strangers or unknown entities, the reason being that they call into question the victim's ability to trust, as well as his or her competence in choosing safe persons or institutions. For example, the parents of a child who has been abused at a school or day-care center of their own choosing may feel more traumatized than if the child were accosted by a stranger. Naturally, the parents chose the school or day-care center as a safe place for their child, and what has happened impugns their judgment as well as their ability to protect the child.

Impact on the Person's Role

If the traumatic event robbed the victim of his or her role or vocation or sense of worth, for example, brought an end to a career or prevented the person from functioning in his or her customary family role, the reaction to trauma will be more severe.

Location of the Traumatic Event

The location of the traumatic event also can have a significant effect: for example, when it happens in the home, a place that is supposed to be nurturing and safe. Whatever the location, if the victim must of necessity return there soon, the fear of doing so followed by the actual returning could heighten traumatic intensity.

Peer Reactions

The effects of trauma can vary according to whether or not being a survivor of the traumatic event is a source of pride or humiliation. The survivors of the 9-11 attacks were traumatized beyond imagining, but they also were witnesses to unforgettable heroism and courage (Hemingway's "grace under pressure"), and they felt overwhelming sympathy for the actual victims. Further, when terror strikes, survivors unite in their anger and indignation, forming a bond against a common enemy. Also, they are not stigmatized as, often, are those who suffered trauma from incest or rape. Factors such as these can ameliorate trauma in terrorism survivors, if not hasten recovery.

Trauma Analysis Protocol

The Trauma Analysis Protocol is a method for organizing information in the development of a strategic, cognitive/behavioral treatment plan. The plan should incorporate both symptom alleviation and systemic issues that the survivor must come to terms with on the way to recovery. The questions comprising the Trauma Analysis Protocol are listed in Table 11.1.

Questions About the Event

When formulating a treatment plan for a survivor, the clinician needs to know how long ago the event occurred. Generally, the effects of a single, uncomplicated event are more accessible to cognitive/behavioral therapy, because treatment will focus on direct symptom relief; also, the client is less likely to have developed maladaptive coping mechanisms or trauma-reactive behavior. If the event occurred recently, treatment can suggest

TABLE 11.1
Trauma Analysis Protocol

Questions about the event:

1. *Time Frame: Did it happen*
(a) within the past 2 years?
(b) within the past 2 months?
In the case of a child victim, did it happen:
(a) during the current developmental stage?
(b) during a prior stage?

2. *Duration: Was it (Were they)*
(a) a single event?
(b) separate events?
  • how many?
(c) a series of events?
  • how long in duration?
(d) more than one series of events?
  • how many?
  • how long in duration?

3. *Origin: Was the agent of the event*
(a) a person:
  • known to the victim when the event occurred?
  • known and trusted by the victim?
(b) more than one person:
  • known?
  • known and trusted?
(c) a political or military group?
(d) an animal, an act of nature, or environmental force?
(e) a mechanical or chemical or other man-made entity?

4. *Intent:*
If the event occurred by human agency, was there intent to harm?

5. *Stigma:*
Was the event one to which a social stigma is attached (e.g., incest, rape, battering, terrorism, war)?

6. *Warning:*
Was there warning prior to the occurrence of the event?

7. *Potential Vulnerability:*
What is the probability that the victim will reencounter the source of the traumatic event in the near future?

Questions about the Survivor:

1. *Status: When the event occurred, was the person*
(a) alone?
(b) one of two or more victims?
  • how did your client view the behavior of the others?

-- Continued

TABLE 11.1
Trauma Analysis Protocol *(continued)*

(c)   in the company of a large group?
• how did the group respond?
(d)   a witness to someone else becoming a victim?
2. *Impact*:
To what extent is the victim aware that the event had a traumatic effect?
3. *Perceived Threat*:
Did the victim believe that he or she might be maimed or killed?
4. *Reactions of Others*:
Did (do) significant others acknowledge that the victim was traumatized by the event?
(a)   then?
(b)   now?
5. *Traumatic History: Had the victim been*
(a)   a victim of a similar type of traumatic event in the past?
(b)   a victim of a different kind of traumatic event in the past?
(c)   a victim of repeated traumatic events in the past?
6. *Clinical History: Had the victim*
(a)   received treatment for previous trauma(s)?
(b)   suffered from a diagnosable psychological condition prior to the traumatic event:
• treated?
• untreated?

appropriate coping mechanisms to relieve symptoms. The course of treatment can be fairly short, ranging from six weeks to a year, depending on the severity of the trauma. Ideally, it will build or rebuild healthy mechanisms of defense. By contrast, if the traumatic event occurred two years or more ago, the client may well have come to rely on maladaptive behavior patterns as the only means to cope. In a case of this kind, the clinician will have to unscramble these patterns before a strategic plan can be implemented; a narrative technique may be useful to help the survivor restructure the event and its sequence. For example, a child who was the victim of a traumatic event in the past may have been in the midst of a different developmental stage from the current one, a fact that makes it difficult to sort out problems that were created then, from obvious problems that the child is having now. A typical example is that of the child who was traumatized during the latency period and is being treated for a delayed response to trauma after the onset of puberty. It is hard enough to deal with the issues of adolescence without having to resolve unfinished business from a stage that seems, at least to the child, "ancient history."

When creating a treatment plan, a clinician must consider the issues that pertain to the origin of the event. In general, people may have an easier time in adjusting to injuries that were not of human origin or, if they were, were not intentionally inflicted. When trauma originates in the environment ("acts of nature"), the principal issues raised concern the person's fate or destiny, and often these can be worked through by means of more direct clinical approaches such as desensitization and relaxation techniques. By contrast, when the trauma was intentionally inflicted, it can reshape (or, in the case of a young child, shape) the victim's whole worldview, as well as damage the dynamic forces that comprise the self. Traumatic injury of this origin may change the psyche of the traumatized person for life.

Some who *witness* traumatic events may be as much affected as are actual victims, having experienced the impact of the event without the protection of defenses available to the victims (denial, repression, etc.). A witness must confront his or her inability to have prevented the event, or to have given help after the fact. This experience is particularly damaging to children.

Questions About the Survivor

If the person was traumatized along with another person or as part of a group, how does he or she feel about the behavior of the other(s)? Is the person willing to work with the other victim(s) to reexamine what happened? Not everyone is brave or strong. Some who were with the victim may have been supportive and some may not have been. This subject could be difficult for a victim to discuss; the facts might not be known for quite a while. Therefore, caution should guide the therapist in bringing survivors of an event together in a group setting before the full story has been revealed. We have found that, at first, some survivors adopt a group façade that eventually disappears.

In many cases of trauma, the victim himself or herself may not define the event as traumatic. This is more likely to occur when the event was one of intrafamilial violence such as physical abuse or incest. Denial of the impact of trauma is also very prevalent in occupations such as the military service, police work, and fire fighting, in which trauma and tragedy are met on a regular basis and rationalized as "part of the job." People in these occupations tend to encapsulate and minimize their feelings. They might be shamed into hiding them, or ordered not to disclose them. There is also considerable encouragement, within the respective professions, for people to deny traumatic impact for fear of being labeled as "weak." When these persons seek treatment, they rarely do so for actual trauma or for traumas suffered in the past. They are outwardly concerned about other matters and see no connection between their present problems and a possibly post-traumatic reaction. Some enter therapy because spouses or supervisors insist that they do so. Hence, it will be the therapist's task to uncover any relevant hidden trauma in a manner that the client can tolerate. Such a process requires great skill and sensitivity, because these reactions may be wrapped in a mantle of denial or dissociation. The lingering wound may be complicated by a long-festering sense of helplessness or humiliation. And, because a survivor's *persona* is so threatened by revelations arising through this process, he or she may withdraw from treatment before the clinician has been able to intervene—unless the clinician is extremely sensitive.

The phenomenon of social stigma should be taken into account when treating a traumatized person. If he or she has endured a traumatic event that is socially misunderstood or castigated, this issue will inevitably complicate recovery. From a systemic standpoint, a client will need to develop appropriate strategies for dealing with those who have applied the stigma. At a deeper level, issues such as being "marked," shamed, outcast, or somehow made to feel different must be addressed. Eventually, issues pertaining to self-image and self-esteem need to be carefully worked through, so that the client does not develop a defensive or self-deprecating trauma response. The goal is for the person to see himself or herself as a survivor, as opposed to a stigmatized victim.

A therapist also must consider the real possibility that some survivors will encounter a similar (or reencounter the same) situation in which they were traumatized; for example, if it was part of his or her job or the event happened in the midst of an aspect of daily life that is unavoidable, such as driving a car, leaving the house, consuming food, or breathing in cases of toxic poisoning. Phobias concerning these activities are often the legacy of traumatic events.

Lethality

The perceived lethality of an event can have marked significance for the severity of trauma. If the person thinks, even for an instant, that he or she could have been permanently injured or killed by what was happening, the resulting terror can be deeply felt and persistent. For some people, this perception is delayed, coming as kind of "aha" phenomenon hours or days later, when they realize, "I could be dead." Some dwell on this morbid thought long afterward. For many, of course, it is the first time they have had such an intimation. Certain people will incorporate it merely as a chastening experience; others will feel dragged, prematurely, to a new level of maturity. Therapy must rest on an estimation of where the client belongs on this spectrum.

An additional complicating factor that should be dealt with when formulating a treatment plan occurs when people who are significant to a traumatized person do not accept the event as having been traumatic. If the victim recognizes the event as traumatic and the others do not, it will be necessary for a therapist to help the client realize that he or she holds a different perception of the situation than do the others. This approach may be difficult, because it may mean that the client will lose or have to alter close relationships.

A client's history of trauma or its absence is a key component of trauma analysis. If the victim has been traumatized before, his or her response to the recent event may be heightened or complicated in some way. This, of course, will be further complicated if the client has denied or encapsulated a trauma response experienced in the past. Even though we believe that the trauma response is frequently overpathologized, we recognize that many trauma victims have preexisting psychological conditions that will affect the present reaction and the ensuing course of treatment. Nevertheless, it is wise not to assume hastily that underlying pathology exists, because normal traumatic responses can masquerade as pathology. The best policy is to treat the trauma and, if an underlying condition exists, it will surface; treatment of the latter can be then interwoven into the plan.

Symptom Checklists

Specific questions that the therapist can ask a survivor, to find out the extent of traumatic injury are listed below. They should be prefaced as follows: "A frightening thing happened to you. After the event occurred . . ."

Symptom Checklist: Adults[1]

1. Did you lose a lot of weight?
2. Did your friends treat you differently because of what happened?
3. Did you feel angry?
4. Did you lose confidence in your work?
5. Was your temper short with family members?
6. Did your emotional state change without warning?
7. Did you feel guilty that it happened to you?
8. Did you have trouble in remembering things?
9. Did you stay away from social gatherings?
10. Did you lose trust in other people?
11. Did you feel sad?
12. Did you try to avoid thinking about what happened?
13. Did you question whether or not life was worth living?
14. Did you experience nightmares about what happened?
15. Were there times when you didn't know what to do next?
16. Did you have difficulty in sleeping through the night?
17. Did you feel "numb" or unable to relate to other people?

18. Were you afraid to return to the place where it occurred?
19. Was your temper short with people at work?
20. Did you feel like crying when you thought about what happened?
21. Did you feel "jinxed" or "marked" in some way?
22. Did you feel threatened by forces beyond your control?
23. Did your sexual desire decrease?
24. Did thoughts about what happened keep returning?
25. Did you feel that you must be on your guard?
26. Did you change your life-style because of what happened?
27. Did you feel that others couldn't understand what it was like?
28. Were there times when you had trouble falling asleep?
29. Did you sometimes feel that it was happening again?
30. Did you feel punished for something that you didn't do?
31. Did you have trouble in concentrating?
32. Did people who know you comment that you had changed or seemed different?
33. Did you gain a lot a weight?
34. Did you feel waves of emotion sweeping over you?
35. Did you "block" when you tried to think about what happened?

This instrument is appropriate for trauma survivors in the age range of 13 and older. For children 8 to 12 years old, the questions below, prefaced in the same way as the adult version, are recommended:

Symptom Checklist: Children[2]

1. Did you eat more than you ate before?
2. Did your friends treat you differently because of what happened?
3. Did you feel angry?
4. Was school harder for you after it happened?
5. Did you get angry with your family more often?
6. Did you change from happy to sad without warning?
7. Did you worry it was your fault?
8. Did you forget things often?
9. Did you stay away from playing with other kids?
10. Did you lose your trust in grown-ups?
11. Did you feel helpless?
12. Did you feel that you have to "watch out" more than before?
13. Did you wonder if life is worth living?
14. Did you have scary dreams about what happened?
15. Were there times when you didn't know what to do next?
16. Did you have difficulty in sleeping through the night?

17. Were you afraid to go back to the place where it happened?
18. Did you get angry with people at school more often?
19. Did you start crying for no reason at all?
20. Did you feel "jinxed?"
21. Did you keep remembering what happened, even though you tried not to?
22. Did you get so angry that you scared yourself?
23. Has your life become different since it happened?
24. Did you feel that others couldn't understand what it was like?
25. Were there times when you just couldn't get to sleep?
26. Did you sometimes feel that it was happening again?
27. Did you feel punished for something you didn't do?
28. Did you have trouble in keeping your mind on things?
29. Did people who know you say that you seem different now?
30. Were there periods of time when you didn't feel like eating?
31. Did you feel guilty because others were hurt more than you were?
32. Did you lose control of yourself sometimes?
33. Did you feel that you needed to be closer to your parents (parent) than before?
34. Were there times when you felt afraid for no reason at all?
35. Were you worried that the same thing could happen to someone else?

Structured Interview for Early Assessment of Post-Traumatic Reaction in Acute or Emergency Situations

The following is a brief assessment procedure designed to quickly identify people who may be suffering from trauma in emergency or disaster situations in which triage decisions need to be made

1. Are you having nightmares?
2. Do you think about it when you do not want to?
3. How many hours are you sleeping?
4. Are you constantly afraid, nervous, jumpy, easily startled?
5. Do you feel numb, detached, estranged?
6. Are you having flashbacks?

If the person answers yes to four or more, he/she should be considered at risk for post-traumatic stress and should be provided with:

- Educational materials
- Community referrals
- Brief counseling or psychological screening

CHAPTER 12

Victims of Violence

The varied psychological phenomena that are associated with the experience of being a victim of violence are discussed in this chapter, and some of society's more typical responses to victims are described. When a person becomes a victim of violence, he or she is psychologically "bombarded" by the acute reality of his or her own frailty, the seeming randomness of life events, and the inevitability of death. Most people arrive at such a crossroad unsuspecting and unprepared. The experiences of few persons will have left them ready for the role of victim in a violent crime. Few, if any, are capable of facing the enormity of such an event without considerable support from others.

It is not a simple task to treat a traumatized person because he or she may resist participating in the emotional process that will lead to recovery. Many people who have been traumatized may view therapy or supportive services as being only for those who are weak, crazy, or who have "mental problems." What needs to be made clear to survivors of trauma is that:

1. Having an emotional response to a trauma is normal.
2. Most people experience symptoms, but they will pass.
3. There are trauma-focused, strategic techniques to treat trauma symptoms that can be effective.

Society has strange attitudes toward trauma survivors. There seems to be a marked reluctance to accept the innocence and accidental nature of traumatic events. This approach to trauma stems from a basic need for people to find a rational explanation for why the traumatic event occurred to the other person. In many cases, even the friends and family of the traumatized person behave in an unsympathetic manner, which can make it difficult or impossible for a survivor to work through the victimization experience. Others close to the person may choose to rationalize about why he or she was a victim, in this way convincing themselves that there was a logical, specific reason for what happened. Furthermore, they may conclude that, because there was a reason, the same fate may not happen to them. When the unfortunate survivor hears such rationalizations, they can only serve to reinforce his or her propensity for self-blame and paradoxical guilt. Many who are victims feel responsible for what has happened, and this feeling may arise even at an early stage of the post-event period.

Another reason that people close to a traumatized person should try to be in control of their emotions is that traumatized people have a heightened startle response. The heightened startle response is involuntary and can be extremely unsettling. Those around a traumatized person must learn how to anticipate and try to avoid startling the person; this can be accomplished in group or family sessions. Significant others should also be advised that startle responses can also trigger traumatic flashbacks that can, inadvertently, retraumatized the person

Traumatized people typically spend hours dwelling on the "If I only . . ." aspects of what has befallen them. When the person's family members or friends or acquaintances indulge in the kind of thinking that shifts blame for the traumatic event onto its victim, by their own efforts they may only serve to deepen the initial shock and retard recovery. This kind of thinking also may lead to the chilling answer, "It was your own fault," in reply to the question, "Why did this happen to me?" Traumatized people ask, of themselves and others, questions such as "why me?" for a long time following a violent assault. A similar mistake, often made by others, that will delay or prevent a person's recovery is to say, for example, "Just forget about it," "Put it out of your mind," or "Pretend it didn't happen." These are examples of classic problem mismanagement, in the sense that belittling a problem may cause it to become more serious. A traumatized person cannot easily put the traumatic event out of his or her mind and make it go away. Such a comment will further alienate the person at a time when he or she deeply needs understanding in full measure.

Those who are close to a survivor can mismanage the situation and block recovery in another way: by overreacting in a hysterical or outraged manner. This can cause the person to mask his or her feelings, because of being afraid of further upsetting a loved one. Within a short time after the event, most survivors become hypersensitive to the anger or other strong emotional responses of those around them. Most are too depressed to express their own anger during this phase, and thus can be frightened by the anger of others. Beneath their fear lies the dread of another attack, in that many obsessively expect assaults from every quarter—even from people whom they know, and especially if they were attacked by a known and trusted person. Hence, survivors need to feel that the people around them are self-controlled and are capable of protecting them. Survivors desperately need to regain a sense of order in their own environments, while attempting to cope with the chaos that the trauma has brought to their lives. It is therefore part of the task of a therapist to treat not only the survivor but also the significant other people in the person's life, in order that the others will not inadvertently say or do things that may block recovery.

Clinicians need to be extremely sensitive to issues surrounding what traumatized people did in order to survive. Many victims of sexual assault had to succumb to sexual acts that they felt were disgusting but acted as though they enjoyed it for fear their assailant might kill them. Hostages and victims of kidnapping may have said and done things to survive that they now feel ashamed of; and, sadly, in facing the horrors of a natural disaster, not everyone was brave. Combat veterans may have had to endure horrific situations and have been forced to make life-and-death decisions in split seconds, and have done things in battle which they may now regret. It will be the therapist's task to help trauma survivors realize that they did the best they could to survive, and to accept the decisions they were forced by circumstances to make. In reality, very few, even those who are trained professionals, are truly prepared for the decisions that must be made during an extreme traumatic situation. Survival is the key issue to focus on with the client, to shift the cognition from feelings of shame, guilt, and victimization to ones of "I did the best I could in the horrible situation into which I was cast by Fate. I survived; what can I learn from this so I can move on with my life? Can I build a better life from whatever wisdom I gained from these events?"

The Trauma Response and Recovery Cycle

Figure 12.1 is a diagram of the process by which people experience a traumatic event and are helped to overcome its effects, on the way to eventual recovery.

The Trauma Response and Recovery Cycle is based on the work of Bard and Sangrey (1980), Sutherland and Scherl (1970), and Everstine and Everstine (1993). For the present discussion, two distinctly different psychological phenomena will be described separately. First, a victim's response to the immediate situation following an assault is discussed, followed by discussion of the Recovery Cycle. Each phase of this Recovery Cycle is described in detail, with suggested methods of treatment for each phase.

The Acute Traumatic Survival State

In most cases, a traumatized person will have been going about his or her daily life when the event occurred in a totally unexpected way. Immediately on the impact of a traumatic event, most people enter a state of shock that will serve to insulate them from the experience, to some extent. This state, with its characteristically dull affect, is often mistaken for a survivor's not being upset about what just happened, or as being "all right." Shock can last from a few hours to several days, or longer, depending on the severity of the trauma that has been suffered and how long the person remained in the traumatic situation. All cognitive functions are concentrated on one issue: survival. In this state, the person's sole focus is surviving or getting through the event; he or she will do practically anything that he or she believes will help. Most victims will be suspended in this "cognitive survival state" until the ordeal of the traumatic event comes to an end.

Severity of Trauma

It has been our experience that the intensity of psychological trauma is related to an interaction of several factors, the first of which is the degree to which the body was violated. Assaults in which the body has been penetrated or damaged in some way (e.g., by rape, shooting, explosion, stabbing, etc.) often prove to be more traumatic than when that has not happened. Another factor is the extent to which a person has feared being killed. Also, the victim's relationship to his or her attacker is an important factor. Contrary to common belief, an attack by someone known (and possibly trusted) by the victim usually raises more complex and serious psychological questions than does an attack by a stranger. People who have complex traumatic histories such as those of child abuse, domestic violence, war, being a refugee, or experiencing a catastrophe will have more

TRAUMA RESPONSE AND RECOVERY CYCLE

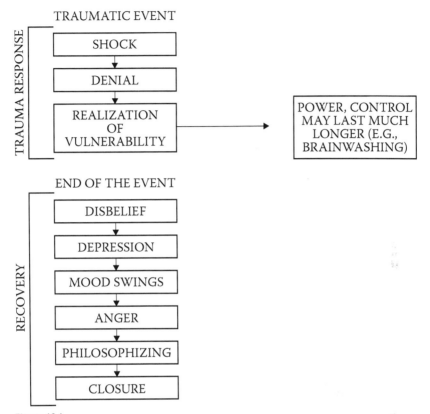

Figure 12.1

severe symptoms and present more serious treatment issues. This has been our clinical experience as well as that of others (Courtois, 2004; Foa et al., 1999). In addition, the victim's past experiences and presently available coping skills are factors in the amount of trauma caused by violent victimization.

Despite the fact that the majority of people experience at least one traumatic or life-threatening experience during their lives (Ozer et al., 2003; Bonanno, 2004), few are truly prepared for it. The authors believe that the Trauma Response and ensuing Recovery Cycle is a normal process that human beings go through after a traumatic event which has nothing to do with mental illness or psychopathology; it is more akin to grief, which is a natural reaction to loss. One should never mistakenly believe that hardy, resilient souls do not suffer—they do. But, they have the capacity to rise, much like the phoenix, and keep going to rebuild their lives and resume their careers.

Finally, the location of trauma can play a role in the degree of trauma experienced by a person. People who, while safely sleeping in their own beds, are suddenly awakened by someone who holds a gun are usually more traumatized than those who are attacked in a public place, such as on a street at night (where they might have been somewhat prepared for trouble). In certain places, people assume that they are safe and protected, and, when one of those places is violated, it is a shattering experience. In fact, a person will probably develop some form of phobic reaction to the site of the victimization, depending upon the contribution of other factors, such as those cited earlier. A woman who has been sexually assaulted in her bathroom at 4:00 in the afternoon will not experience a long, hot shower as being comfortable and relaxing for some time to come.

Initial Impact After the Traumatic Event

After the traumatic event ends, the vicitm will be overcome by disbelief, the mind reeling in a desperate attempt to cope with the situation. The sensation of disbelief occurs because the mind, in a primitive way, tries to dispel the confusion by pretending that the event was not real. But, when cold reality descends on the victim, there often occurs a stage during which the person's affect becomes quite frozen or "flat." After this stage, many people enter a depressed or subdued stage, chiefly because very few are capable of expressing anger just after being traumatized. Toward the end of this depressed phase, a survivor usually experiences mood swings. Moreover, during these early stages, the person may feel considerable anxiety about his or her mental stability and whether he or she will ever be "normal" again. He or she may be experiencing flashbacks, thoughts, and feelings the likes of which he or she never dreamed possible. Throughout this period, the clinician needs to reassure the survivor that what is happening is part of a normal process, which will pass more quickly if he or she tries not to resist it, but accepts it as normal. At this stage, we have found psychoeducational written information to be very useful.

Following a depressive phase, the survivor usually enters an actively angry phase, which can be quite destructive if the person(s) who committed violence has (have) not yet been apprehended and brought to justice. This is a time when the survivor may displace anger onto some "safe" object such as a loved one or friend, and these significant others will need considerable help to understand why they are being attacked by the survivor—especially as this phase usually occurs a while after the traumatic assault. Although this period of anger can be difficult, it should be welcomed by a therapist because it usually marks a turning point in the Recovery Cycle. At this time, family or couple's therapy or treatment with significant others may be necessary. Following the angry phase, many survivors, if properly guided in therapy, become more resilient and enter a somewhat philosophical period in which they review what the event has meant to them. During this reflective phase, a survivor realizes (if the rest of the cycle has gone well) that he or she is no longer the same person as before the traumatic event occurred, and reflects on what this will mean for the future.

Next, a person moves into a period of "laying-to-rest" and moving on, in which the experience is relegated to that of an ugly memory. In the process, the person *accepts* that his or her life has changed because of the event. A survivor of violence will never be able to forget what happened, and each will have lost some of the protective fantasies on which we all rely. But, if the person has gone through the entire Recovery Cycle, he or she is likely to be successful in putting the event in perspective.

It has been the experience of these authors that the end result of trauma is not necessarily a negative outcome. In fact, it has been our experience, as well as that of others (Bonanno, 2004) that many people can emerge from the traumatic experience more resilient, and with a deeper appreciation for life and its positive experiences. Some trauma survivors utilize the experience to make positive life changes, whereas some are not able to do so. It is the role of a clinician to guide the client through the traumatic experience, utilizing appropriate interventions such as these:

- Psychoeducational information
- Strategic cognitive/behavioral therapy
- Desensitization techniques
- Narrative reprocessing therapy
- Supportive psychotherapy or counseling
- Religious counseling when needed
- Hypnotherapy
- Couple's and family therapy
- Medication referral

The treatment plan and the method or methods utilized to treat traumatized people, especially those whose experience involved violent human intent, need to be chosen with great care. Complex and serious traumatic issues may lie dormant, encapsulated behind what may appear to be a fairly simple current traumatization. This subject will be discussed in greater detail in Chapter 13 on treatment.

The Criminal Justice Process

Although the decision of whether or not to report a violent crime is left to the victim, we usually encourage the victim to report it for several reasons. Above all, we know that few people who commit violent crimes only do it once. They will do it again and again in the future, and there is a likelihood that subsequent assaults may be progressively more violent. Each new case presents the logical possibility that this person has attacked in the past, and any evidence provided by a current victim may be information that is useful in apprehending the person or strengthening an existing but weak case against a suspect. In addition, there is a certain symbolic value in the victim's making a report of the attack to the police and asking society for justice. The potential significance of reporting to the recovery process should not be overlooked, even though many of us tend to forget the significance of symbolic or ritualistic behavior in our own lives. In the case of an assault, even if the assailant is not caught or slips through the criminal justice system by some means, the person will know that what he or she did could right the wrong that was done. Finally, if the person can witness the man or woman who made the assault being brought to justice, the experience may aid in recovery and help the person to regain a sense of reason and strength in his or her life. A more detailed description of this process will be found in Chapter 15.

CHAPTER 13

Treatment for Trauma

How do we provide survivors with the help that they need? First of all, mental health practitioners should refrain from considering post-traumatic stress a "disorder." It is not; it is a normal reaction to a horrible, sometimes catastrophic, life-changing event. But, by categorizing it as a disorder, it leaves clinicians with a totally false mind set; it leads them to assume that people who experience post-traumatic stress have an illness that needs to be "treated." This simply is not true in our experience, and there is considerable support for this view. (Henry et al., 2002; Knowlton, 2004; Bonnano, 2004; Litz et al., 2002; Linley, 2003; Maddi, 2002, 2005).

Many people who have recently experienced a traumatic event are frightened by their subsequent emotional reactions to it. Hence, most trauma survivors will benefit greatly from clear, concise, educational information about post-traumatic stress, what to expect, how long it usually lasts, what they can do about it, and where to seek help if their reactions last longer than should be expected. Hence, educational information should be made available to emergency service personnel such as police, firefighters, and paramedics; schools, community agencies, and emergency room staffs should be trained to screen for post-traumatic stress and provide practical advice to trauma victims. Even today, with all the attention given to trauma, we are disappointed to learn that emergency room staff members screen for physical injuries and often ignore the emotional effects of traumatic injury.

Also, witnesses to traumatic events should be provided educational information. All too often, the victims of the event are tended to and the stunned, horrified witnesses are ignored. Sadly these witnesses may have been more visually and sensorially traumatized than the actual victim, who may have been knocked senseless, or so adrenalized that he or she may not have been fully aware of what had happened. The witness may have seen or heard or smelled terrifying stimuli; his or her traumatic experience may be quite profound but go unnoticed because he or she was not a direct victim.

We also suggest describing such services as these for trauma survivors as opposed to "victims' services" or "mental health services." Many people will avoid services if they are labeled as mental health, because of the stigma. The term "survivor" reframes the experience in a significant, positive way, that people can accept as a first step back. The following is an example of an educational brochure that we developed after the Loma Prieta Earthquake in San Francisco.

Information on Reactions to Traumatic Events

An emotional reaction to a traumatic event such as the one you have just experienced is quite natural. Many people feel "strange" or unlike themselves for varying periods after events of this kind, often from 1 to 6 weeks. The most common responses to traumatic events are:

- Anxiety about the possible recurrence of the event or a similar event
- Emotional distress caused by events or objects that remind you of the traumatic event
- Confusion, difficulty in concentration, memory problems, or an inability to estimate time accurately
- Flashbacks of the event that may be visual or may take the form of reliving the event emotionally
- Temporary mood swings, general changes in temperament, irritability
- Sleep problems or nightmares
- Feeling depressed or detached or estranged from others
- A change of appetite or eating patterns
- Shortness of temper, angry feelings, or lack of patience with yourself or others
- Diminished interest in significant activities (work, social, or family)
- You may experience some or all of these symptoms. If you have a question about one of them or if it continues for more than 6 weeks, consult your doctor or one of the services listed below that provides counseling for people who have experienced a traumatic event.

[A list of community agencies can be appended.]

Intervention at the Scene

More and more, clinicians are called to the scenes of disasters and other traumatic events, or asked to see people shortly after such events have occurred. Strategic early intervention such as educational and supportive services, as well as clinical follow-up, can play a significant role in lessening the severity and duration of the post-traumatic response. When first considering working with traumatized people, a clinician needs to be keenly aware of personal biases toward fate and causality, and to examine how he or she has been taught to cope with loss and suffering. A therapist must be able to accept the fact that there are truly innocent victims of fate, even though some people "tempt fate" or "set themselves up" to be victims. In no other field of clinical practice does a therapist experience his or her own vulnerability as acutely as when treating trauma survivors. Save for a stroke of luck, the clinician could have been driving the car that was struck in an intersection, could have been living in the town ruined by flood or earthquake, or could have been the person who was robbed at gunpoint. Only when a therapist is clearly in touch with his or her own mortality can he or she focus effectively on the reality of the traumatized person.

The first step in treatment of a traumatized adult is for the therapist to enter the shattered reality of the survivor and see it through the survivor's eyes, while maintaining a clinical perspective. To do this, the clinician needs to be secure within himself or herself, as well as supported by colleagues. This inner security will enable a therapist to help the trauma survivor regain a sense of emotional control. Immediately after a traumatic event, a person's cognitive and analytical faculties are usually in a state of disarray; often, the survivor functions solely at a primitive, instinctual level. For this reason, he or she may be acutely "tuned in" to the perception of feelings such as fear, disgust, or blame on the therapist's part, even though the person may not be able to voice this sensibility at the time. One consequence of such a development could be that the client will simply "fade away." In some cases, the client may not be able to articulate clearly why he or she feels unsafe with the therapist, or has decided to leave treatment.

Steps Toward Recovery

One of the primary roles of a clinician who treats trauma survivors is to facilitate the traumatized person's entry into the recovery process, a natural psychological passage that is similar to grief. This process may be fairly brief and focused on symptom alleviation, or it may be long and complex, depending upon the nature of the trauma. Furthermore, one must assist the person in moving through the various stages of this process in such a way that he or she does not become arrested or blocked in one of the stages, and is able to rebuild a healthy identity and worldview.

As noted earlier, much of theory in psychotherapy is rooted in models of pathology, that is, maladaptive behavior or interactions. Many traumatized people exhibit conditions such as anxiety, depression, or even paranoia, but these symptoms are *reactive* to the traumatic event and not necessarily the result of underlying pathology. In fact, anxiety, depression, and paranoid or hypervigilant thinking are, in many cases, quite understandable when one considers what the survivor has experienced. These reactions should, in fact, be considered normal responses to an "insane" situation or series of insane situations. Even so, many traumatized people are embarrassed by their feelings because they are afraid that they are losing their minds. By using the pathology model, a clinician runs the risk of retraumatizing someone or driving the survivor away from therapy, by confirming the person's worst fear that he or she has been made crazy by the event.

As an illustration of this point, some seriously injured or disfigured survivors develop a trauma-reactive form of paranoid thinking. Their injuries have caused them to be hospitalized for long periods of time, isolated from mainstream society. Next, they undergo long periods of rehabilitation at home or in an extended-care institution. When they emerge, they have been out of touch with day-to-day, "normal" life for a long time. Simple tasks that the average person takes for granted, such as getting on a bus, going shopping, or going out for a meal, become complex and difficult for those on crutches or in wheelchairs or those who have, or believe they have, obvious disfiguring scars. People stare; the world becomes a hostile obstacle course on which they cannot compete. They begin to see themselves as being in a battle of some kind with the privileged, "normal" world. Such a viewpoint is not the product of a delusional system. It is the reality of disabled or disfigured people, into which fate has cast them. If a therapist is to help these people find their way out of this angry, cloistered place, he or she must first see the world from their perspective, trying not to mistake their reality for pathology.

We do not deny the existence of significant pathology in some trauma survivors, but if a clinician begins treatment by looking for the manifestations of illness, he or she usually will miss the mark. If there was preexisting pathology, it will surface as the client proceeds through the recovery process and can be dealt with as a part of the course of treatment. In fact, dealing with the person's underlying pathology will be a *necessary* aspect of treatment; nevertheless, this must wait until after stabilization has occurred and the survivor has entered the treatment phase.

Early Interventions

Many traditional clinical intervention strategies are not useful when working with acutely traumatized persons. One reason that these approaches are not appropriate to the acute stage of trauma is that they require a higher level of intellectual functioning than is possible for severely traumatized people at this stage. For example, the "reflective" or problem-solving techniques, often taught as crisis intervention strategies, employ a level of abstraction and cognitive reasoning that is beyond the acutely traumatized person. This reflective or problem-solving approach will only add to the fears, confusion, and frustrations of someone who is acutely traumatized, by demonstrating how much his or her thinking is impaired. This can be a terrifying "double bind" for the survivor because, as a result of that same cognitive impairment, he or she will not be able to *explain* being incapable of reflection or analytical thought. In such instances, a traumatized person will become anxious, confused, or will merely "shut down."

Above all, the use of methods designed to induce catharsis is contraindicated in cases of acute trauma. These methods encourage a survivor to "let go" and to "vent" his or her feelings, at a time when the person is struggling to regain composure and to make sense out of chaos, horror, or excruciating loss. Clinicians should be sensitive to the fact that emotions may be the only aspect of themselves over which trauma survivors can exert control. When a therapist pushes a person to express his or her feelings prematurely, especially negative ones, the person may feel that the therapist is attacking the last bastion of sanity in a nightmare world. In effect, traumatized people who are reluctant to show their emotions should be approached with great sensitivity and caution. Even though an acutely traumatized person may sob, scream, or autistically moan and rock, this should not be confused with the emotional ventilation that occurs naturally in a course of psychotherapy. It is a primitive, reflexive response to psychic distress, much like a startle response; this kind of display is neither the qualitative nor the quantitative equivalent of a "release." Often, there must be a considerable period of healing and rebuilding before a survivor can give vent to emotions in a constructive way.

Stabilization

In our work with acutely traumatized people, we utilize a trauma stabilization process, based partly on concepts of constructivism as advanced by Watzlawick (1984), and partly on Ericksonian hypnotic techniques (Erickson, 1980a, 1980b, 1980c, 1980d). A fundamental premise of this stabilization process is that, in the acute trauma stage, one's concept of reality is profoundly altered. By "concept of reality," we mean that each person "constructs" a world view that is primarily rooted in assumptions forged by past experiences, by fantasies, and by faith, and that is informed by a modicum of external data. From this, each person spins a web of illusion that bolsters his or her beliefs about what is reasonable or just in life, as well as a view of relationships with others and with society. When someone is acutely traumatized, this edifice of belief collapses, and the survivor feels a horrible loss of control over his or her role in a world created by others. Because of that upheaval, a clinician's first task is to help the person reconstruct this lost view of reality on functional, healthy terms.

The trauma stabilization process is designed to assist a trauma survivor to repair and revise his or her connection with reality and, in the process, regain the faculty of abstract thought. The survivor must recapture a sense of fundamental safety and control before moving on to the more complex, introspective tasks that are required of a typical client in psychotherapy. If the person does not receive assistance with these fundamental processes, he or she may possibly acquire maladaptive trauma response behavior. In cases of moderate to mild trauma or uncomplicated severe trauma, the restructuring process may be accomplished in a relatively short period of time after the traumatic event; in cases of severe, complex trauma, the process may take months; in cases of complex, catastrophic trauma, the process may take years.

Shock and Denial

We begin by attempting to understand the traumatic experience from the survivor's point of view, even if that viewpoint appears strange or misguided. It is absurd to try to force acutely traumatized people to change their minds, because their mode of thinking is too concrete. One step toward overcoming the mind set of a survivor is to imagine his or her perspective on the situation and then gently alter this orientation. The following are two examples of cognitive redirection as part of the stabilization process.

In the first case, a moderate trauma was suffered by a colleague of ours. He was kicked by a horse and knocked to the ground, receiving a bloody head injury of unknown severity. At the time of the accident, he had been bringing his horse back to the stable to groom her. After he was kicked in the head, a friend told him that he needed to go to the hospital to be "checked out." Even though he was a physician and knew that someone who sustains a head injury should seek immediate medical attention, he refused, insisting that he must return the horse to the stable and groom her. The more adamantly his friend insisted upon taking him to the hospital, the more adamantly he resisted, It wasn't until the friend had joined him in taking the horse to the stable and begun to help him groom the horse that he could be persuaded to leave for the hospital. This case is an example of how rigid traumatized people are, and how they can become fixated on what they were doing prior to the traumatic event. Even if continuing with the activity is foolish or dangerous, the survivor may resist changing a course of action until someone joins him or her in the framework of the trauma experience. A therapist can play that role by entering into the "reality" of the survivor.

A second example showing the advisability of understanding the survivor's experience of the trauma is that of an elderly woman who was kidnapped and brutally gang-raped by four men. Although she was seriously injured and required medical attention, she refused to allow any of the medical staff at the hospital to touch her. She sat on the examining table, rocking and mumbling; when a nurse or physician attempted to touch her, she would become extremely agitated. It was clear that she would attempt to flee if anyone persisted in trying to examine her. When the clinician arrived, she knelt in front of the survivor and said, in a loud but calm tone of voice, that she was a doctor and that she knew that the woman was hurt and afraid. Then in a rhythmic tone, she repeated that the woman was hurt but was in a hospital and was safe; the repetitions were timed to follow the woman's autistic rocking. When it became clear that the woman was in too much pain to hear someone speaking in a normal voice, the therapist spoke in a louder voice each time she repeated the phrases, "I am a doctor. You are hurt. You are in a hospital. You are safe now." She kept repeating the phrases until she was sure that the woman could hear and understand what was being said; this took a few minutes. Then the therapist interspersed other phrases among the original ones, such as, "I'm a doctor. You are in pain. Doctors will help you. You are in a hospital. You are safe now. Look at me. You are safe in a hospital."

In a while, the survivor focused on her as she repeated the same phrases, each time inserting more information. Then the clinician sat next to the woman who continued to rock back and forth on the table. Eventually, she was able to put her arm around the woman's shoulders and gently move her backward so that she was lying down on the table. While this happened, the therapist continued saying the phrases rhythmically, adding that the doctors needed to examine her to help her. Then she asked the woman to say the phrases, "I'm in a hospital. I'm safe." When the woman had repeated them several times, it meant that her frame of reference had been sufficiently altered from the acute traumatic survival state to one that enabled her to permit a doctor to touch her. Eventually, she was able to repeat, "I'm in the hospital. The doctors are taking care of me." Throughout the examination, the clinician made sure that the survivor looked at her, while she held the woman's hand and talked to her reassuringly. The purpose was to keep the survivor outside the acute traumatic survival state long enough to permit the medical staff to examine her. This constant contact with the therapist prevented the woman from experiencing traumatic triggers during the exam which would cause flashbacks to the traumatic incident that, in turn, would have forced her back into the acute state again.

Both examples demonstrate the necessity of entering an acutely traumatized person's frame of reference. The second case illustrates that severely traumatized people can be out of touch with their surroundings; they can be either so flooded with emotions or in so much pain that someone attempting to help them must literally cross a barrier of chaotic thinking, including triggers, without adding further trauma. The key, in both cases, was to "join" the survivor and then to direct him or her into doing what needed to be done. One may wish, in some cases, to raise the volume of one's voice to penetrate pain or confusion, but this should be done gradually. An exception occurs in *very high risk* cases, when quick action needs to be taken to prevent further harm, or when events have accelerated out of control so that someone is in imminent danger.

When the situation is volatile, a therapist must act swiftly and decisively to "break through" to the traumatized person; often, making a very loud, startling noise can accomplish that. Next, the clinician should speak in a loud voice (or even yell), but with a hypnotic tone; the aim is to match the clamorous intensity of the survivor's reality. For example, when a seriously injured man who needed immediate medical attention was fighting with emergency workers, a therapist slammed a metal pan down on an adjoining table; then she shouted, in a loud rhythmic voice, "Chest hurts . . . chest hurts bad . . . look at me . . . chest hurts . . . look at me . . . chest hurts . . . breathe slowly . . . chest hurts. . . ." While shouting, she grabbed hold of the man's hand so tightly as to cause pain. In rhythm with his breathing, she continued to shout, "Chest hurts . . . breathe slowly . . . hold my hand . . . breathe slowly." Then she slowed the cadence of her commands. In a matter of moments, the therapist had broken through the man's formless terror and escalating pain and had refocused his attention so that he could breathe normally. She was then able to induce him to cooperate with the medical staff.

When clinicians intervene in cases of severe trauma, it is important to be cognizant of the fact that traumatized persons, especially during the acute stage, may not be totally aware of their surroundings and may not realize who the helping professionals are. Hence, it is wise, in these situations, to make sure that the person knows who you are and what your role is, so that your very presence does not add to the chaos. Medical practitioners, in particular, should consider the fact that some necessary medical procedures may be similar enough to the traumatic experience to cause the survivor's trauma to intensify. For example, in the case of the elderly woman described above, the medical staff needed to touch her and, eventually, have her lie down in order to suture her many wounds and treat her gynecologically. Her first perception of these procedures was that people were holding her down again, just like the men who had repeatedly beaten, raped, and sodomized her. In this flashback, she believed that she was being attacked. She had no idea that she was in a hospital. The lesson to be learned is that medical procedures implemented after a traumatic event should be done with considerable caution, to ensure that the survivor recognizes the surroundings and is cognizant of what is being done.

As noted earlier, trauma survivors' thought processes are concrete on the one hand and suffused with emotion on the other. Hence, their ability to *absorb* information is very limited. The clinician should, therefore, not be hesitant about repeating himself or herself until quite sure that the intended message has been received and understood by the survivor. During this initial stage, a clinician can have only limited expectations about what acutely traumatized people are able to retain. He or she should be prepared both to repeat what was said and to write significant information down for the person to review, as an *aide memoire,* at a later time. Trauma survivors, especially those who have any form of head injury, simply do not recall much (if anything) that is told to them during the acute stage. For example, we placed a large card in a prominent place in the hospital room of a young woman who had been in a very serious auto accident; the card bore the message that her husband and son were safe at home and that everyone in the car had survived. Many survivors awaken alone (or fade in and out of consciousness) in a strange hospital room; they know that they are injured, but have no clear recollection about what happened to them or anyone who was with them. Such an experience adds to trauma and only serves to deepen the person's sense of helplessness.

When possible, it should be arranged that a trauma survivor will not have to regain consciousness alone in a dark room. And, because of the common experience of short-term memory loss in such situations, the person may need to be told about his or her medical status, and that of any other survivors of the same event, more than once. Nevertheless, it is unfair to assume that nurses will be there each time the patient regains consciousness to convey this information, because of the demands of their duties. Survivors can, therefore, be given basic information relating to trauma in writing, and this applies even to those who are being released to return to their homes. Added to this can be a standard description about traumatic reactions and their duration, including what symptoms may occur.

Following a traumatic event, traumatized people often have a very strong wish to return to their normal activities. This usually stems from their need to feel a sense of control in their lives, as well as a desire to prevent the experience from intruding any more than it already has. In this situation, a clinician should assess how much of his or her regular activities a trauma victim can realistically do. The survivor can then be encouraged to attempt to resume as many ordinary activities as is reasonable, and can be dissuaded from attempting activities that may aggravate trauma.

In our experience, even mild concussive syndrome is accompanied by psychological symptoms that can be very frightening and, by themselves, traumatize. If survivors do not know what symptoms are the natural components of traumatic reactions, they may think that they are losing their minds or have something wrong with them medically, when they are suffering normal trauma or concussive symptoms. Hence, insufficient information can serve to make a traumatic situation even worse.

Communicating with acutely traumatized people can be a delicate process. Because they are overwhelmed, what one says to them should be as uncomplicated as possible. Questions posed should be of the sort that can be responded to by "yes," "no," or one-word answers. In this way, the clinician will obtain the information that he or she needs and the survivor will experience a sense of competence. Open-ended or complex questions such as "How do you feel?" or "Tell me about your feelings" should be avoided during this acute period, because responding requires a level of analysis and communication skills that a survivor rarely possesses. Often, acutely traumatized people respond to questions of that kind with "It's okay" or "I'm all right"—not because they are, but rather in an attempt to convince themselves that they are. Another motive for answers such as these is an effort to get the questioner to leave them alone. They feel that the questions are, at best, too complicated to answer straightforwardly and, at worst, intrusive. The message is, "Please go away. You are asking too much of me."

Despite its success in research and popularity among academics, exposure-based therapy (Foa, 1999, 2000) is neither widely used nor accepted by frontline clinicians, especially those who treat severe, complex trauma. Some are of the opinion that it is too focused on reducing symptoms, for example, Gold (2000) and Courtois (2004), and does not consider the larger issue of the whole person, his or her relationships with others and social systems, or the more philosophical and spiritual issues raised by trauma.

Education and Validation

The communication process between an acute trauma survivor and a clinician should be focused on providing *information* about the event and what may happen in the future, as well as the person's likely reactions to the traumatic event, so that he or she can begin to feel more in control. It is the clinician's task to break down such information into portions that are sufficiently clear and simple enough for the survivor to grasp. For example, phenomena such as flashbacks, sleep disturbances, startle responses, temporary problems with memory, mental confusion, and phobic reactions, as well as other trauma-related symptoms, should be explained to the survivor as being typical reactions. In addition, the person needs to know what to expect in the immediate future. The main purpose of explanations such as these is to help a survivor realize that he or she is going through a *process* that has a structure and follows a sequence, so that the person feels less helpless and can think of himself or herself as still being within normal limits. Survivors need to understand that most traumatized people experience these phenomena; they are normal and they are treatable. Practically all traumatized people question their sanity at one time or another after a traumatic event. They usually believe that they are the only ones who have experienced phenomena such as flashbacks or startle responses, and see them as signs that they are going crazy or are weak or incompetent. That is why the therapist should play an educational role, so that the trauma survivor is aware that such phenomena are expectable, understandable, and run a predictable course.

In review, this process of trauma stabilization is a natural precursor to actual treatment. The process is necessary for the trauma survivor to reach an equilibrium in his or her perception of reality, before engaging in the more complex conceptual tasks of treatment. In guiding a survivor to stabilization, the clinician becomes a sort of teacher or guide who provides realistic information about traumatic reactions. In our experience, as well as that of Litz (2004), trauma survivors have limited capacity to retain information, or to explain fully how they feel immediately after a traumatic event. This stabilizing process of providing realistic information, support, and validation of the survivors' experience in clear, simple, written form, is essential.

A therapist will recognize that a survivor has stabilized when he or she can begin to think in the abstract and can talk about the event, to some degree, without reliving it; further evidence of stabilization is when the traumatized person's defense mechanisms begin to function in a more integrated way as opposed to the survival mode, and he or she can begin to accept the reality of the experience.

Because lack of sleep as a result of nightmares, night terrors, or anxiety about experiencing them can retard stabilization, the clinician should carefully monitor a survivor's sleep patterns. If sleep is seriously disrupted, the client should be referred for medication, even though many survivors resist taking medication for trauma because of issues of control, as well as the stigma associated with taking psychiatric drugs or fear of dependency. But, the negative effect of sleep deprivation on recovery and physical health can be very serious, and the survivor should be made aware of this.

The Medical Recovery Period

It is not uncommon for the emotional sequellae of a traumatic event to lie dormant during the medical recovery period, such as when an injured person is convalescing in a hospital. There can be several reasons for this, for example:

1. The trauma survivor is in a sheltered environment, that is, the hospital.
2. The person, in many cases, is totally focused on his or her physical recovery and is reacting to medical procedures.
3. The survivor does not have to cope with demands of day-to-day life, nor is it likely that he or she will face triggers to memory of the traumatic event.
4. In cases in which the event was caused by another person, the survivor may not have to encounter unfriendly strangers while being cared for either in the hospital or at home.

Another reason for delay in the trauma response may be that those who are close to a traumatized person are more attentive, sympathetic, and protective while the person is physically disabled. Because many support people are not as comfortable with or aware of the invisible psychological wounds of trauma, their support may rapidly fade when the physical injuries heal. Often these support people want to forget, to go on with their lives, and to put their own terrible memories of the event behind them. This can occur just when the traumatized person has begun to recover physically. So, these people may mistakenly expect the survivor to be fine and get on with his or her life, now that the physical wounds have healed.

The clinician should take note if a seriously injured traumatized person is unable to acknowledge emotional or psychological issues during this physical recovery period. But, by no means should psychotherapy be postponed until after medical treatment is completed. It is important that the survivor view therapy as a part of the fabric of trauma care, not as an indication of a weakness or pathology. Even though it is quite logical to expect that psychological symptoms may not always become apparent until after medical treatment is completed, many trauma clients are profoundly startled by the onset of such symptoms. Many were so relieved to survive the event that, during physical recovery, they did not think about what returning to their day-to-day lives might entail. Hence, if the treatment process begins during the physical recovery period, the clinician will have an opportunity to prepare the client for the struggle that lies ahead. Initially, it may take the form of supportive therapy and education of the survivor and his or her family, because the survivor may not be willing or able to work toward treating symptoms directly in this phase.

People Who Resist Intervention

Many trauma survivors are reluctant or resistant to treatment for a number of reasons. They may have been healthy, functional people before the traumatic event, and seeing a psychotherapist is yet another indignity. As Mollica aptly put it, many traumatized people associate psychotherapy with a "broken mind or spirit" (1988, p. 301). Because post-traumatic reactions are still linked with mental illness, weakness, cowardice, malingering, or avarice, many survivors do not wish to be identified with them. Others resist therapy because they simply don't want to talk about the traumatic event or its aftermath. For instance, people who do not understand what psychotherapy is may assume it to be some sort of endless reanalysis of the trauma experience. They fear losing control or being flooded by their emotions if they engage in such a process. In many cases, a survivor will talk obsessively to a friend, a relative, a spouse, a priest (rabbi, minister), a lawyer, or a physician, but staunchly refuse to see a therapist because of not wanting to be labeled as "odd."

Many trauma survivors frustrate or annoy medical practitioners with a sequence of complaints that have no medical basis; for these people, the only socially acceptable way to express emotional injury is through some sort of physical discomfort. (This is especially true in regard to ethnic groups such as Hispanics and Asians.) Other survivors may be suffering from a conversion reaction of the classical clinical kind. In either case, what is needed is treatment for the emotional reaction instead of suspicion or annoyance.

There are some trauma survivors who exaggerate their symptoms, but it has been our experience that the majority minimize or hide them. The popular stereotype of the histrionic weakling or mendacious malingerer, serves as a societal rationalization that helps to protect the general public from facing its own vulnerability to trauma. The logic of this protective device is: "If only the weak or avaricious suffer from symptoms such as these, I shall be spared because I am neither weak nor avaricious." We generally tend to blame traumatized people for their own symptoms as a form of emotional damage control against human frailty. How does one deal with this kind of resistance and stigma? Above all, emergency service professionals as well as medical practitioners need to be trained about the realities of the trauma response. First-responder physicians should be given further training on how to cope with trauma survivors who exhibit symptoms that have no medical basis. When a traumatic reaction can be identified as a normal phenomenon having typical characteristics in every person, helpers will make wiser decisions about it when it occurs.

The Dynamic Systems Point of View

Trauma can affect virtually every aspect of a person's being—both the conscious and unconscious aspects of the psyche, as well as one's interactions with external systems. Therefore, the scope of the systems affected by the trauma should be calculated, as well as an assessment of the severity and type of traumatic injury suffered by the survivor. Treatment will be focused on the person's interactions with family, work, and other external systems, as well as on emotional and cognitive processes occurring within the person. For example, for the survivor of domestic violence, the very definition of "family" has been inexorably changed. The survivor of an industrial accident may not only have to adjust to a changing role in his or her vocational system (or to the loss of this role entirely), but also cope with a loss or change of role in the family system, from that of provider to one who is taken care of; this can be a difficult adjustment for the entire family system.

A case in point is that of a man who was seriously injured in an automobile accident, in which his femur and pelvis were broken and in which he sustained considerable back injury. Not only was this man traumatized by the shock, pain, and horror of the accident, he also suffered several systemic losses:

1. He was unable to fulfill his role as breadwinner for his family.
2. While at home during his long period of recuperation, he felt helpless and inadequate; but, when he attempted to assert himself with the children, his wife intervened because she felt that he was intruding on her role.
3. Driving, once a much-enjoyed activity, became something that he feared or avoided.
4. If members of the family were a few minutes late, he exploded at them.
5. After a short period, friends from work rarely visited him.
6. He often awakened late at night and felt the need to have a drink to relax and feel better; soon, alcoholism became a problem.

Trauma and History

Although a traumatic event is rooted in the "here and now," the survivor's history is a factor in the trauma response, because in the past the person has learned coping tactics for dealing with life's disasters. Another legacy of the past is a person's belief system concerning fate and his or her "destiny." When therapy begins, its aim is to speed recovery at the deepest levels of personality organization, some of which are wholly beyond the consciousness of the survivor. This early work proceeds through the medium of precise repair of the most primitive mechanisms of cognition, as described in the section on the neurobiology of trauma (Chapter 10).

Even before this fundamental cognitive work has been completed, the effort to repair damage to the survivor's personal systems (family, close friends) should begin. And while both efforts are underway, an attempt to reintegrate the survivor into his or her primary social systems (work, community, etc.) should be started. By coordinating and timing these parallel activities, a therapy plan can be designed to lessen the impact of the invading traumatic element and, eventually, reintegrate the survivor. In summary, treatment for trauma proceeds as simultaneously as possible at both internal and external levels, for the purpose of assisting the healing process to complete the tasks of resolution and moving forward. This treatment plan needs to be strategically designed to meet the specific systemic, emotional, and developmental needs of the client (Everstine and Everstine, 1993; Gold, 2000; Courtois, 1998, 2004).

In a case that demonstrates this approach, a mother of four young children suffered a significant injury at her factory job. Before the accident she had been an active, outgoing person who was devoted to her family and had an excellent work record. Her main goal in life was to be a good wife to her husband and to raise healthy, successful children. There was no evidence of a preexisting condition. One afternoon, a piece of machinery at the factory malfunctioned and fell over. In an attempt to avoid the falling equipment, she fell and seriously injured her back. At first she thought herself lucky to be alive; she focused her attention on two co-workers who had actually been hit by the equipment and were obviously very seriously injured. After a while, she realized that something was very much wrong with her. She suddenly collapsed and was taken to the hospital, where it was discovered that she had a significant back injury that would require at least two surgeries.

Although the subsequent surgeries were essentially successful, she still had some significant restrictions. After the second surgery, the surgeon became concerned about the woman's increasing symptoms of depression, and put her on antidepressant medication that he thought would help the situation; he expected the depressive symptoms to fade shortly after the woman returned home, because he knew how important her family was to her. At home, her husband was supportive; he and the children did the best they could to shoulder the household tasks during her convalescence. Even though the woman made good physical progress, she continued to become more and more depressed. When she recovered physically, she still had significant problems such as limitations on bending and lifting, a limited range of movement, and she would periodically drop things. Although she was cleared to return to work in a part-time, sedentary job (away from heavy machinery), her symptoms of depression were such that she was unable to do it. The family physician referred her to a therapist when she broke down in his office and said that she was "worthless," "no good for anything," and did not "want to live."

When this trauma survivor began therapy, her primary symptoms were periods of intense depression with suicidal ideation, difficulty in sleeping, nightmares when she did sleep, loss of her sense of self-worth, withdrawal from friends and family, and intense fear that she would become reinjured or that a member of her family would be injured. Even though she had been medically cleared, she was not emotionally ready to return to work.

At first, the therapist thought that the primary issue in treatment would be the traumatic injury that the woman suffered at work. She displayed the classic post-traumatic symptoms of flashbacks, social withdrawal, depressed mood, irritability, sleep disturbance, and nightmares. As a part of the initial evaluation, the clinician met with the woman's husband and children. The husband said that he felt helpless and lost; no matter how hard he tried to be a good husband and help his wife, she seemed to withdraw from him more and more and to be getting worse. He went on to say that, even though he never complained, it was hard for him to do "women's work." He sadly shook his head as he reiterated that the more he tried to do things to help his wife at home, the worse she got. He said that his wife was even resentful of his mother when she would visit the home to help; now, his mother sent prepared food but would not come herself.

As the therapist continued meeting with the client, it became clear that she was exhibiting the internal dynamic processes of depression, but was also suffering from a systemic loss. To treat this woman successfully, both conditions would have to be treated. Because what she valued most in life was her role as a wife and mother to her family, the woman took immense pride in performing these roles well. In her mind, her main reason for working was to help her family have a better life. Seeing her husband and children doing her routine tasks humiliated her and made her feel worthless and, as a result, she obsessed on her traumatic accident. When the husband brought his mother to help with the housework and cooking, the situation got worse because it made her shame and failure manifest to the rest of the family. The final blow was when her doctor gave her the pills for "crazy people." She took the pills because he said so; she would not disobey her doctor. But the message she took from the prescription was that she was not only worthless—she was crazy. At one point, she sobbed that she would not mind going back to work if she knew that she would be killed in the next accident. That way, her husband could marry a woman who could take proper care of him and the children.

This woman's industrial injury had caused her systemic as well as psychic trauma because it had damaged her role in the family system; in turn, this had stimulated the symptoms of depression. And the members of her family system were, in a manner described by Watzlawick et al. (1967), making the problem worse in their attempts to make it better. The clinician continued seeing the survivor individually to help her with trauma-specific anxiety and fear; for this purpose, desensitization, Ericksonian waking-trance cognitive reprocessing, and relaxation techniques were utilized. The therapist also helped the woman to deal with the internal forces that caused her depression. She was taught to articulate her needs more clearly, in particular to feel less threatened by her negative, angry feelings and to express them more appropriately. She also was helped to develop a healthier self-image and to have more realistic expectations of herself as a wife and mother. Because her views on what the "good" wife and mother should be were so rigidly held, considerable working through was required before she could see that even a good wife and mother might accept help from others.

Concurrent with these individual sessions, the therapist began meeting with the woman and her family. In the family sessions, the therapist was very careful not to discount the husband's efforts. Instead, an attempt was made to "reframe" the family situation in such a way as to credit the husband with having to make yet another noble sacrifice for his wife, namely to let her struggle with most of the household chores—especially the cooking—and only to help her if she asked for help. The clinician knew that this would be difficult because the husband felt that it was his duty to take care of his injured wife; nevertheless, the sacrifice would be absolutely necessary for her recovery. It is worth noting that the therapist only made this intervention after checking with the woman's physician to make sure that it was medically safe for her to do household chores. The physician said that it would be difficult, in fact more difficult than some of the activities required of her by her job, but that she could do it with some effort. The therapist also explained how the client perceived the antidepressants, and asked whether or not they could be discontinued; the physician said that, if he saw sufficient improvement, he would discontinue them when he saw her next, in about six weeks.

After a series of meetings with the client and her family, the clinician began to note improvement. Her self-esteem increased, she had more energy, and her sleep pattern improved. Even though the husband complained about how it caused him pain to see his wife struggle with housework, he could acknowledge that it was useful for her to try. At first, she asked for his help very rarely, but as she began to deal with her own identity issues in individual therapy, she was able to ask for help more often. The therapist continued to be supportive to the husband, reminding him that she knew how hard this sacrifice was for him, but that it was necessary for the good of his family. The wife continued to improve and, when she visited her physician, he took her off the antidepressant medicine.

When the therapist was certain that the client had returned to her proper role in the family, the family was seen once a month for three months to reinforce and maintain changes within the family system. The survivor continued her individual visits to discuss trauma-specific issues, as well as issues pertaining to identity, self-esteem, and depression. After about 6 months, she was able to return to work on a part-time basis. Four months after she had returned to work, she and the therapist agreed that she could discontinue weekly therapy and come back on an as-needed basis.

During the early stages of therapy, clinicians should be cautious about focusing too closely on getting the traumatized person to express anger—or other emotions, for that matter. Clearly, most trauma survivors have considerable reason to be quite angry. Such anger, although obvious to the clinician, may be masked from others by primitive defenses such as denial, dissociation, or magical thinking, because it may be too threatening. If this is the case, the therapist should not aggressively attempt to bring the anger to the surface. If a clinician persists in such a course, the survivor may well feel that he or she is being forced to experience something too dangerous, and may retreat from therapy. (Similar caution should be used when considering the use of exposure-type therapies early in the treatment of traumatized persons.) Or, in such a situation, the person might develop a masochistic transference with the therapist, and symbolically, repeat the traumatic experience in a therapy session. This may provide for emotional sessions, but it rarely proves to be truly cathartic or even clinically constructive for the trauma survivor. Instead, the clinician's efforts should be directed toward helping a client regain the ego strength that will enable him or her, eventually, to express anger through normal channels of ventilation. Anger usually arrives spontaneously at one of the stages in treatment (see Chapter 12), but well after other aspects of the trauma response have run their course.

Before anger can be ventilated in healthy ways, trauma survivors must struggle with some shattered fantasies about life, that is, the faith that there is justice and that this is a rational world. Many people hold notions about being able to vanquish an attacker or how they would bravely cope with disaster, but often, when a traumatic event strikes, its reality mocks these fantasies. Therefore, it is the task of the clinician to help a trauma survivor come to terms with, and to accept, what he or she did to survive during the event. Some clients need to obsess for considerable lengths of time over what they did or should have done. Throughout this process, the therapist tries to reorient them to the more self-accepting position that the event was horrible and that they did the best they could to cope with it.

The Interaction Between Power, Trust, and Trauma

Although a therapist may view the treatment relationship with a trauma survivor as one of care and nurturance, he or she must always be aware that some traumatized people—particularly those who were survivors of violent crime, domestic violence, child abuse, war atrocities, terrorism, or those who have been held hostage or were political prisoners—may have experienced indescribable pain and torment at the hands of other people. Such experiences may not only change how the survivor views human beings in general, they may also scar how the person functions in relationships, as well as how he or she interacts with the greater social system. Issues such as control, influence, and power within a relationship can send these people into a panic or into renewed cognitive survival state behavior. They may flee, adopt a rigid, hypervigilant attitude, assume a placating, dependent role, or attack angrily in a manner that is akin to identification with the aggressor.

The psychotherapy relationship is a very powerful one, and its power may be expressed both directly and in subtle ways. Hence, therapists must be observant of client reactions to issues of trust, vis-à-vis control or influence, when treating those who were traumatized by other people, to ensure that the power inherent in transference does not evolve into a neurotic, dependent form of interaction. (Another reason therapeutic techniques that rely on exposure should be used with great care, is that they may raise serious questions of power and trust.) In masochistic transference, a trauma survivor may turn the therapy relationship into yet another form of abuse. Some traumatized people literally act-out or, in other ways, provoke their therapists to be angry or punitive toward them. Such behavior is usually a form of repetition compulsion and should be treated as such. The role of the therapist is to focus attention on why the person is acting-out as opposed to getting into a power struggle over sanctions for the acting-out itself.

For example, if a survivor is engaging in some form of trauma-related, risk-taking behavior such as provoking fights, the clinician can either concentrate on issues such as rebuilding self-esteem so that the patient will take better care of himself or herself, or try to find out what message the client is attempting to communicate by such behavior. One way to do this is simply to feign being perplexed by such aggressive or provocative behavior on the part of a client who, himself or herself, has been the survivor of violence. The therapist should attempt to help a survivor work through this form of compulsive expression within the therapy process, until the person is able to bring the acting-out or risk-taking behavior to a stop. Unfortunately, in some cases of severe trauma, the acting-out may be so dangerous to the client or to others that the clinician may need to utilize external types of control, such as hospitalization or close observation by family or friends.

Clinicians should be alert to the possibility that risk-taking clients or those who repeatedly set themselves up to be victimized may be struggling with a heretofore undisclosed trauma or with some form of survivor guilt. Moreover, *because* of the new trauma, there may be aspects of the original trauma that the survivor is unable or fearful to disclose. The person may be acting-out feelings that cannot be described or that he or she believes to be "deserved."

Flashbacks and Intrusive Memories

Flashbacks and intrusive feelings or images are common symptoms of the trauma response, often starting just after the traumatic event. In most cases, initial flashbacks are frequent and of overwhelming intensity. They usually represent a key moment or moments excerpted from the traumatic experience. The content often deals with the instant when the person realized that he or she was totally helpless to prevent the event (or protect someone from being harmed). In other instances, the flashbacks or intrusive feelings are symbolic of principal sequences in the person's traumatic experience. Flashbacks and intrusive images or feelings can be so terrifying that they give the person the feeling of being about to lose his or her mind. Because of this, from the beginning of therapy, clinicians need to educate traumatized people about the nature and course of these symptoms, helping the survivor to understand that the symptoms are a natural part of the recovery process: they *will* fade and there *are* interventions that can diminish their intensity.

As a part of the trauma response, people can suffer flashbacks in any sensory mode—visual, auditory, tactile, olfactory, or gustatory. In cases of very severe trauma, the person may experience "flooding" in every mode, literally reliving the traumatic moment. The most common medium of the flashback is visual, and these sensations are often mingled with the auditory. Because of the popular notion that only crazy people see or hear things that are "not there," many traumatized people are terrified when they first experience flashbacks. It is not uncommon for them to deny or attempt to conceal the fact that they are having a flashback, for fear that someone will think them crazy. Moreover, in some ethnic groups, seeing or hearing things is associated with being "touched" by the devil with the curse of madness.

Simply put, flashbacks seem to occur when one or more sensory modes are overwhelmed or overloaded with sensations. As a consequence, these sensory channels become hypersensitive to trauma-related stimuli from the environment. When something that happens in the environment (even out of conscious awareness) is somehow reminiscent of the traumatic incident, it stimulates this sensory mode, acting like a trigger to reactivate the already overloaded sensory channel, which "flashes back" the traumatic experience. These experiences can be vivid enough to terrify someone who may not comprehend what is happening; the typical reaction is that the person feels that his or her mind has gone out of control.

When treating a survivor who is having flashbacks or other kinds of intrusive traumatic memories, one should first explain, clearly, what causes flashbacks, so that the traumatized person understands that there is a rational basis for these phenomena. Flashbacks are not caused by emotional weakness. Instead, a clinician should explain that flashbacks have a neurological, biochemical basis that has nothing to do with strength or weakness. Next, the person should be helped to understand that flashbacks and intrusive memories are stimulated by things that occur around him or her that are reminiscent of the traumatic event. It may be useful if, initially, a survivor tries to avoid places or situations that might act as triggers, if possible. That advice is not always realistic, of course, and all manner of things could happen that would catch the person by surprise and trigger a flashback. Even so, a therapist should encourage survivors to be gentle with themselves about staying away from situations that could rekindle traumatic feelings. The concept of immediately getting back on the horse that threw you is an example of folk wisdom that can cause harm. Clinicians also should be very sensitive to the fact that there are cultural issues associated with people "seeing things" or having "visions." As a consequence, they may be afraid to disclose the fact that they are having flashbacks.

A trauma survivor should not try to block or arrest flashbacks once they have begun to occur. Trying to stop this process may only serve to intensify it. Instead, clients should be told to say to themselves, should they suddenly have a flashback, "I am having a flashback; it will pass." They should be told to say this until the sensation subsides. Flashbacks and intrusive memories should be treated in the context of cognitive/behaviorally oriented psychotherapy; also, relaxation techniques and hypnotherapy can be very useful augmentations: Cardeña (2000), van der Hart (1989) (1990), Spiegel (1990). For example, a person who has visual flashbacks can be taught hypnotic exercises such as focusing the eyes on a spot, staring at a pendulum or crystal, or the Spiegel eye-roll (Spiegel, 1974). We have found that traumatized people are more at ease with waking trances, such as those taught by the Milton Erickson school of hypnosis, because the client has his or her eyes open and feels more fully in control. Those who experience tactile or kinesthetic flashbacks or intrusive feelings can be taught progressive relaxation. People who have olfactory or gustatory flashbacks can be taught focused breathing exercises focusing on positive smells or tastes.

Clients should be encouraged to practice these exercises at least three times a day for a minimum of 5 minutes each, even if they are not having a symptom. The exercises are soothing in themselves; people usually like them and they often quickly provide survivors with some relief. Learning these exercises can also give the traumatized person a corrective experience, in that he or she knows how it feels to have some control over the symptoms should they occur. Next, the client and therapist can work together to develop two or three simple, direct narrative messages, specific to the trauma but positive to recovery, that will help the client counter the negative feelings in the flashback; for example, "The accident is in the past;" "I am safe now;" "I am a survivor." Of importance is that these messages be short and direct, that they place the trauma in the past, and that they give a survivor key information that he or she can use to move beyond the trauma experience. Although simple, they should be *carefully* crafted by the therapist in collaboration with the client.

In summary, the primary focus of these procedures is to teach the survivor a skill by which he or she can gain a sense of mastery over some of the more unpleasant symptoms of trauma. Because this process involves close analysis of key moments of the traumatic event itself, it is likely to bring up clinical issues at many levels. Hence, it should be done within the framework of an entire psychotherapy process. The goal of this approach is far more comprehensive than mere symptom reduction.

Dream Dynamics

The range of emotions that is manifested during the traumatic event itself is often reflected in the dream process and sleep patterns of traumatized people. Initially, many trauma survivors are only able to sleep for very brief periods of time (15 minutes to an hour), sometimes awakening with a startle response or in a panic that they may be traumatized again. If, after about a week, a traumatized person is sleepless for increasingly longer periods of time, the clinician may wish to consider a referral for medication to help the client sleep enough to function. We have found that sleep deprivation, so common in survivors, may seriously exacerbate other symptoms of trauma. Hence, trauma clients rarely begin to be clinically stable until some regularity is achieved in their sleeping patterns.

At first, the dreams of many traumatized people reflect the chaos, terror, and helplessness that were aroused by the traumatic event. Others may block the entire content of the dream because it is too threatening; many awaken with the feeling that they have dreamed something horrible but can't remember what it was. Still others relive the traumatic event in their dreams, often with details of the actual happenings changed. For example, a person who narrowly escaped death in a train accident is killed again and again in various types of crashes in his dreams. Soon, the actual dream content will probably take on symbolic forms that represent issues of survival, betrayal, loss, and so on, that were raised by the event. Very rarely, in our experience, do people relive the event itself in their dreams for a long period of time. (In fact, one may begin to suspect that there could be a form of malingering or an exaggeration of symptoms in those who have exactly the same reenactment dream over and over.) Why most people only relive the event in dreams for fairly short periods of time, until the dreams evolve into permutations of the event and then on to more symbolic themes, is not fully understood. Perhaps the psyche simply cannot bear repeating the event while, at the same time, it seeks release for feelings that the event has produced. Therefore, by employing the defense mechanism of repression, it replaces the real with the symbolic.

Often there is a hiatus in the dream process, between the vulnerability-anxiety dreams and the angry dreams of a later stage. During this interval, a survivor may have few or no dreams that relate directly to the event. Then, suddenly, the person starts having violent, sometimes horribly graphic dreams that may catch him or her very much by surprise. In other cases, there is a slower progression through the fear and anxiety dreams to the angrier ones. Frequently, traumatized people are ashamed or afraid of the grisly, gory content of their dreams. Because a survivor may be shocked and horrified that such thoughts existed, he or she may hide them from the therapist, wishing to be viewed in a favorable light. Hence, it is wise for the clinician to prepare a client for the likelihood of such trauma dreams—especially violent ones—well in advance. It is worth noting that angry, violent dreams, in many cases, usually begin *before* the survivor enters the anger stage of recovery. For that reason, they may be incredibly confusing or frightening to a person who is still in the depressed phase of the cycle. Preparation by the therapist may make it easier for the client to disclose this frightening dream content when it arrives. Violent, angry dreams will probably continue for a considerable period of time. During this period, the client may reexperience difficulty in falling asleep because he or she simply dreads the dreams that are to come. The clinician should point out that such dreams are a natural part of catharsis and release.

Some severely traumatized people, such as hostages, survivors of war atrocities, or terrorism, may suffer from horrific dreams for years; some will have nightmares all their lives. Therapists should warn clients who were the survivors of violence to screen, carefully, what they read or watch on popular media: for example, they should try to avoid television shows or movies that have violent content as well as news stories about violent crimes or atrocities. These sensationalized accounts may prove to be extremely upsetting and result in a recurrence of nightmares. As one young woman, who was a rape survivor, put it, "Violent movies are no longer entertaining because I know the true horror that the people in the movie suffered."

As the client makes progress through the recovery cycle, violent dreams eventually turn to themes of mastery and resolution. When these latter themes emerge, a survivor is usually approaching or has entered either the philosophical or the closure stage of recovery.

Repression and Distortion

The strategies described here pertain to traumatic memories. (Techniques for working with adults are presented here, although they are equally applicable to treatment with children or adolescents.) Bringing traumatic memories to the surface or changing severely distorted traumatic memories should be handled with extreme caution and sensitivity. A clinician should bear in mind that the trauma survivor may have distorted or blocked an original thought, because the psyche could not tolerate the memory. In extreme cases, he or she may have created a different personality or reality to deal with the emotional distress.

Whenever possible, the repressed or distorted memory should be brought to light with great care. One way of doing this is to present the client carefully with new information about the event, in a narrative process.

(If possible, it is best to do this through conscious processes, i.e., not by hypnosis; there is too much risk of suggestion, perhaps of a false memory, in the hypnotic state.) The client can be a sharing participant in the process and, therefore, will feel more in control. The experience can become one of mastery and thus more deeply corrective. Also, when the process is a conscious one, the therapist can judge whether or not a client's defenses have healed enough for the information to be assimilated fully. In cases involving blocked or distorted memories in the more distant past, a therapist may wish to find photos, videotapes, or audiotapes that were made of the client at or around the time of the traumatic event. These can be used clinically as a kind of strategic chronological probe, or reality check, to help retrieve lost or to revise distorted traumatic memories.

It cannot be emphasized too much that a clinician should make absolutely certain that a survivor has recovered sufficiently from trauma to have developed functional defenses for coping with newly uncovered information, and that he or she is capable of being a willing participant in this process. Many acutely traumatized people do not know how to express, to a therapist, that they are not ready to deal with certain thoughts and feelings. Also, some traumatized people slip easily into a victim role or adopt a form of learned helplessness, in which they automatically tend to defer to those in authority—out of fear. If the person is not ready for the process of revealing traumatic memories, an experience of doing so will not be one of recovery; instead, it will amount to trauma at the hands of the therapist. As noted earlier, one of keys to helping people recover from trauma is the development of healthy, adaptive defense mechanisms.

Strategic Narrative

When beginning to treat traumatized adults, adolescents, or children, to help them reintegrate and reprocess the traumatic experience, a clinician needs to exercise great care to be sure that reexposing them to facts of the traumatic event will not retraumatize them. Therapists should be careful to bring forth only as much event information as the client is capable of confronting without creating or triggering traumatic symptoms. A secure baseline should be established from which to move forward with a strategic form of narrative in which new information is reintegrated into the traumatic experience by the therapist. We have found that the use of a narrative process (Neuner et al., 2004) has yielded good results. It is also wise to be sure to place the traumatic memory in a "clear container" that provides some emotional distance. The client can imagine that he or she is watching the event on a video, or looking at it in a book; either will close at the end of the specific segment. Often, counterphobic clients will push clinicians to delve into many traumatic memories prematurely, insisting that they want to "deal with it all right now." Clinicians should *not* comply with such urgings, because the client's insistence is more rooted in maladaptive defense mechanisms such as the counterphobic wish to prove his or her prowess, as opposed to good sense.

Before beginning this technique, a therapist should tell the client exactly what information will be used during the process, to help him or her feel secure about retrieving the memories and working with them appropriately. In this way, the process is less likely to startle or confuse, and the client will feel safe and in control. Ideally, the new, higher-level information that is needed for understanding and resolution will be smoothly folded into the experience of the traumatic event by the strategic introduction of new information via narration, with as little dissonance as possible. He or she can continue discussing information from the narration until it has been fully integrated. In the case of the severely traumatized client, the therapist may have to break traumatic memories down into very small segments, so that the person will be able to cope with each one in turn.

In some more complicated cases of trauma, clinicians may need to spend considerable time with the person to reveal and resolve traumatic memories through this narrative reintegration process. Only a few sessions may be sufficient to resolve the symptoms of an uncomplicated traumatic experience. Even so, these kinds of interventions may not always be applicable to survivors who are "flooded" with severe traumatic memories or who have experienced intense flashbacks early in the trauma experience. With people who are in the early stages of severe trauma, a therapist should focus on interventions that are aimed at stabilizing the client and reducing those symptoms that do not involve reexposure.

Guilt and Shame

In addition to agonizing about their inability to prevent the traumatic event or feeling that they are somehow being punished for past misdeeds, many traumatized people feel immense anguish because others suffered more than they did, or died during the event while they were spared. Therapists need to be extremely sensitive to this kind of issue. For example, one should be careful not to comment on how fortunate the person is to be alive or to have been spared more serious injury, lest by doing so the person is silenced or further shamed. Here is another instance in which one must use the traumatized person's view of the event, and its reasons for occurring, as a starting-point. A therapist should be especially mindful of the possibility of survivor guilt in trauma survivors who cannot move beyond the depressed stage. Furthermore, this form of paradoxical guilt may lurk beneath the surface when traumatized people engage in risk-taking or self-destructive behavior.

Issues of guilt, shame, and responsibility will surface many times and in many ways during the recovery process. Each time they do, the clinician will be called upon to help the survivor cope with them, placing the guilt and shame where it truly belongs. It has been our experience that traumatized people are rarely able to lay these issues to rest until they are past the anger stage of the recovery process and well into the philosophical stage.

Mood Swings

The mood swings stage of the Recovery Cycle is a confusing and turbulent time for trauma survivors. Although the clinician, who is aware of the changes that occur in recovery, views this stage in a more positive light because it is one in which the client's depression is breaking apart, the person who experiences it finds little solace because it often feels as though he or she is on an emotional roller coaster. The survivor catches a glimpse of psychological stability, feels good for a while, thinks, "I'm finally through the horror." Then, something happens, and the person is slammed back down into the gray pit of depression. Many fear that, once back in the depressed state, they will never be able to climb out again. During this stage, clients require a lot of reassurance because they often have the sensation that they are about to lose their minds. A therapist should look on the turbulence of this period as an early warning sign of the arrival of the anger stage.

Anger

The anger stage often arrives quite suddenly, much like an eruption, catching family, friends, and lovers quite by surprise if they are unprepared, because this period usually begins long after the traumatic event ended. So, when the survivor's anger finally surfaces, the significant others in the survivor's life have probably worked through much of the trauma themselves and often want the "horrible thing" to be "over and done with." This lack of synchronicity between the arrival of the traumatized person's anger and the state of mind of significant others can frequently lead to painful conflict and misunderstanding. For this reason it is wise, as noted earlier, for clinicians to meet with significant others very early on, to educate them about the various stages as well as the probable length of the recovery process. Certainly, the therapist should meet with them before the anger stage, if possible, because they will need considerable guidance and support through this difficult but necessary time.

The therapist's role during this crucial period is to help the trauma survivor to articulate and vent his or her anger in an appropriate manner. In this way, the client will avoid the experience of further pain caused by damaging important personal, social, and professional relationships through hostile outbursts. As one survivor put it, "Sometimes I want to say and do horrible things, but I don't want to hurt anybody." Many trauma clients are sufficiently aware of their angry impulses, having had preparation for them in therapy, to be able to redirect these impulses into the therapy process and, thus, deflect them away from key people in their lives. Nevertheless, some clients need to be monitored *very* carefully, because they could lose control and harm someone, or previously unresolved identification with the aggressor could surface and lead to violent acting-out. (It is a serious clinical error to assume that, because a person has been the victim of a violent traumatic event, he or she would not act out to harm others. This is simply not the case, especially if the victim of violence leaves treatment suddenly, is self-medicating with drugs or alcohol, or has suffered an injury that bears a stigma or doesn't evoke sympathy.) One should never underestimate the amount of consternation and rage in need of expression that is characteristic of this period. It is the task of the therapist to utilize his or her clinical skills to see to it that this anger is channeled in such a way that, when released, it leads to healing and recovery rather than to further calamity.

Traumatic anger is a form of free-floating, random rage that seeks out objects to attach itself to. There is often a logic to the choice of an object as the target of this emotion; in other instances, it can be a pure, amorphous wish for vengeance. Some survivors may fear their own aggressive impulses and utilize obsessive-compulsive rituals as a defense against them. Others withdraw socially, because they fear that they may lose control in a social situation. An example of this is a rape survivor, normally a quiet, soft-spoken young woman, who became nearly agoraphobic as a result of the following incident: She was leaving a store with two friends, when a male passerby whistled at her and made some suggestive, inappropriate remarks about her figure. Suddenly, she ran after the man, screaming obscenities and shouting that he had no right to assault her. She had to be physically restrained by her friends to keep her from attacking the man. When she had calmed down sufficiently, she was so horrified by this loss of control that she refused to leave her house except to go to work.

The anger of some trauma clients is more predictable when it is focused on the cause (or symbol of the cause) of the traumatic event. An example is that of a woman who was held hostage on a plane when she was on her way to visit her native country. She had once taken great pleasure in traveling, and particularly enjoyed going home. After the hijacking, she developed a vehement dislike for anything associated with the native country—people, food, customs, and clothing. She broke off all relationships with people she had known there, even relatives. She also developed an almost paranoid hatred of big businesses, which she associated with the airline. Her belief was that the hijackers were able to gain entry to the plane because the airline, "a big business," had been too cheap to provide adequate security.

Many survivors express intense rage at those persons or institutions who, they perceive, were "failed protectors:" for example, an airline that did not keep hijackers off its plane, the police who could not catch a perpetrator, the district attorney who failed to convict a criminal, manufacturers of the auto that malfunctioned, the flood control system that failed, the spouse or a lover who was not there to protect the person at a crucial moment. The failed protector category can incorporate almost anyone. Even if the protectors did, in reality, all they possibly could have done, this logic is rarely appreciated by a trauma survivor at the outset of the anger stage. It will be the task of the clinician to help the client, eventually, to adopt this logic.

Of course, certain survivors did, in fact, suffer because of the negligence or inattention of others. In cases in which there was an actual failure to protect, the client's anger may follow a much longer course. Sometimes it can be helpful if this anger is directed toward a legal resolution. Even so, a therapist should be quite careful about how this is done, because if the traumatized person's anger is unleashed inappropriately in the legal system, that strategy can bring even more pain and humiliation. In our experience, clinicians who are unschooled in the realities of the legal system may unintentionally encourage a survivor to have unrealistic expectations about legal retaliation; they may, in the short run, enable their clients to vent some anger, but do harm in the long run.

If legal redress is not available to the trauma survivor, a clinician may wish to direct the person toward symbolic forms of release within the therapeutic process itself. For example, a therapist may use the guided fantasy technique or a structured hypnotic process, in which those who were negligent or directly responsible for the trauma are "brought to justice." A client also may be invited to utilize the empty chair technique to say what needs to be said to those who have wronged him or her. If a version of psychodrama involving other people is used, the clinician should be sure that the survivor is in sufficient control of his or her impulses so that no one gets hurt in the process. The client's need for revenge and meting out punishment is most powerful during this angry period, and its expression should be carefully monitored.

Acts of nature such as tornadoes, floods, and earthquakes also raise complicated questions regarding guilt, blame, and punishment. Sometimes, survivors of natural disasters are able to bond together in a support system that may permit them to see the disaster as the tragic whim of fate. But, other times, the anger is displaced onto builders, planners, and other public officials who, they believe, could have or should have done more than they did. Traumatized people have a powerful need to see those who were responsible for the traumatic event punished. If the retaliation of "an eye for an eye" is not possible, a survivor may displace these angry feelings onto safe objects such as friends, relatives, spouses, or lovers. This is another situation in which a therapist may need to involve people who were not survivors in the treatment process, because in many cases they may not understand why, a long time after the traumatic event, the survivor is suddenly "turning" on them. Often, and rightly so, significant others feel that they are being unfairly treated by the traumatized person, when this rage or need to punish reaches *them*. In such instances, the support and guidance of a therapist can help these people to realize that even anger is a part of the process of recovery; it will pass, and they needn't take the attacks personally.

Displaced anger may take a form in which the survivor has very limited tolerance for being told what to do, or for allowing another person to have any control over him or her. One of the reasons for this intolerance is a core element of the trauma experience, namely, the sensation of total helplessness and loss of control. Hence, if the survivor believes that someone is trying to exert control in some way during the anger stage, there is a possibility that he or she will lash out at the other person. This may even be the case in situations in which the person has made a request of the survivor in very reasonable, polite terms. For example, one evening a young man who had been the victim of a brutal armed robbery was leaving his house to do some shopping. As he left, his wife said, "Dear, while you are at the store, could you pick up some laundry soap and bleach? We're almost out." At once, he angrily turned to his wife and yelled, "You are so thoughtless and inconsiderate. How dare you take advantage of me. You are always taking advantage of me with your thoughtlessness," slamming the door on his way out. As the man recounted the incident during therapy, he said that he had not heard the request as being polite. What he experienced was that someone was again trying to control him and he had to fight back. He added that, when it happened, he was convinced that he was right: trying to reason with him at the moment would have been useless. Not until several hours after the incident did he realize that his reaction had been totally inappropriate. Such outbursts of displaced rage are very common with trauma clients and, if significant relationships are to survive intact, they usually require the significant other to participate in the client's treatment, so that such behavior can be put into perspective.

Some other forms of trauma-induced rage may appear even more irrational but are, nonetheless, very logical to the survivor during the anger stage. Some people will be quite ashamed of such irrational eruptions, whereas others feel justified in their rage. For example, a survivor may feel anger toward those who died during the traumatic event because they "abandoned" him or her. Conversely, clients may feel an unacknowledged resentment toward those who were *not* injured or traumatized to the degree that they were.

This angry period, naturally difficult for the traumatized person as well as the significant people in his or her life, will pass in time. This is a time when strategically-focused family or couple's therapy can be very helpful in the recovery process. Eventually, the person will move toward the philosophizing stage that precedes closure.

Philosophizing and Closure

Most survivors need to pass the anniversary date of the traumatic event, especially if their trauma was severe, before they can begin to bring the trauma response to closure. Often it is only after this anniversary (or subsequent anniversaries) that a survivor can begin to move outside of the experience and see it as something that *happened to* him or her, but that fell short of being an overwhelming or engulfing experience. In order to achieve closure, a survivor's defenses must be rebuilt. Furthermore, the person's cognitive processes must be sufficiently restored so that he or she can think abstractly enough to observe himself or herself as an object. In that way, one can see oneself in relation to the event and to the others who were involved in it. This process of externalizing the traumatic event as something that happened to (past tense, passive voice) the person is the talisman that permits entrance to the last stages of recovery. As the trauma client approaches closure, the therapist can help him or her to form a newly realistic and adaptive self-image. The therapy process is vital in shaping the eventual contours of such a self-image, preferably one on which the client can build a healthy future.

In these final stages, it will be useful to reevaluate the survivor's own role in the traumatic event—not in a way that will bring up feelings of guilt and shame, but "framed" in a question such as this: What should the person reasonably do to protect himself or herself from future trauma? This is part of the work of rebuilding feelings of self-worth, because one component of a healthy self-concept is self-care and valuing oneself enough to avoid taking unnecessary risks.

Not only do traumatized people come to view themselves differently if they move appropriately through the sequences of the recovery process, they will come to view life differently, as many people do when faced with their own mortality. If handled well clinically, this can be a positive time, when the client looks over his or her values and reassesses what he or she truly wants from life and what life should mean. Through the stage of closure, the person can find new meaning as a survivor, and go on to choose a future path. Some trauma survivors are able to make positive life or career changes out of a renewed sense of value in life. Tragically, not all trauma survivors are able to achieve this successful completion of the ordeal. Many struggle with the emotional ravages of trauma for the rest of their lives.

Survivors of Prolonged Terror

In this section, techniques are suggested for treating people who have been the survivors of protracted terror or violence, such as those who are kidnapped or taken hostage. Of course, many survivors of rape and sexual assault fit within this category because they, too, have experienced prolonged violence and terror; in many cases, they exhibit symptoms similar to those that are discussed in this section. Yet, because of the complexity of rape and other forms of sexual assault in adulthood, those subjects will be discussed in greater detail in another section.

A therapist who wishes to treat survivors of prolonged terror and violence must be sensitive to the psychological forces that interact to create the sometimes strange and contradictory behavior of the survivor. People in general have many fantasies about what they would or should do if they are attacked. Some believe that they would be able to run away or otherwise use their wits to escape the situation, but these common escape fantasies are seldom achieved in reality.

In most cases, when people are attacked and held captive, there is no real prospect for escape. Few survivors are capable of overpowering their attackers, lacking the strength or a weapon to do so; and, even if they were capable, the reaction of most persons to an attack is one similar to shock. Bard and Sangrey (1980) and Symonds (1980a) have referred to this kind of response as "frozen fright." During such moments, a victim usually tries to undo the reality of the assault with thoughts such as, "This must be a dream," or "This could not really be happening." One survivor of a bank robbery that became a hostage situation put this denial reaction into graphic terms by saying, "When I saw the men coming into the bank with guns drawn, my first thoughts were that the men were police in plain clothes. Then I wondered why they had their guns drawn. It was only after the robbers forced me and the other people in the bank to lie face down on the floor that the fact this was a robbery came to my mind. And, from then on, the only thing that concerned me was how I was going to get out of this alive!"

After the initial shock and disbelief pass, many victims enter into a psychological state of frozen affect, and adopt a false demeanor of calm. While the victim's behavior is outwardly quite cooperative, at the same time the cognitive functions have become channelled in the direction of survival. The neurological correlates of this kind of behavior have been confirmed by the research of Van Der Kolk (1994, 1996). This manifests itself as a key component of the phenomenon known as "identification with the aggressor" or as the "Stockholm Syndrome." In this state, a victim develops a pathological identification with, and attachment to, his or her captor or captors. Another component of the Stockholm Syndrome is that the person who has been kidnapped or taken hostage perceives that the captor had an opportunity to kill him or her but chose not to do so. Whether this was true or imagined, the effect is a powerful one and the person's appraisal of his or her captor may undergo a profound change: that is, the captor may be seen as a protector who has "saved" the survivor's life. Contrary to popular opinion, this kind of change in a victim's perception of a captor can occur within a short time, perhaps minutes. Despite myths portrayed in the media, people, unless trained otherwise, quickly become passive and their cognitive processes become concretely focused on survival. Among the crucial factors that can bring about this perceptual transformation are the degree of perceived helplessness, the degree of physical vulnerability, and the closeness to death that a victim has experienced. Identification with the aggressor can occur when there are: (1) threats to the self; (2) a deluded view that the captor has spared his or her life; and (3) a distorted perception of the captor as the only one who is capable of saving the victim.

The concept of "failed protector" is equally useful to an understanding of the etiology of identification with the aggressor. A victim begins to view the captor as a "true" protector, and the family, police, and community at large as failed protectors. In this misperception, the captor is seen as one who permits a victim to live, while the family or police are those who may kill the person or cause the person's death by their carelessness. This belief may be given impetus by the captor's own rationalizations about why the victim was chosen.

Behind these distortions of reality lies a victim's anger (enhanced by the concrete cognition of the Traumatic Survival State) toward those who are normally expected to provide protection—for permitting this terrible assault to occur. An example is the case of a person who was held hostage during a house invasion burglary and brutally assaulted for hours, who could later describe the assailant as being "kind" to him "at times;" the victim was subsequently angry at a neighbor who had called the police, and refused to see family members after being admitted to a hospital for treatment of severe injuries. This shows that, within only a short time, a sequence of events similar to those that led the kidnap victim, Patricia Hearst, into becoming a fugitive and a revolutionary, can begin. Such seemingly paradoxical behavior can be more fully understood when viewed in the light of underlying dynamics, as outlined above. Once these dynamics are understood, a therapist can begin to take some of the following steps, in treatment, to help a survivor of protracted terror recover from the event.

First, it is vital that the clinician attempt to create a supportive atmosphere in which the survivor of prolonged violence can feel safe and protected. There are schools of psychotherapy that view defense mechanisms in a negative light, and use extremely confrontational or intrusive therapeutic methods to break down a client's defenses; the aim is to reach the "true feelings." This approach cannot be opposed too strongly for several reasons. Many survivors have been through terrors that nonsurvivors, in their worst nightmares, can only have imagined. During this ordeal, their defense mechanisms served to insulate and shield them from disintegrating into madness. If a therapist attacks (or is perceived to attack), or "floods" what a survivor feels was a source of strength that protected him or her in an hour of deepest need, the person may well decide to leave the therapeutic relationship. A survivor may feel that the therapist has assaulted him or her more violently than did the captor.

The therapist's task is to facilitate, in a nurturing way, the balance between a survivor's defense mechanisms and what his or her ego can tolerate. In time, the goal will be for the survivor to face and integrate the many facets of what has happened, and for the ego to heal its wounds. A clinician certainly should support healthy, adaptive defense mechanisms, while at the same time being careful to prevent the survivor from acquiring self-destructive or maladaptive defense mechanisms. The client may need to learn that some defenses that served well during the traumatic ordeal, may be maladaptive in the process of recovery and moving forward with life.

After determining the pace at which a survivor can comfortably proceed, the clinician should work on reversing those psychological factors that caused the traumatic identification with the aggressor, if they are

214 • Strategic Interventions for People in Crisis, Trauma, and Disaster

present. If at all possible, a therapist should try to work with the survivor's family and loved ones, bringing them into the therapy process to assist the survivor's recovery. It is wise to view the survivor's family and loved ones as survivors as well, because someone one they care for has been hurt and they were helpless to do anything about it. After a survivor's release from capture, these significant others are often bewildered recipients of the survivor's displacement of anger—because they are safe objects. The anger that a survivor is incapable of directing toward his or her captor may be directed toward them for being failed protectors. For this reason, most significant others need some therapeutic support to help them deal with their own feelings, in addition to guidance in dealing appropriately with the often paradoxical and confusing behavior of their loved ones.

It has been our experience, as well as that of others, that when family members are involved in the treatment of a survivor, recovery is almost invariably hastened; but, it should be done with care. A clinician should interview the significant others to be sure that they understand the true emotional condition and perception of the survivor, and what that person is capable and not capable of understanding. For example, the loved ones may want to make sure that the survivor knows the real truth about what happened. But, if the person was truly brainwashed or formed an identification with the aggressor, he or she will reject this information and the bearer of the message. This new information should, instead, be broken down into elements that the survivor of prolonged terror can assimilate when becoming free of the traumatic cognitive distortions.

To begin this process, a therapist should learn how the survivor viewed the captor(s), those who were failed protectors, and the eventual rescuers. One should not be surprised if the survivor's views are quite unusual or distorted from those of other observers. Nevertheless, this is where one must begin the process of restructuring the cognitive distortions resulting from a protracted traumatic event. An example of this was when one of the authors began to treat a young girl who, along with her younger brother, witnessed her father murder her mother. The father fled with the children and went underground and was able to avoid apprehension for almost 7 years. During this time, the children were physically and sexually abused and the girl was used in child pornography videos. When the father was finally apprehended, he was convicted of murder, kidnapping, and several counts of sexual and physical child abuse. Both children were placed with relatives of their mother, their aunt and uncle, in a happy, well-adjusted family with two other children. This family welcomed the two traumatized teens. The new parents were quite surprised to find that, rather than being happy to be freed from their abusive father and pleased to be with a normal family, the teens were "shut down" emotionally distant and, at times, hostile. Finally, the daughter was referred to us for therapy. When her aunt and uncle brought her in, they described in detail the horrible abuse inflicted on her and her brother by the father, while she sat glowering sullenly at them. The uncle seemed to be genuinely concerned but baffled as to why this girl was so angry. What the therapist noticed was that her relatives were defining the trauma experience for her, and they were doing it in a way in which they were unknowingly silencing her. They also were clearly establishing themselves as rescuers/protectors without finding out how she felt about the situation first—a common occurrence with loved ones.

When the clinician first met with this girl alone, she asked about her experiences with her father. It was an attempt to present a neutral, open-ended question. She looked at the therapist coldly and said, "You already know all the bad stuff." In reply, the therapist, realizing how distorted the perceptions of people who suffer prolonged trauma can be, said, "Well, there must have been some good stuff, too. It must be hard for you at your uncle's because he's so angry at your Dad; you can't say anything good about your Dad or even talk about him without feeling judged." She looked at the therapist with an almost trance-like look on her face; her eyes were full of tears and she started to talk about her "daddy" in baby talk, about his swinging her on a swing and how much she missed her "daddy" who loved her. The clinician realized that, if she was going to treat this girl, she would have to begin with this view of reality. Then she would slowly add new information at a pace that the girl could tolerate. The addition of new information would be accomplished in an Ericksonian-style narrative process, incorporating cognitive restructuring and behavioral techniques such as desensitization in conjunction with family therapy.

Many family members also make mistakes in judgment that, although well-intended, can cause additional problems for the survivor. An example of this mistaken judgment is when a loved one's need to see the survivor as "all right" interacts, in a pathological way, with the survivor's "facade of competence." (The latter is a residual of the survivor's frozen affect just after the traumatic event.) This need to perceive a survivor as being "all right" is a mistaken interpretation of the facade, by means of which loved ones try to reassure themselves that the survivor is, in fact, doing fine. This, in turn, influences the survivor to avoid dealing with the trauma and makes it difficult or impossible for him or her to reveal—to these significant others—that he or she is having problems. We have also observed this phenomenon in soldiers returning from war, whose loved ones want to see them as heroes who are doing well. Thus, the façade will be maintained and a tragic pattern of behavior begun which is hard to stop, because it serves to seal the survivor's trauma and leave it festering beneath the surface. Considering this sequence of events, it is not surprising to learn that many love relationships end in the wake of trauma. Survivors of protracted trauma that is not heroic in nature sometimes break off close relationships and isolate themselves from others who, they feel, do not understand. Their isolation may be further compounded by the fact that many people tend to shy away from, or even ostracize, persons who have been victims, finding reasons to rationalize why it happened to someone else and not themselves. This reaction is very likely a primitive means to deny our vulnerability to seemingly random catastrophes.

Those who work in the helping professions should do their best not to alienate or block the traumatized person's access to help. This can occur when professionals do not realize how vulnerable a person may be after a prolonged trauma response. In many cases, a survivor is unable to express his or her needs directly to a clinician even though, at the same time, he or she expects those needs to be met. This often places a therapist in the difficult position of having to guess about the survivor's needs. It is vital to realize that many survivors are not "all right," even though many cannot admit it, and that survivors may have enormous needs for nurturance and protection. The therapist can help to prevent a second injury by trying to create an environment in which the survivor will feel safe to ask, eventually, for what he or she wants. This is especially true in the case of returning war veterans, or police and emergency service personnel who may have complex issues about asking for help or being vulnerable. Many returning veterans have suffered complex trauma and are in emotional distress, whereas friends and loved ones place social expectations on them that cause them to hide their traumatic experiences beneath the hero façade.

From the beginning of the therapeutic process, a clinician should strive to help a survivor of prolonged terror regain lost feelings of competence and control over his or her life. One cause of the loss of these feelings is an overwhelming sense of helplessness, which needs to be countered by giving the survivor a measure of control over the therapy situation. Survivors are extremely sensitive to any form of intrusiveness, insensitivity, or perceived coercion in their therapist's approach. Consequently, a wise clinician will be cognizant of issues of power and authority in the therapy relationship. As therapy evolves, a therapist acquires considerable authority in the relationship, and even if a therapist's intentions are totally benevolent and humanitarian, he or she must take care that a survivor does not project (onto the therapist) aspects of the captor's *abuse of authority*. If this occurs, the survivor will either develop an unhealthy, dependent transference to his or her therapist or flee from the therapy experience. In effect, the usual limits concerning permissible levels of inquiry in therapy do not apply with survivors of prolonged traumatic events. A clinician should be extremely patient with the survivor until a solid trust relationship can be established, and this process may take as long as several months in cases in which the person has suffered severe or complex trauma.

During an early phase of treatment, a therapist should help the survivor to realize that he or she is not the only person who has been traumatized and that his or her feelings and experiences are consistent with those of other survivors. A clinician should be cautious not to demean the person inadvertently or to imply that his or her experience was any less terrible than someone else's. Instead, a survivor should be aided in understanding his or her behavior during and after the traumatic event. The person needs assurance that he or she was (and is) reacting normally to an abnormal situation, and many need frequent reassurance of being accepted by the therapist. Even if others do not fully understand or accept what the traumatized person had to do in order to survive, it is vital that a therapist does both.

Many survivors of prolonged traumatic events need to review, obsessively, the events that occurred during their periods of captivity, analyzing and working through their reactions and what they had done. In this phase, it will be helpful for a clinician to focus attention on the concept of survival, that is, that what was most important was that the survivor survive the ordeal. By focusing on the person's doing what he or she needed to do to be a survivor, a therapist can utilize cognitive/behavioral techniques to reshape how the person fundamentally views himself or herself on the continuum from negative victim to positive survivor.

Even so, if the person will be a witness in any aspect of the criminal justice or civil legal system, a clinician should be very careful not to use any therapeutic technique that could compromise the person's testimony. Some cognitive restructuring techniques have caused victims of violent crimes to be excluded from testifying in court, because his or her memories are considered as "altered" by these techniques and thus unreliable.

The survivor may eventually be questioned by those who are trying to apprehend and prosecute those responsible for the traumatic events, and will very likely be cross-examined by the defense attorney. The questioners may be less than sensitive to the psychological trauma that results from prolonged victimization. Therefore, the survivor may have additional doubts and questions about his or her thoughts and responses as a result of the criminal-legal process, that will have to be addressed in therapy. Until one is sure that the entire criminal-legal process has been completed and the client will not be required to testify or give further evidence, one should avoid therapeutic approaches that involve any form of cognitive restructuring or are considered to be reality-altering such as hypnosis or guided imagery. Instead, one should utilize therapeutic interventions focusing on symptom reduction such as progressive relaxation, breathing exercises, desensitization, relaxation, and meditation tapes.

During their captivities, traumatized people may have done things that actually helped their captors, and sometimes much is made in a court case of this behavior. It is a therapist's role to help the survivor put this kind of "second attack" into perspective, if it happens. Sometimes a survivor may not reveal accusations by significant others of compliance, because of feelings of shame. The therapist may need to inquire tactfully, from time to time, whether or not significant others fully understand what he or she had done in order to survive being held captive. As stated earlier, the message that the person did only what was necessary to survive may have to be repeated many times, in many ways, until it can be accepted.

Another subject that needs to be explored with a survivor of prolonged victimization concerns the fantasies that he or she may have about why the capture occurred. It is very difficult for most people to accept the *randomness* of such a catastrophic event in their lives, and people frequently have fantasies that they are being punished for past wrongs. This is a particularly relevant subject for exploration in cases in which there may have been some social or political motive connected with the victimization. When drawing out a survivor's feelings on this subject, the clinician should be quite cautious concerning what he or she says about a captor, because the person may still believe that his or her life is owed to the captor. It is wise to avoid using logical argument to contradict the person about this misconception. In time, this belief will fade, but first a person needs a considerable period of freedom from the captor to express his or her feelings about the captor, as well as angry feelings about a failed protector(s).

During the first stages of treatment, it is vital for a therapist to: (1) adopt a nonjudgmental approach in which the person is permitted to express feelings freely; and (2) provide the person with as much information as he or she can tolerate about the reality of what occurred, and the true roles and motives of the various participants. In many cases, the only information about what was taking place in the "outside world" was provided to the survivor by his or her captor, who may have distorted the information to suit the captor's needs. During the recovery stage, a therapist must help the survivor assimilate and understand what had actually taken place, using cognitive reprocessing and desensitization techniques at a pace the person can tolerate. A survivor needs this missing information, but only in a context that he or she can acknowledge and accept. If the information is presented too bluntly or too rapidly, a survivor may become angry and defensive about the captor, believing that failed protectors are rationalizing in order to justify their own behavior.

In many cases, there will be a direct relationship between the survivor's ability to perceive the events of a traumatic situation accurately and the amount of control that has been regained over his or her life. Even in the recovery process following a crime of brief duration, considerable time may pass before the person will be capable of expressing anger at a perpetrator. But, as noted earlier, when the anger eventually is expressed, it should be welcomed as a significant turning point in the survivor's recovery process. A survivor needs to be encouraged to express his or her anger toward an attacker, and the clinician should provide reassurance that this anger will not bring on any counterattack or reprisal.

In short, a therapist may view the treatment of a survivor of prolonged terror as the process of welcoming back a friend, in which the therapist assists in guiding the person to a healthier perspective on his or her relationships with other people.

CHAPTER 14

Sexual Assault on Children and Adolescents

Researchers estimate that about 10 percent of boys and 25 percent of girls in America have been sexually abused.[1] This chapter reviews some of the commonly held assumptions and prejudices concerning children and adolescents who have been victims of sexual assault. Certain of these assumptions have resulted in young victims being treated as if they were guilty persons rather than victims, and some sources of those unfortunate misconceptions are identified here. The first section describes how the trauma of a sexual assault can manifest itself in children's behavior and is illustrated by two case studies, one concerning a 5-year-old girl who was raped by a stranger, and the other concerning a 9-year-old girl who was molested by a neighbor.

The Child Victim

This discussion is focused primarily on children, but the principles that are referred to here are valid for young people in general. The section does not completely exclude the subject of incest, because so many sexual assaults on children are made by family members; but, a clear distinction will be drawn between incestuous and nonincestuous types of assault. Confusing the symptoms of these two types can result in misinterpretation of the child's behavior or that of the child's family members. The classic father-daughter incest relationship was described in Chapter 8.

Many of the primitive prejudices that are commonly held about adult survivors of sexual assault, which tend to ascribe guilt or blame to the victim rather than to the perpetrator, are also held about child survivors. Many adults tend to think of children as either unreliable or naughty, and this stereotype often predisposes them to view a child as the "guilty party." Because of this tendency, many real incidents of sexual assault against children are dismissed as products of the imagination or as fabrication by a bad or difficult child. A recent incident in the court system brought this point home to the authors: a jury failed to believe four little boys who did not know each other but described exactly the same sexual abuse by a local businessman. When the jury was asked why it found the man not guilty, to a person they replied that they could not just "take the word of children" against an adult.

Some adults show more concern with the role of children in "bringing on" the assault, or whether or not children tell the truth, than with a victim's psychological well-being. This predisposition to doubt that a child can actually be considered a victim is indefensible in the light of facts. For example, a study of 250 children who were known to have suffered sexual assault showed that 60 percent had been coerced by force or the threat of force (De Francis, 1969). (See also Arata, 1988; Hansen et al., 1998; Lamb and Edgar-Smith, 1994 for further assessments of the degree of force or coercion used in child molestation.)

Adding insult to injury, many perpetrators of assault have defended themselves by claiming that the child was provocative, seductive, or extraordinarily mature (sexually) for his or her age; the adult thus attempts to shift responsibility for himself to the child. Meiselman (1978, 1991) has shown in detail how some parents will place the blame for incestuous relationships on their children—by describing them as sexually mature and seductive when, in fact, the children were neither. Meiselman (1978, 1991) and Everstine and Everstine (1983) also pointed out how clinically important it is to stress that self-control is the responsibility of an adult, even if the child may be behaving in a sexually inappropriate manner.

Although children sometimes behave in a seductive way toward adults, their actions differ greatly from those characteristic of adult sexuality. Children who act-out in this way are incapable of comprehending what could actually result from their behavior. When an interaction of this kind results in abuse, the child is left feeling shocked, confused, and betrayed. In most cases, the child had been seeking recognition or affection from the adult and was not aware of the potential consequences of his or her behavior. One of the authors asked a 9-year-old client who had been sexually abused by an adult to describe the difference between a good touch and a bad touch. She said: "A good touch is when a grownup touches you to make you feel good because they care for you and you feel good. A bad touch is when they touch you to make them feel good and you feel awful."

Because the details of incidents of sexual assault on children are in many cases shocking and repulsive, many adults unconsciously prefer not to hear them or dismiss them as exaggerated fantasies or "fibs." The tragic legacy of this mistrust and disbelief of children, combined with the child's helplessness and fear, is that many child sexual abuse cases go undisclosed (London et al., 2005). And, although disclosure rates are increasing, Sas and Cunningham (1995), Elliot and Briére (1994) and Henry (1997), it often takes a while before a child will be able to make a full disclosure of abuse.

A child cannot describe sexual behavior clearly and in detail unless he or she has been exposed to that kind of sexuality itself. So, it is essential that the child's account be documented in detail and not dismissed, no matter how bizarre or repulsive. The role of the clinician is solely to document and report an account of abuse to the proper authorities. It is not within this role to investigate what may have happened or to determine whether or not abuse occurred.

From our work with adults in psychological emergencies, we have learned that childhood sexual trauma, if treated improperly, may remain as an unhealed wound that reveals itself years later and can cause serious problems in adult life. Furthermore, undisclosed child sexual abuse can be seen as an emotional time bomb that may explode at any time in the victim's future.

The Effects of Sexual Abuse

Children initially respond in one of two ways to being molested: (1) a delayed or "silent" reaction, usually depressive in nature or "sealed over" with a façade of normalcy (in some cases, this façade only dissolves after the abuse has been reported; when this happens, the adults may wrongly blame the disclosure or the investigation of the report for the child's distress, instead of the abuse itself); (2) overt symptoms may be displayed immediately after the assault, including changes in personality, mood swings, uncharacteristic anger, panic attacks, or social phobias; there may be gastrointestinal disturbances, sudden changes in toilet habits, sleep disturbances, or enuresis (in the youngest children). Child victims frequently withdraw from their accustomed activities and relationships, sometimes by refusing to play outside the home or by becoming school-phobic. Burgess and Holmstrom (1974c), De Francis (1969), and Boney, et al. (1998) noted in their studies that a majority of child victims had at least mild to acute post-trauma symptoms. Peters (1975a, 1975b), De Francis (1969), and Everstine and Everstine (1983), also observed that many parents tend to underestimate the degree of psychological trauma that their children have experienced as the result of an assault. Their underestimation is probably caused by the parents' wish that the horrible event had never happened. This kind of thinking can lead parents to believe that the child does not require treatment because he or she has been unharmed by the event. Thus, a wishful fantasy on the part of the parents can serve to prevent a child from obtaining needed treatment. Another form that parental denial can take is pretending that, no matter what has happened, the child will just forget about it. This misguided attitude by parents can lay a foundation for more serious problems later, because the child cannot forget about it. Moreover, the parents' "Let's keep it quiet" attitude may imply, to the child, that they are ashamed of the child or of what has happened.

Because some child victims are often quiet and emotionally bland, they may be thought of as unaffected by the assault when, in fact, they are depressed. We have found that a fairly lengthy period of play therapy sessions, in which the child is reassured that it is all right to express his or her feelings and to be angry with adults, is required before the child will be able to express anger toward the perpetrator. Often it is only after this outward expression of anger that the child's depression will begin to lift and the child will be able to describe, fully, what was done to him or her. (Goodman, et al., 1992; Sas and Cunnigham, 1995; Henry, 1997). Some children find it particulary difficult to express their feelings toward adults. They may have been taught to obey adults and not to "talk back" to them. Considering the fact that 60 percent of molesters were previously known by the children whom they assaulted and 30 percent were relatives, it is clear that molestation can often place a child in a double-bind situation. The child was assaulted because of obeying an adult, but he or she cannot express angry feelings because speaking out against adults is forbidden. This kind of conflict can cause a child to suffer deep depression. The conflict may be further compounded if the parents react by severely restricting or excessively supervising their child after the molestation, which the child may perceive as a form of punishment for having been molested.

The following is a list of common symptoms of sexually abused children:

- Sudden or gradual behavioral or personality change
- Sleep problems; for example, nightmares
- Depression or withdrawal from friends or family
- Seductiveness
- Openly sexual behavior that is not age-appropriate
- Attempting to engage other children, adults, toys, or animals in sexualized behavior
- Saying that there is something wrong with his or her body or that his or her body is dirty, damaged, or injured in the genital area
- Refusing to go to school or engage in normal social activities
- Delinquency or other problems of conduct
- Secretiveness
- Sexualized drawings
- Uncharacteristic or bizarre behavior
- Risk-taking or self-destructive behavior or suicidal talk
- Bouts of unexplained crying or moodiness
- Statements such as "No one understands."
- Bedwetting or soiling, that is, loss of sphincter control

Role of the Parents

Because young children are still emotionally and physically dependent upon their parents for care and protection, they often reflect the parents' own feelings about something that has happened. As a result, it is vital that the mother and father of a child sexual abuse victim obtain the support and guidance that they themselves may need, so that they will be able to respond appropriately to their child. In some cases, it is difficult for parents to grasp what the assault has meant to their child in terms of the child's developmental level; and, if they become involved in their own feelings, they may not be able to respond to the child on the child's terms. For example, parents may become angry with their child for having gotten into a car with a stranger or having gone to a neighbor's house, in spite of having been told not to go there. As they become more involved in this anger, they may forget that the child has experienced a painful and terrifying ordeal. In reality, the child may have been a curious (or even somewhat willing) participant in the event. He or she may have been flattered by the molesting adult's attention and may even have experienced some sexual pleasure through the initial stimulation. But when the parents, on discov-

226 • Strategic Interventions for People in Crisis, Trauma, and Disaster

ering the molestation, overreact and possibly misdirect their anger toward the child, the child may be prevented from expressing his or her true feelings about the event for fear of receiving added adult condemnation.

Assessing the Impact

Our experience is that the amount of post-traumatic stress that a child suffers is usually correlated with the amount of violence or terror associated with the event, in addition to the degree of physical assault that the child has experienced. Usually, children who were victims of rape were more severely emotionally damaged than were child victims of other types of sexual assault. But, we have found that molestations in which the child was seduced and manipulated, can be just as psychologically damaging. Furthermore, assaults on children by people whom they knew and trusted are more traumatic than are assaults by strangers. It is also clear that the way in which parents, relatives, teachers, and other adults respond to the child will have a significant effect upon the child's recovery. In simple terms, children whose parents respond in an understanding and loving manner will have a better prognosis. In addition, the child's age is a significant factor in determining how traumatic an assault has been and how successful will be the child's recovery. A younger child is more vulnerable to trauma and more likely to be overwhelmed by the experience.

To review, the psychological aftereffects of molestation depend on the following variables:

1. Age of victim: younger children are more vulnerable than are older adolescents to permanent damage.
2. Emotional maturity of the victim: child victims who have had previous emotional problems may experience more subsequent problems, and those problems may be longer lasting.
3. Type of assault: the amount of violence experienced by the child is positively correlated with degree of trauma.
4. Psychological manipulation associated with the sexual abuse: children who are emotionally manipulated as well as being sexually abused may suffer more lasting trauma.
5. Repeated assault: repeated assaults cause more psychological damage than do isolated assaults.
6. Stranger versus known offender: sexual abuse by someone whom the child knows, in some cases, will cause more lasting damage than will rape by a stranger.
7. Reactions of others: negative reactions on the part of police, parents, teachers, friends, can contribute to permanent damage.

8. Therapy and support: as with adults, child victims of sexual assault who receive therapy are more likely to recover completely than are those who do not have treatment.

In conclusion, there are numerous factors that determine how traumatic a sexual assault on a child or adolescent will be. Our clinical experience strongly suggests that the most significant factor in how well a child or adolescent recovers from sexual assault is the nature of the response on the part of his or her parents, as well as that of significant other people in the child's life.

The Case of Lisa

Lisa, aged 5, was raped by a stranger on her way home from school. The policeman who responded to the initial call thought Lisa would feel safer if he talked with her when her parents were present. That was an unfortunate decision because the parents became extremely upset when they heard the details of the rape from their daughter, and ordered the policeman to leave their home. Before the policeman left, he suggested that the parents call a therapist for some counseling.

Because of the severity of the trauma, the therapist visited the hospital where the child was being examined, within an hour. She suggested that she would like to talk with the parents first, so that they could speak freely. The parents were extremely angry, and they displaced some of this anger by thoroughly questioning the therapist concerning her educational background and how much experience she had had with child rape victims. The therapist described her qualifications and experience, and attempted to reassure the parents. At first, she wanted them to ventilate some of their anger about what had happened to their daughter. Then she began trying to help the parents understand what the experience may have been like for Lisa, and to show them that Lisa might interpret their expression of angry feelings as anger directed toward her. The therapist explained that a child of Lisa's age could not fully understand the sexual aspects of what had happened to her. Instead, Lisa could only know that terror and pain had been inflicted on her by an adult, while until that time she had trusted most adults.

The clinician explained to Lisa's parents that their child's primary need, at this moment, was to feel as protected and loved as possible. Furthermore, they should be careful not to do or say anything to Lisa that she might misinterpret as anger or as blame. By the end of the session, the parents were able to admit that they had been so hurt and angry that they felt like striking out at everyone. They promised the therapist that from now on they would try to focus on Lisa's needs. Also, they decided to press charges against the rapist, with the thought of preventing the molestation of other children in future. As the intervention proceeded, the therapist said that, if Lisa felt comfortable with her, she would accompany Lisa the next day, when she had to return to the Police Department for more questioning. The parents were greatly relieved, admitting that they needed support to keep focused and to keep their emotions under control.

When the therapist asked if she could talk with Lisa, Lisa's mother brought Lisa into the living room and introduced her to the therapist. Lisa was quite small and fragile in appearance. She spoke softly and clung to her mother the whole time. After the clinician had made light conversation with Lisa for a while, she asked Lisa to show her her room, and Lisa agreed. The therapist talked with her for about half an hour in her room, utilizing the Trauma Analysis Protocol (Chapter 11) to assess the scope of Lisa's trauma. The therapist asked Lisa if she would like to come to her office and play with the toys that are there, and Lisa said that she would like to if her mother would take her.

On the way to the office, a few days later, the therapist asked Lisa if she would come in by herself, or if she would prefer that her mother come in with her. She said that her mother could wait outside. The therapist noticed some apprehension on Lisa's face, and asked if she would like her to leave the door to the office open. Lisa seemed immediately relieved, and said "Yes, please, would you leave it open for me." The therapist told her that she could have the door open as wide as she wished. (It is worth noting that giving the child choices and focusing on the child's sense of safety can help to establish a structure for the therapy to follow. Here, a cognitive/behavioral process can help the child relearn a sense of mastery and create a base from which the child can move forward to desensitization and other, cognitive work.) During this meeting, the therapist was careful not to walk rapidly toward Lisa or to touch her unless Lisa initiated it. She permitted Lisa to set the pace and closeness of their interaction, in this and subsequent play therapy sessions. The next office appointment was arranged for three days later.

The Trauma Analysis Protocol, given to Lisa at the therapist's first meeting with her, yielded this information:

Timing:	immediate (violent)
Degree of Injury:	bodily penetration
Origin:	stranger
Intent:	yes (direct, obvious intent to inflict harm)
Stigma:	yes

Warning:	none
Status:	alone (vulnerable child)
Impact:	terror (fear body is damaged, fear for life)
Perceived Threat:	severe
Reactions of Others:	intense anger
Potential Vulnerability for Future Trauma:	low
Traumatic History:	none
Clinical History:	none

During the second session, the therapist administered a symptom checklist (Chapter 11), to learn which traumatic symptoms Lisa was currently experiencing. The checklist rated her traumatic reaction as acute, including symptoms of avoidance, fear, and anxiety; she was having problems in sleeping as well as night terrors; she was depressed and withdrawn.

When the therapist met with the parents, she asked them to complete the same checklist themselves. Their description of their daughter's traumatic symptoms was consistent with Lisa's responses, as well as the therapist's observations of her. The therapist reviewed, with them, her treatment plan, consisting in strategically focused, cognitive/behavioral play therapy with a narrative exercise directed toward alleviating Lisa's symptoms. She also suggested a night light and, perhaps, a tape playing music to help Lisa with the night terrors. If Lisa could not fall asleep, a parent should stay with her until she fell asleep, but she should not be encouraged to sleep in the parental bed.

During the first three sessions, Lisa played out scenes in a doll's house involving a little girl doll. Each story told of a girl who got hurt or was sick; she would have to go to the hospital and, later, her mother and father would have to take care of her. Throughout these sessions, Lisa appeared emotionally "flat" and depressed. She would narrate lengthy stories about the hurt little girl while remaining largely expressionless. In each session, the therapist used narrative technique to guide the theme of the play in a direction of positive cognitive restructuring; for example, the parents of the girl found a doctor or nurse to make the sick child healthy, because the parents loved her very much. Lisa brought some of her own toys to the third session, and it was then that she asked the clinician why she had not asked her about the "bad man." When the therapist replied that they could talk about the man if she wanted to, Lisa abruptly changed the subject. The therapist did not push her to talk about him further.

Lisa brought more toys from home to the fourth session. The therapist waited to see if Lisa would bring up the subject of the "bad man," but she didn't. The therapist mentioned him once, but Lisa changed the subject again. Later on, the theme of play therapy changed, to include elaborate scenes of her being fed and protected by her parents, for which the therapist provided a positive narration. Before the next session, the therapist learned, from Lisa's mother, that Lisa was still refusing to play outside the house because some older children had teased and frightened her. Two more sessions of play therapy involved complicated feeding scenes, as well as scenes of a child being hurt and rescued. After each feeding scene, the children would be taken home by their mothers and put to bed. At each session, the therapist attempted to create narrative themes directed toward the cognitive goal of helping her regain her sense of safety. She also started to introduce, indirectly, treatment for symptom-specific issues, using the medium of play therapy. For example, she taught Lisa relaxation and breathing techniques to help lessen her startle responses by showing her how the nurse dolls helped the sick, hurt, or scared doll. By special ways, nurses and doctors teach children to take deep, strong breaths, so they don't feel scared.

Eventually, the play therapy sessions became more interactional, in that Lisa would create scenes of children playing together or watching television together. As her play became more interactional, so did her behavior with the therapist. She sat closer to her and touched her at times. She also began to involve the therapist in the play as a participant. Before, the therapist had been more like a narrator at the side, who could comment, interrupt, or direct Lisa's play, but was not actually an active part of it. Now, the therapist could directly involve Lisa and the story's characters in symptom-relieving strategies such as relaxation techniques and desensitization, as well as more direct cognitive/behavioral corrective and mastery experiences.

The scenes then totally changed to those involving the bedroom and the toilet. By now, she was actually interacting directly with the therapist as part of the play. The therapist saw this as a very significant shift, and believed that important work could soon begin. The toilet scenes consisted in Lisa's thoroughly examining both the male and female dolls and their using the toilet. The therapist learned, when she spoke with the parents that same week, that Lisa was now willing to come home from school by herself, even though she would run the entire way home. To the next session, Lisa brought a doll who wore no panties, and, when Lisa commented on this fact, the therapist asked if the doll had left them at the hospital. Lisa replied with a definite "no." She buried the doll in the sandbox, but then suddenly uncovered it and picked it up. As the sand was falling from the doll's hair, Lisa quietly said "like rain. . . . She's clean now," caressed the doll and very carefully wrapped it up and put her in her backpack.

Although the therapist was tempted to ask Lisa what she had meant by what she had done, her intuition told her that the child had made a very private cleansing ritual that needed to be respected and left private.

The next session began with innocuous play, and then Lisa suddenly grabbed an adult, male doll and began burying him angrily. She said that he was crying for help, but no one would help him because he is a bad man. "Help me bury him; let's bury him, he's bad." Then, with obvious pleasure, Lisa stuck the scary animals around him in the sand. As she did this, the therapist created a cognitive/behavioral intervention to help Lisa begin to have the sense that she was no longer the bad man's victim, and that she had a right to punish him. The therapist reiterated that she was a good girl, and what the man had done was in the past and had not changed her. The grownups will punish him for what he did to her. Pushing his doll under the sand, she triumphantly pronounced the man dead. After this, she carefully removed the scary animals and put them away. Then, she dug the man out, put him in a box and shut the lid, referring to the box as "his coffin." The therapist tried to show Lisa that she, the therapist, accepted this anger, and tried to reassure her that it was all right for her to be angry and to bury the man.

Following this session, Lisa's mood changed dramatically; her manner became much more animated and her depressive symptoms began to lift. She continued to work through the anger that was still felt toward the man by repeatedly burying him or feeding him to ferocious animals. Slowly, her anger began to subside and her play scenes became interactional again, in that she would once more create family scenes and scenes of children playing. The therapist continued to meet with Lisa's parents for supportive therapy, but also to involve them in supporting the therapeutic work that was being done during the therapy sessions; for example, their reminding her to use her "strong-girl breathing" (deep-breathing relaxation exercises), when she felt anxious. The parents needed some help in understanding why it took so long for Lisa to become angry, and why, at times, it was directed at them. The therapist explained that they were the people with whom she felt safe enough to express the rage. This made sense to them, and they were also relieved to learn that, once vented and properly directed and validated, the anger would, in time, pass; it did.

The therapist learned that Lisa's behavior at home and with her peers had returned to normal. By then, the clinician had begun to believe that Lisa had confronted as much of the rape experience as possible for someone at her stage of psychological development, and thus decided to conclude the play therapy sessions. When meeting with Lisa's parents, the therapist explained that Lisa had worked through the rape experience as well as possible for the time being, adding that renewed therapy might be appropriate when Lisa became an adolescent.

The Case of Marie

The mother of 8-year-old Marie brought her to the local police department's Sex Investigation Office because she thought Marie had been molested by a neighbor. The mother had learned that Marie had gone to visit, on several occasions, a neighbor without her permission, and had started to behave like a completely different child after the visits. When she arrived home after the last visit, Marie ran at once to the bathroom, locked the door, and would not answer her mother who could hear her crying inside. When she finally came out of the bathroom and was asked where she had gone that day, Marie answered, "I thought Mr. Smith was a daddy," and ran to her room, once more refusing to talk with her mother. From that moment, according to the mother, Marie's entire personality changed: a once well-behaved, friendly little girl, who loved to help her mother and had done very well in school, suddenly became moody and secretive and was afraid to leave the house—even to go to school. She withdrew from her father and brothers, with whom she had been very close. She also would have sudden, unexplainable tantrums and at times say odd things such as, "I thought only mommies and daddies did that," and run out of the room when her mother would try to question her. Marie had frequent nightmares as well, and often would wake up screaming.

In his questioning of Marie at the police station, the Sex Investigation Officer asked her what had happened at Mr. Smith's house. Marie looked away and said, "I forgot." The officer then asked Marie's mother to step outside so that he could talk with Marie alone; he attempted to reassure Marie before asking her again what had happened. This time, Marie began to tremble and cry, and her repeated answer was "I don't know. I can't remember." By this time, the officer felt convinced that something had happened to Marie, but he was not sure exactly what. Thinking that a therapist who specialized in children might be of help, he suggested that the mother call our office. He added that some therapy might be worth trying if, in fact, Marie was blocking something from her mind, or was too afraid to talk about what had happened to her.

A therapist met with the officer, Marie, and her mother that same afternoon. After getting acquainted with Marie and her mother, the clinician decided to find out whether or not Marie would talk about what had happened. The counselor used a "guided imagery" technique in which Marie was asked to make a "journey" to a beautiful, safe place. In this safe place, she would be able to sit on a cuddly, teddy-bear-policeman's lap and remember what had happened, because the teddy-bear-policeman loved little children and would protect her. Although Marie seemed comfortable in her safe place and even appeared to be enjoying it, as soon as the subject of remembering Mr. Smith's house was brought up she began to tremble and big tears rolled down her cheeks. When the therapist asked her again what she remembered, Marie replied, "Nothing. I forgot. I can't remember." Then, she began to cry once more. At this point, the clinician believed that Marie had suffered some traumatic experience on the last day she had visited Mr. Smith, but what it was remained a mystery. Furthermore, she believed that Marie actually remembered what had happened, but was afraid to tell. The therapist decided to ask Marie to return, later on, for play therapy. She explained to Marie's mother that the therapy would move forward at Marie's pace, and reassured Marie that she would not be forced to do or say anything she did not want to do or say.

During the next session, Marie and the therapist made drawings together. When Marie was engrossed in a drawing of her brother, she spontaneously commented that "Mr. Smith only showed me pictures of naked people from here up," gesturing that she meant from the neck up. The therapist thanked Marie for sharing that with her, and added that she knew that what had happened to Marie must have been scary and embarrassing. But, it was not Marie's fault, and no one would be angry with her if she told the rest. When Marie did not reply, the therapist dropped the subject and continued drawing with the girl.

Marie and the therapist began the next session by drawing pictures; but, then, Marie noticed a doll's house in the room and asked if she could play "mommy and daddy." When they were playing with the doll's house, the therapist asked, "What do mommies and daddies do?" In reply, Marie began enacting a very detailed scene in which daddy asked mommy to come inside and clean the house. As she continued with the fantasy of the mommy-doll cleaning the house, Marie became quite anxious; she abruptly stopped the cleaning in the dining room and went back to drawing pictures.

Next time, Marie returned to the doll's house and began playing mommy and daddy again. But, when the mommy-doll was in the dining room, the daddy-doll took off her pants and made her lie on the floor while he rubbed himself against her leg. As Marie played out this scene, she constantly looked toward the clinician to see what her reaction would be. Because the therapist remained calm and accepting, Marie continued. She said, "He rolled her over and put his fingers up her bottom and it hurt." The therapist asked if that was what Mr. Smith had done to her. Marie began to sob and said "yes;" she added that she was pregnant and that her parents would send her away, because Mr. Smith had said that's what they do to bad little girls. The therapist reached out and held Marie's hand and assured her that Mr. Smith was a bad man and told lies. She explained that Marie could not be pregnant because she was too young, and that her parents would not send her away because of what had happened. She continued to reassure her that her parents loved her very much, no one was mad at her, and that it was not her fault.

The therapist then went to find Marie's mother, and, on the way back to the playroom, explained that Marie had revealed what Mr. Smith had done to her. The therapist suggested that it was important for the mother to be very loving and supporting if Marie were to tell her about what had happened. When the mother entered the room, Marie—crying all the while—told her mother that Mr. Smith had asked her to come in and help him clean the house. He took her into the dining room and showed her some pictures of naked people, and then he told her to take her pants off. Marie had done what he said to do because she was so scared. Mr. Smith told her not to tell anyone because, if she did, her parents would send her away to be locked up because she was pregnant. Marie's mother reassured her that Mr. Smith was a liar and a bad man, and that she and Marie's father loved her very much and would never send her away. Her mother also reassured her that she could not be pregnant.

The next day, Marie and her parents returned to the police station and told the Sex Investigation Officer what had happened in the incident. After Smith was arrested, it was discovered that once before he had been accused of molesting young children (in exactly the same manner) in another state. Later, when Smith was released on bail, Marie saw him from time to time in her neighborhood, and that frightened and confused her because she was afraid he would come back and "get" her. Because of this, Marie's parents felt that it would be best for her if they moved to another part of the city.

Once the nature of Marie's traumatic experience was learned, the therapist reviewed the case according to the Trauma Analysis Protocol, with these results:

Timing:	immediate
Degree of Injury:	body penetration
Origin:	trusted neighbour
Intent:	yes (intent to harm)
Stigma:	yes
Warning:	none
Status:	alone (vulnerable child)
Impact:	very much aware

Perceived Threat:	fear
Reactions of Others:	parents supportive
Potential Vulnerability for Future Trauma:	low
Traumatic History:	none
Clinical History:	none

Next, the therapist administered the children's symptom checklist with the result that Marie indicated experiencing different symptoms than those she had revealed at home. The parents said that she was expressing more symptoms of anger and social alienation at home than she had in the therapist's office. At home, her demeanor was quite depressive and avoidant. The parents and therapist surmised that this discrepancy was caused by the fact that the molester had been a neighbor. This confirmed the parents' decision to move away.

The decision to move was reflected in Marie's play therapy sessions, in which sick or hurt children had to "go away" to get better. After Marie's court appearance, her play sessions displayed considerable anger. She had several tantrums, during which she threw things around the playroom. Her drawings consisted in angry people fighting each other. The therapist would intervene with narrative strategies to problem-solve or resolve conflicts. With time, Marie's anger slowly subsided. She and the therapist began role-playing scenes involving her friends as well as grownups, and focused on how to handle scary or bad people. The therapist also enlisted the parents—especially her father—and her brothers, to help lessen the effects of triggers and startle responses; they were to announce in advance when they were entering a room or approaching her if she did not see them. Her parents made it very clear that teasing Marie would not be tolerated. The therapist taught Marie "strong girl" breathing exercises that she could use when she felt uncomfortable or anxious.

As therapy drew to a close, the clinician conducted several family sessions in which Marie's parents and brothers attempted to let her know that they were proud of her for being brave and telling the truth. By the time therapy had concluded, Marie had started playing with her brothers again and felt at ease with her father once more.

The cases of Marie and Lisa serve to illustrate some typical behavior patterns of the sexually assaulted child. In our experience, some of these children appear at first to be emotionally bland or depressed, while others show symptoms immediately. Even so, each victim will need considerable support and reassurance before he or she will be able to express feelings, as well as the full extent of the abuse (Goodman et al., 1992; Sas and Cunningham, 1995; Elliot and Briére, 1994; Henry, 1997). Unfortunately, adults often misinterpret the flat affect of the abused child as showing that the child was undisturbed by the event. It is also our experience that victims of childhood sexual abuse do not always need long-term therapy; instead, strategically directed play therapy is recommended to assist the child in working through the trauma as it was experienced. We believe, as do Cohen and Mannarino (1996, 1998, 2000, 2003) and Deblinger et al. (1996), that therapy focused strategically on the issues with which the victim is struggling, using cognitive/behavioral techniques, is the most effective mode of treating sexually abused children and adolescents. Later on, further strategic therapy will probably be useful during critical developmental stages, such as the onset of puberty or leaving home for college.

The Adolescent Victim

Violence against adolescents is far more prevalent than many realize; one in three adolescents experiences violence during dating (Bureau of Justice Special Report: "Intimate Partner Violence," May, 2001). One in eleven teenage girls have admitted to being forced to have sexual intercourse when they did not want to do so (Center for Disease Control and Prevention, "Youth Risk Behavior Surveillance," 1999). In fact, 67 percent of rape victims were of high school or college age when raped (U.S. Department of Justice, 2002). These statistics clearly indicate that adolescence is not only a time of "pushing limits" and risk-taking but also a period of enormous vulnerability. Certain aspects of an adolescent's rape trauma are unique, and even though many of the treatment principles for these victims are the same as those for adults (see next chapter), the experience itself merits description in this section.

As a result of adolescent exploration or acting-out, a girl may place herself in jeopardy of being the victim of rape. For example, she might think of hitchhiking as daring or adventurous, and dismiss her parents' warning against it as stuffy or old-fashioned. If she does become a rape victim as a result of disobeying her parents, she may tend to blame herself more intensely than would some adult victims. Or this may lead her to hide the fact of being raped for fear of admitting it to the parents.

Sadly, many adolescent victims do not tell their parents directly about the assault, but the secret is often betrayed by their behavior. For example, sudden and inexplicable changes in the habitual behavior of a teenage girl may be a sign that the girl was the victim of a hidden, undisclosed rape. Such changes in behavior patterns may take one of several forms, for example, (1) a rapid drop in school attendance and school performance, (2) flagrant and repetitive promiscuity, (3) withdrawal from peers and peer groups, (4) self-destructive or suicidal behavior, or (5) self-medication with alcohol or drugs. Any one of these changes can be the manifestation of a teenage girl's wish to keep secret the fact that she has been raped. Even so, this relatively sudden change in behavior on the part of the girl will call attention to itself eventually, and the secret may come out as a result. In retrospect, one can say that the adolescent's rapidly changing behavior patterns represent a "cry for help."

A key to working with adolescent victims of assault is to realize that they have many of the same emotional needs as do children who have been molested. This is especially true with respect to the need for nurturance and support on the part of parents. Even though an adolescent girl may have reached a similar stature to that of an adult and have attained the physical attributes of an adult, she is still in many respects a child. Her striving for independence from the parents may mislead an adult into thinking that she is more mature than is the case. Indeed, the parents themselves may be misled to the belief that their teenager needs less of their tender concern than she did when she was in elementary school. Sometimes, when an adolescent reports to her parents that she has been raped, they in turn focus their attention on her risk-taking behavior and the poor judgment that she may have shown. Some parents express their concern about the possible public scandal that might arise. In this kind of myopic view, the parents lose sight of the fact that their daughter has suffered a terrible trauma and needs to feel loved. Above all, she needs to believe that she will be protected. When parental concern "gets lost" and parental anger "spills over" onto the rape victim herself, it only serves to instill in her a sense of guilt or worthlessness that may lead to greater loss of self-esteem. Furthermore, this too often becomes a motive for self-destructive acting-out on the part of the adolescent. Although the parents may believe that they have done "what is right," in the process they may have contributed to exactly the kind of behavior they most fear.

An alternative form that post-traumatic behavioral changes may take is that the girl may react by trying to avoid social contact with boys as much as possible, and for a considerable period of time. This kind of withdrawal should be respected at face value. A clinician should help the parents to realize that, because their daughter has been deeply and overwhelmingly frightened, they must let her find her own way back to a "social life." The mentality of "After a fall, put the rider right back on the horse" is not the way back but patience and desensitization is. The therapist must accept responsibility for helping the parents, siblings, and other important people in the girl's life to permit the wounds to heal in a manner which validates her sense of competence.

There will be cases in a therapist's practice when he or she learns that an adolescent client has been a victim of undisclosed rape. When this happens, it is important to try not to react in a judgmental way. A clinician should focus immediately on the girl's need for care and protection—for example, should she have medical treatment or a pregnancy test? Next, the therapist should attempt to get her consent to inform the parents about what has happened. If the rape was committed by an adult, and not reported, the girl may need assistance to do so. The therapist should inform her that rape by an adult is a crime and must be reported. But the therapist will support her through the process.

Even if an adolescent wishes to keep the rape secret from her parents, a clinician can encourage her to report it anonymously to the police. The therapist can say that he or she would like the person who committed rape to be punished and prevented from finding another victim. Most Sex Investigation Officers are well aware of the fact that many adolescents who are raped do not report the assault right away. Another possible reason that the girl may not have reported being raped is that the rapist may have been an adolescent from her peer group, and she may have well-founded fears of ostracism or revenge by others in the group if she reports the assault.

In summary, although the case of an adolescent survivor of sexual assault contains factors that are similar to cases of both adult and child-hood assault, there are unique elements as well. In terms of psychosexual development, adolescence may be the most stressful phase of the entire life cycle, and sexual abuse during this period can have a lifelong effect. Although the authors do not believe that all parents will react to their daughter's trauma with insensitivity or indifference, we are convinced that how the adolescent's significant adults respond after the assault will be a key factor in her recovery.

Finally, it should be noted that, in some cases of adolescent rape, being raped is the girl's first sexual experience. Although most adults can clearly understand the difference between consensual sex and rape, an adolescent survivor may have difficulty in making that distinction if she lacks prior experience. This is a subject that the therapist will need to explore with an adolescent survivor, in order to help her unravel some of the possible mis-understandings about sex that may be part of the aftermath of rape.

CHAPTER **15**

Adult Victims of Rape

Rape is a severe and complex form of assault, and there are many elements of this traumatic event that warrant special attention when planning treatment for a rape survivor.[1] Too often, therapists and counselors focus primarily on the sexual aspect of an assault, and do not help the survivor work through other profound psychological questions that she may have had to confront during and after the assault. Being raped is a brutally destructive attack upon the survivor's sense of personal integrity and competence, as well as her basic trust of others. Furthermore, rape is an assault on the survivor's sense of territoriality, as the body is the person's most basic "territory."

We are extremely territorial beings: consider, for example, how it feels to be in an elevator crowded with strangers. We express and experience our sense of territoriality in myriad everyday situations, and it is so basic that we rarely think consciously of "territory" as such. People have a region of very private "space" around them, with a radius of about a foot-and-a-half to two feet. People in different cultures have differing critical areas of space;

for example, Northern Europeans and North Americans generally tend to have a larger region of personal space than do Latin Americans. A profound source of trauma in sexual assault is the devastating breach, and temporary destruction, of the woman's basic feeling of territorial boundaries.

People who have been robbed experience a similar sort of territorial breach, but to a much lesser extent. An example is the case of a client whose apartment was broken into. Although nothing of value was taken, she came home to find her clothes and other possessions strewn around the apartment, and for several weeks she felt uneasy in her own home. The apartment had become "violated" space, and it was much later before she felt safe about returning home in the evening. This feeling, compounded a hundred times, might describe the emotional state of someone who has been raped. For not only has something intruded into the rape survivor's space, but her very skin—the ultimate personal boundary—also has been invaded. There are only a few circumstances in which people's bodies are penetrated against their will, that is, a stabbing, a shooting, or a rape.

A concept that is helpful in understanding rape and other forms of sexual assault is that the survivor's sense of integrity is temporarily destroyed. Her basic feelings of wholeness, strength, and self-control are lost. With them, a person loses confidence in the ability to say "no." Most of us are secure enough, within ourselves, to believe that if we say, "I don't want you to do that" or "Stop that," the other person will likely stop. We began to learn that when we were 2 years old, in the stage of discovering the word "no." Suddenly, as an adult, the woman's attempt to stop the attacker has not worked; she was powerless. For a rape survivor, this feeling of powerlessness is devastating to her sense of being competent to interact with others and to have some measure of control over her life.

Sexual assault can greatly damage the survivor's feelings of trust in others. These assumptions of trust are vital elements upon which personal relationships, as well as society itself, are based. Few of us are consciously aware of how much implicit trust we have in other people with whom we share social relationships. We assume that people will not intentionally harm us. Then, in one horrible moment, a survivor realizes how vulnerable to others she has always been. Although the assault is sexual, the most severe wounds that are inflicted upon a rape survivor are not physical but invisible, psychological wounds. These psychological effects, combined with the physical assault, leave the survivor in a profound state of shock. The authors are of the opinion that it is instructive, from a clinical point of view, to make a sharp division between two major stages of the traumatic process—hence, the usefulness of the Trauma Response and Recovery

Cycle, which describes two distinct processes separated by the survivor's release from his or her assailant (see Chapter 12).

Survivors have a strong need to ask "Why?" That is, "Why did this happen?" "Why me?" "What did I do wrong?" For example, even in a case such as that of a woman who is alone in her home, asleep in her bed, when someone breaks into her home and rapes her at knife point, the woman is likely to ask why it happened to her. Human beings are basically rational and need to have some kind of plausible explanation for an event, especially one so traumatic as sexual assault. Most of us have some religious background and believe in at least a form of destiny or divine judgment, a fact that may explain a survivor's asking "Why should I be punished?" or "What did I do to deserve this?"

If, as is often tragically the case, a survivor may have done something prior to the attack that she feels guilty about or regrets, she may infer that the attack was some sort of punishment for a past deed. An example of that sort of misunderstanding is this case of a rape survivor: she was quite reluctant to see someone for treatment, but her family insisted because of her unusual behavior. She had not wanted to report the rape herself, even though she had been badly beaten by the rapist. She seemed to be curiously resigned to the rape and was extremely uncooperative with the police once it had been reported by the family. She refused to give a description of the rapist or to look at mug shots of suspects, despite having told her parents that she knew what he looked like. After the clinician had seen this woman for a while, it was discovered that, until about a year before the rape, she had been through an acting-out period of nearly 2 1/2 years. During that time, she had associated with the "wrong kind" of friends, had been sexually promiscuous, and had experimented with drugs. However, for the past year she had stopped seeing these "bad" friends and had stopped using drugs. Hence, following a period of time during which the girl had changed her behavior, gotten a job, and was in a positive, stable relationship, she was brutally raped. She intuitively believed that this was God's punishment for having once been a "bad" person. Once this secret belief had been discovered and discussed with her family and boyfriend, she was able to work through the rape experience successfully by means of both individual and family therapy.

Each of us lives with problems and fears and sorrows, but usually there is an undercurrent of order and reason to our lives. Suddenly, an inexplicable, devastating event takes place, an event which occurs beyond the compass of our usual conceptual framework. Because many sexual assaults are committed by unknown assailants, they are (from the point of view of the survivors) virtually random occurrences. In fact, they are typically "crimes of opportunity" (e.g., "The window was left open;";"She was walking down the street without suspecting any danger;" "She was driving, and when she stopped at a stop light with the passenger door unlocked, he jumped into the car with a weapon"). In the randomness of a moment like that, questions about destiny and injustice are inevitable.

Survivors of rape, like other survivors of violent crimes, experience a state that resembles acute grief, because of their severe psychological losses (as described in the classic study by Lindemann, 1944). They need to go through the Recovery Cycle of disbelief, depression, mood swings, anger, philosophizing and, finally, "laying to rest." The order of these phases may vary somewhat, but it is basically one unified process. What takes place in this cycle involves the same dynamic processes that function to reconstruct the ego after any personal tragedy or mind-shattering event.

Treatment Techniques

When we begin working with a rape survivor and her family, we usually take both a more directive and a more educational approach than is taken with most clients. The rationale for this approach is that the survivor usually has a need for basic information, a need to have answers to questions about what she is experiencing, and a need to be reassured that she is not "going insane" and that her questions are reasonable ones. For example, many survivors can be helped if one explains what ego defense mechanisms are, how these mechanisms are acquired, and how they work. Once the survivor's shock wears off, she will probably be attempting to utilize certain of these mechanisms as vital components of the recovery cycle. The purpose of explanations such as these is that the woman gains some perspective on the total process, and the loved ones gain an understanding of what is going on inside the survivor—even though she may not be able to explain it herself.

Many survivors don't realize that they were in a state of shock when they were being raped or assaulted. Hence, they may feel some guilt or misunderstanding about their seemingly strange behavior. This doubt may find expression in questions such as, "Why didn't I fight?" Some survivors describe the attack in terms such as these: "It was like I was under water;" "Everything was going in slow motion;" or "I couldn't even speak." Quite frequently, a rape survivor will say something like that and then describe feeling guilty for her inability to fight. A good way to resolve this guilt is to explain to the survivor that, because she was in shock during the attack, she was incapable of fighting—or even of keeping track of time—and that her state of consciousness could be likened to that of a deer in headlights.

The following case will serve to illustrate how much support and information-giving is necessary, as well as to describe the problems that may arise if relevant explanations are not provided to the survivor. A young woman who had been raped by a man who broke into her apartment when she was asleep was referred to us by the police after a serious suicide attempt. She had previously been in therapy, for about a month, with a nondirective clinician who was competent but didn't have much training or knowledge about working with trauma survivors. During her course of nondirective therapy, the person would say things such as, "I don't understand why, when I was raped, I couldn't fight; it was like everything was a bizarre nightmare." The therapist would respond by asking questions such as, "Well, why do you think you didn't fight?" What the therapist unwittingly had done was to put responsibility for the rape back on the survivor. Instead, a simple explanation of shock and how it affects a person's ability to respond would have resolved the issue.

By the end of a month of this sort of treatment, the woman had attempted suicide because, as she put it, "If I knew why I didn't fight, I would have told him [the therapist]. I began to feel the rape was my fault. I felt so worthless I didn't want to live." A rape or violent assault is not the kind of event that the survivor can reflect upon calmly or analyze logically. Instead, it is a totally irrational reign of terror in which the survivor's primary goal is to survive. A survivor needs clarification of what has happened to her and why she reacted as she did.

As an initial intervention, our strategy is to explain shock to the survivor, as well as the possibility that she may block out bits and pieces of what has happened. We also describe the basic defense mechanisms of repression, denial, projection, and displacement, in order to help her gain a perspective on what she is experiencing. Sometimes these mechanisms can be more easily explained to a survivor by analogy to physical defenses: for example, "Just as your body has a defense against bacteria called 'antibodies,' so your mind has defenses against too much psychological pain; your mind uses these mechanisms to protect itself." The clinician can continue by clarifying other aspects of the Recovery Cycle; for example, by telling her that each crucial event in our life carries a number of emotions with it that need to be expressed. Giving birth has a quantity of emotion attached to it, a birthday has feelings that go with it, a divorce has strong outpourings of emotion, and so has rape an intense emotional component. No matter what kind of event it is, the relevant emotions will need to be worked through.

Some of the personality changes that a survivor will experience, such as bouts of depression or anger or sudden bursts of exhilaration and energy, represent attempts of the psyche to cope with this recovery process and eventually put to rest the traumatic event. A survivor should be encouraged not to fight these vital processes, but some will vigorously resist allowing their feelings about the attack to show for various reasons. For example, some rape survivors have great difficulty in expressing the profound anger that they feel toward the rapist himself because they are usually too fragile or fearful, until they move well into the recovery cycle.

As mentioned in a previous chapter, many survivors have a need to prove that they are "all right." For them to admit their feelings and the fact they are not all right would be, in the logic of magical thinking, a way of permitting their attacker to "know" how much he injured them. Another reason why many survivors resist showing their feelings and working through their grief is that they are concerned about the possible reactions of friends and relatives. In many cases there is also a strong desire on the part of a survivor's family and friends to wish "the whole thing never happened" or to think, "Let's just put it out of our minds." People can be very sympathetic and understanding when it comes to a person's need to talk about physical wounds, but they are often impatient or unsympathetic (or even cruel) with a survivor's invisible, psychological wounds. The woman's family members may also be obsessively concerned about a social stigma or "what the neighbors will think;" because of this, they may be insensitive toward her. The concept of the invisible psychological wound is too complex for many people to understand, but that kind of wound can be more serious and long lasting than a physical one. It, too, requires a healing process.

When a rape survivor begins the angry phase of the Recovery Cycle (see Figure 12.1 , Chapter 12), she may benefit from an explanation of the defense of displacement, in which anger is vented on another, "safe" object. A clinician could explain this defense by telling the survivor that she may not wish to be "nice" toward men—or even want to be close to them—for a while, because she has been so terribly injured by a man. Some version of this comment may prove helpful: "You have a right to be angry about what happened, and some of your anger may be projected onto your father, your brother, a male friend, or some person who is equally 'safe' ." It is well to remember that the survivor also may harbor unconscious resentment toward her husband or father for not "being there" to protect her. A therapist must help the woman balance her need to ventilate anger against the necessity of preserving the most significant male relationships in her life. In addition, a therapist should explain to these significant other(s) (father, husband, lover, uncle, or brother) that the survivor may displace anger upon them as a part of the recovery process and that this understandable reaction, if dealt with appropriately, will subside and pass away. It is a good idea to present this concept to each significant other in a separate session when the woman is not present, so that each may give vent to some of his own feelings. This may also be a time for some focused couple's or family therapy with the survivor.

After a rape, it may take from six months to a year and a half of therapy before the survivor will begin to work through the trauma and recover her confidence and self-esteem. The typical length of time required for treatment varies from 6 to 10 months. In this connection, it is worth noting that the unfortunate assumption is often made that a survivor of sexual assault is a person who has few other problems and will necessarily be cooperative in treatment. It is possible that a survivor may have had serious personal difficulties before the assault took place; for example, she may be a member of a dysfunctional, unhappy family or she may have been experiencing a miserable marriage relationship or prior abuse. A sexual assault may interact with and exacerbate these kinds of preexisting problems. Also, women who are going through life crises may be more susceptible to being chosen as survivors of rape, for the reason that their thoughts may be more directly focused upon internal problems than on external safety.

The family of a rape survivor can be of enormous help as a tangible source of support, or it can contribute additional problems. Moreover, it is important to be aware of the social system in which a survivor lives and to draw as much support as possible from that system. Both relatives and friends can assist in the recovery process, or they can cause the assault to be a lingering illness that never heals and is never discussed. The family must understand that *a survivor needs to talk, but should not be pushed to talk.* One reason why those who are close to the woman should accept this wish to talk is that their characteristic impulse is to avoid listening to the grim details over and over again. But, if they can see the importance of letting her tell about the assault many times, she may perceive them as more understanding. Sometimes a survivor needs to tell her loved ones the most gruesome details; in a symbolic way, she is asking a loved one to reassure her that, despite what was done to her, she can still be loved. Other survivors, by contrast, do not want loved ones to know any details of the assault. In either case, it is the task of a therapist to discover and respect the woman's wishes.

When therapy with a survivor begins, it is helpful to refrain from asking about details of the rape; this recommendation applies especially to male therapists. The woman has already been asked to tell her story too often, to too many people. Eventually, when she trusts the therapist, she will tell about the assault, usually in great detail; indeed, as mentioned earlier, some rape survivors need to repeat the description of what happened again and again. A clinician can say something such as this to the client: "I don't need to know any details of what was done to you, but we can talk about it if you want to. Whenever you want to talk about it, that's all right with me . . . but I don't want to push you to talk about anything prematurely, or get you to tell me something that you would feel uncomfortable to talk about." It is more important for the rape survivor to describe how she *feels* than to describe the painful and humiliating details of the assault. In fact, many survivors are more "open" to therapy once they realize that discussing the actual events of the assault is not essential to treatment. Successful cognitive/behavioral and strategic work can be done without the client's having to recount specific details.

It is important to try not to pressure the survivor into doing or saying anything that she does not want to do or say. Instead, try to convey the message that a therapist's first role is to help her recover and to regain a sense of personal integrity and independence. This advice may seem to contradict previous suggestions about being directive, but there is a difference between being directive and supportive (while giving a clear explanation of the psychological processes that a survivor is experiencing), by contrast with pushing the person to deal with thoughts that she may not be ready to confront. Because survivors of sex crimes have been forced to commit acts against their will, it is vital that similar coercion does not occur in therapy, so that a strong trust relationship can be established. What the woman needs above all is to regain a feeling of control over her life. Thus, in therapy it is important that she work at her own pace (not the therapist's), as a means to establishing some control within the context of the therapeutic relationship. Many assertive interventions that a therapist would make with other clients are simply out of place when working with a rape survivor.

In psychotherapy it is sometimes necessary to "confront" a client, but this should be avoided with a rape survivor. A therapist may say, for example, "I think you need to realize that you may not be dealing with feelings that you should try to acknowledge, but I am not going to force you to do so." An event that actually occurred in counseling will make these points clear. The woman was being seen as a psychotherapy client. She was quite fragile and getting ready to face the stress of facing the man who raped her at the criminal trial. On the day before a scheduled third therapy session, she called the office and asked to see the therapist right away for an emergency visit. When the woman arrived, she was obviously deeply shaken and, when asked what had happened, began crying uncontrollably. Haltingly, through the hour, she told the following story. A few days before, a friend had called and asked her to accompany him to a weekend group with a "life coach." The client didn't want to tell this friend about the rape, so she just said, "No, thank you," adding that she didn't feel like going out on the weekend, and said "goodbye." Later that same evening, the friend called again and repeated his invitation. This time he was more forceful, insisting that the group experience would be good for her and arguing that she should change her mind and go. When she said "no" again and he continued to badger her, she finally put down the phone. The woman said that she was sincere in not wanting to tell her friend about the rape. (In fact, she did not feel comfortable in talking about it with anyone other than the therapist at this time). Finally, the friend called a third time, at about 12:30 a.m. He was very aggressive and said that she was a coward and a chicken for not wanting to go with him. This time she was half-asleep and blurted out, "Leave me alone; I have just been raped." Then she put the phone down sharply.

After that incident, she felt as though she had been raped a second time. She was sobbing as she ended her story: "I didn't want to tell him . . . he kept after me, and after me, and made me tell him. It was like being raped all over again. . . . Have I lost control over everything? I can't say 'no' to anything!" This example serves to emphasize how important it is for survivors to reestablish the ability to say "no" again, and to feel that they have control over their lives once more.

Some resistant rape survivors may need to leave therapy for a period of time, even though they have not completely worked through their traumas. The clinician can deal with this by saying, for example, "I really don't think you have come to terms completely with your feelings about what has happened. And, I think there are more issues that you need to work through. But, if you want to stop for now, that's all right. I understand. If you decide to come back in a while, you will be welcome to return." The woman will appreciate it if a therapist respects her decision in this regard. Most will return to treatment, usually within two or three months.

An example of this was the case of a young woman who tried to go to work the day after she had been brutally beaten, raped, and sodomized. She arrived at work but immediately felt compelled to run to the women's room, hide for about 20 minutes, and then go home. She had felt a great need to prove to herself—and everyone else—that she was all right. She refused to cry or to show any negative emotions, believing that if she allowed herself to show how badly she was hurt, she would be permitting the rapist the satisfaction of knowing, in some symbolic way, how much he hurt her. She resisted expressing her feelings in therapy for a considerable time and finally decided to leave treatment. When discussing this decision, the therapist told her that she was resisting working through some feelings and that she would be welcome to return at any time.

When she resumed treatment approximately four months later, in the first session she said that she was now ready to work on her feelings. During the first series of visits, she had been struggling terribly just to survive from day to day. If she had been forced to express her feelings, which the therapist could have accomplished very easily, she would have run out of the office and never returned because she would have considered it another form of assault. She remained in therapy for about five months on this occasion, and successfully resolved the emotional and sexual conflicts that once she had refused to acknowledge. It cannot be emphasized too strongly that rape survivors must be allowed to proceed, in therapy, at a pace that they feel is on their terms and under their control.

Sexual Factors in Rape

It is important to be aware that rape is not a sexual act in the usual sense. Instead, it is an event in which one person hurts another *by means of sex.* Thus, in essence, it is an assault. Of course, in most cases, the rapist is sexually aroused when committing rape, but what motivates him is not sexual desire but the impulse to hurt another person. The desire to humiliate or destroy is that which produces arousal. Quite frequently, habitual rapists become increasingly more violent from one rape to the next, getting as much involved in the attack on the woman as in the sexual act. Moreover, it is not unusual for a rapist to have difficulty producing an erection until he actually hurts the survivor or forces her to do something bizarre or humiliating, that is, when the rapist sees his survivor's face distorted with pain or disgust.

In some cases, a survivor who has been forced to do extremely degrading acts will be reluctant to tell anyone, including the police, the details of what happened. For instance, a survivor may have been questioned repeatedly by both the investigating officer and a district attorney, yet not until she is on the witness stand, under oath, will she reveal having been forced to commit oral sex, having been sodomized, or doing bizarre sexual acts. A possible cause of this reluctance to provide details of vital importance to the criminal case is that the woman may not yet have encountered a nonthreatening person to whom she could tell her story candidly. In many cases, what a survivor is willing to say at first differs markedly from what she will say later on when she feels safe and accepted by her therapist. In fact, a clinician may discover that many things other than being raped were done to her. Unfortunately, the formal legal process tends to discourage rape survivors from revealing the full details of what was done, especially because the woman will be questioned repetitiously by what may seem an endless parade of strangers. However, police attitudes have changed considerably in recent years, mainly because officers have learned that, through more sensitive questioning of survivors, they will get more cooperation and will be able to solve more cases.

In this discussion of sexual factors in the rape assault, it will be useful to clarify the "rape fantasy." Fantasies about being forced into having sex are created and controlled by the woman who has the fantasy; that is, the person who is having the fantasy decides who is going to commit rape, where the rape will occur, and specifically what sexual acts will take place. The important consideration is that the woman who has such a fantasy has decided that she *wants* to be raped in this particular fantasy. In an actual rape, the rapist is probably an exact opposite of the person in the woman's fantasy and, in every respect, as repugnant as a creature from the most terrible nightmare. In an actual rape, there is real fear and real violence, not the kind of romanticized force that a woman may include in her controlled fantasy. Hence, real rape bears the least possible resemblance to rape in fantasy, because the purpose of the former is to cause physical and psychological pain. Instead of seeking physical pleasure or sexual gratification, the rapist's primary motive is to inflict harm.

Another misconception that is related to this rape fantasy concept is the view, shared by some, that women enjoy being "taken by force." This belief is a consequence of the passive social roles that women have been trained to adopt, and the way in which women are portrayed in some of the popular media. For example, some rapes have occurred because the woman has simply done what the rapist told her to do, instead of running or screaming for help. Moreover, many sexual misunderstandings occur between men and women because the woman, when a child, was not taught to make clear that "no" means what it says. When a man believes that "no" does not always mean no, he will question its meaning even though he hears it repeated a second or third time.

One reason for the view that a survivor of sexual assault may be complacent about the experience can be found in the paradoxical guilt that is typical of rape survivors, as described earlier. A survivor, by asking questions such as "Why did this happen to me?" and "Am I being punished for something that I did in the past?" may foster this kind of suspicion unwittingly, while in fact she is just trying to sort out her thoughts and restore some balance to her image of herself. Many of the same women who interpret being raped as a punishment often have an accepting or passive nature that may easily be misunderstood by the observer.

The Support Network

If the rape survivor has a "significant other," such as a husband or lover, it is advisable for the therapist to schedule at least one visit alone with that person. Too often, the feelings and needs of these important people have been overlooked during the initial shock after the attack. Because of their pain and feelings of helplessness at seeing someone they love so dreadfully hurt, they may blurt out questions to the survivor such as, "How could you let him do it to you?" or "Why didn't you lock your car door?" An unthinking outburst of this sort can serve to deepen the woman's misguided sense of guilt and intensify her feelings of self-doubt. In addition, an accusatory question of that type, in a moment of psychological crisis, can create an irreparable tear in the fabric of the relationship. Few love relationships can withstand the trauma of sexual assault. According to a representative of Women Against Rape in Santa Clara County, California, in about half the cases of rape, the woman's primary love relationship or marriage comes to an end. Yet, many of these relationships could have been saved by providing the loved one with counseling and support at the time of the emergency, as well as during the recovery period. Ideally, a clinician would arrange two or more sessions with the survivor's loved one and at least four sessions with both persons jointly.

During individual sessions with a loved one, it is important to give the man plenty of time to express his feelings of hurt and anger about the event; he may not have been able to show these feelings in the presence of the survivor. A therapist should try to give him some insight into what is happening to the woman psychologically, explaining the Recovery Cycle that a survivor needs to experience in order to heal after having been raped, and why the woman may be behaving in what appears to be a paradoxical manner. A therapist also may discuss the importance of not pushing the woman to talk about the assault, because even though she may need to talk, she must be permitted to do so at her own pace. Although the woman feels intense anger or even rage, she may not be able to express these feelings for some time to come. This apparent lack of angry feelings in the survivor can cause unfortunate suspicion (or at least confusion) to arise on the part of a significant other. A clinician can explain to the loved one that she may not be capable of expressing anger at this time because her defense mechanisms (psychological healing processes) are completely engaged in reconstructing her crushed ego.

During these sessions with a significant other, the therapist can help him resolve some of his stereotyped misconceptions concerning rape survivors such as, "Only bad women (or women who are 'looking for it') get raped," or chauvinistic thoughts such as, "Did she enjoy it?" In these individual sessions, a loved one can learn to express and work through his anger toward the survivor for not having been "more careful." The next step is to help a loved one look beyond the sexual factors in rape itself and come to terms with some of the larger issues that the woman is struggling with—for example, those of personal worth and integrity. In this respect, it is a good idea to dissuade the loved one from making sexual advances toward the survivor—in a misguided attempt to "undo" the attack too soon after it occurred. He should be counseled to let the woman indicate when she is ready to resume sexual activity. Even when she makes that indication, the loved one should proceed slowly and sensitively.

The Criminal Justice Process

In most cases, the police will take a victim to the nearest hospital or medical clinic for an examination, for the collection of physical evidence, for treatment to prevent venereal disease or pregnancy, and documentation of injuries inflicted. A clinician should advise the rape victim to take a change of clothes to the hospital, because the clothing in which she was assaulted must be held as evidence. Questioning by the police may take place either at the scene or in the hospital emergency room. The police officer will make a tape recording of her statement, and, while it is being spoken, the therapist will be able to provide much emotional support by being there.

On the following day, in many cases, the survivor will be questioned by a specially trained detective. The officer will have to ask many detailed questions that are necessary to the investigation of an assault. Answers to these questions regarding a rape are particularly important, because each rapist acts differently from every other, and the way in which a man rapes is often an identifier as distinctive as a fingerprint or a signature. Some rapists tie their victims in a unique way; some say or do things to each victim in a certain order; and, some have a special way of stalking or surprising their victims. Indeed, one case was solved because the victim was able to describe a type of knot that the rapist had used in tying her up, as well as certain details of a speech pattern that proved to be unique to a certain suspect. The therapist may be able to prepare a victim for this questioning, and his or her very presence may encourage the survivor to be more frank about details. In addition, a clinician's skills in communication and counseling may assist the officer in obtaining necessary information, with less risk of added trauma for the survivor. During this interview session, an investigator will review the tape recording of the survivor's original statement and ask her if there is anything that she wishes to change or to add. Most investigators are aware that the original statement will have been given when the survivor was in a state of shock and thus may contain omissions, incorrect information, or confusion.

There may be subsequent meetings with the investigator to clarify details of the incident, as certain leads are followed to a conclusion. A survivor also will be asked to assist in making a composite picture of her attacker's face, by means of a computer program used by the investigator. This program contains specimen drawings of parts of the face from which a survivor selects those features that most resemble the attacker's. The survivor also may be asked to look at pictures of suspects and, probably, to witness a lineup (through a one-way-vision window) that will contain one of the suspects. Going to the lineup can be a frightening and even traumatic event for the person in many ways—some direct and some symbolic. A potential source of trauma is that this may be the first time the survivor will see again the person who attacked her. That can be a powerful and painful moment.

Survivors often have a feeling that an attacker is omnipotent while they are helpless. In some cases, a clinician will be called upon to reassure the survivor that a perpetrator cannot escape from the lineup and attack her again because she has reported the crime to the police. A survivor may need to be reminded frequently that plenty of people will be around to protect her and that she will never be left alone during this necessary procedure. (In fact, it would not be wise to leave the survivor alone at all during any aspect of these police investigation procedures.)

It is also worth noting that a survivor should *not* be accompanied to the room where the lineup will be viewed by a spouse, lover, or parent, because the survivor's emotional reaction to seeing the attacker again may well be quite strong. This reaction could upset the loved one and lead to more complications. For example, a survivor may have tried to be brave and to maintain her pride in front of the family, and yet, when she sees the assailant, she may be obviously shaken or hysterical. Should a loved one see this, he could become upset and, when the survivor realizes how much she has upset her loved one, she may become even more distraught. A therapist will find that survivors usually want family members to be nearby, but not actually present with them during that possible "encounter" with the assailant. Seldom are we turned down by a survivor when we offer to accompany her to the lineup in place of a loved one. Although some may not accept the offer, it is well worth making. On many occasions, a survivor has expressed relief that we offered to go with her, because she was too afraid or embarrassed to tell family members or loved ones that she did not want them in the room with her.

After the police lineup, it is a good idea to schedule some time to be alone with the survivor. Or, if the therapist has not accompanied her to the lineup, it may be wise to arrange an appointment that same day or evening. Key issues will probably arise in this session: for example, if the assailant was not present in the lineup, a survivor will probably be depressed that he wasn't there. Memories of the attack will surface again, and her fears of an attacker's omnipotence will be renewed because the police have not been able to catch him. In fact, there may be recurring fantasies about the assailant's returning for revenge because the survivor has called in the police. Conversely, if the attacker *was* in the lineup, another issue may arise that will require help—namely, now that the survivor has identified the assailant, will he be able to get out of jail and will he try to murder the survivor or assault the survivor again for revenge? Survivors sometimes ask, even though they have just seen their assailant in a jail uniform and in hand-cuffs, questions such as, "Are you sure there isn't some way he can get out and get us as we are leaving?" Sometimes, this kind of question is stated in an embarrassed, half-joking manner; but, in fact, the person is not making a joke at all. It takes considerable time (in some cases long after conviction) before many survivors feel safe from revenge in the form of another attack by the same assailant.

If the person who committed the crime is never apprehended, or is found but for some reason not convicted (a frequent state of affairs), the fears described above will persist even longer. It is difficult for a survivor to comprehend that what was such a terrible personal affront and wounded her so deeply could have been a totally impersonal incident to the assailant. Even so, whether the attacker is apprehended or not, a therapist will do well to devote a significant amount of time to helping the survivor reestablish a basic feeling of personal security and protection. For example, the clinician may suggest that they ask a police Community Relations Officer (or the person in charge of crime prevention in the local police department) to inspect her home and give advice about how to make it as secure as possible. Most departments are willing to provide this service, which includes instruction about which locks are the best for certain purposes.

There are groups that sponsor personal safety and self-defense courses for survivors of assault, and these can have clinical value in helping the survivor to realize that she does not have to be passive; in addition, she will learn that, if attacked again, there are methods that she can use to escape. Many such seminars are effective in teaching a survivor to "think defensively," so that she will try to avoid certain high-risk situations in the future. Another suggestion, which may seem trivial but has proven useful if the survivor is fearful of the dark or has trouble sleeping, is that the survivor buy a little night-light of the sort that fits into a wall plug. Many will remember these lights from childhood; they reminded us that we were safe in our parents' home, and also gave just enough illumination to make it possible to survey the room if suddenly awakened from a nightmare. Leaving a radio on, or playing a hypnosis or relaxation tape once she is tucked into bed, can be helpful to a survivor as well.

If the survivor has been successful in identifying the person who assaulted her, the assailant will be formally arrested and charged. Later, the suspect will be arraigned, that is, the defendant will appear before a judge and plead guilty or not guilty to the charges that have been brought against him. At the arraignment, a date for the preliminary hearing of the evidence will be set. A defendant has the right to have this hearing within 10 days of arraignment, but he may waive the right if he chooses; this commonly occurs if the defendant is not in custody, because a common defense strategy is to drag things out as long as possible. A survivor's next participation in the court process will occur at this preliminary hearing of the evidence, and the required waiting period is likely to be filled with disquieting fears and concerns about what will happen at the hearing. During this time in therapy, strengthening assertiveness skills by means of cognitive/behavioral techniques aimed at anxiety reduction can be helpful. Survivors can also be taught breathing exercises as well as progressive relaxation techniques. But, clinicians should be extremely cautious not to utilize any narrative, hypnotic, cognitive reprocessing, or exposure techniques that could be possibly construed as altering the survivor's memory of the events of the crime, in any way prior to testimony. Treatment interventions such as these could alter the survivor's memories of the crime and cause her testimony to be inadmissible in court. The result of this could be emotionally damaging to the survivor and permit the assailant to go free. It is advisable to make sure that the survivor is aware that the hearing is not a trial but, instead, a review of evidence that will enable the judge to decide whether or not an actual trial should take place.

At the hearing, a survivor will be asked in detail and under oath about what took place during the assault. A therapist can assure the survivor that the defense lawyer will not be permitted to ask many personal questions about past life history or about sexual orientation. A lawyer may try to do this, but such questions will usually be objected to and disallowed. The survivor can prepare for this first court experience by means of role-playing in which she learns to answer questions slowly, thus permitting the district attorney enough time to object if necessary. In general, the purpose of the hearing in a case is to (1) establish the elements of the crime necessary to prosecute the case and (2) identify the accused as the person who allegedly committed the crime. During this hearing, the judge also will examine any medical evidence and question any other witnesses pertaining to the case. The survivor's therapist is the most suitable person to help her become as ready as possible, psychologically, for the hearing. If she is psychologically prepared and given support through this first phase, the actual trial will, in most cases, be easier for her because she has been somewhat desensitized to the distressing court process.

The preliminary hearing and the trial, as with the previously discussed lineup, are situations in which the presence of relatives and loved ones should be carefully thought through. No matter how well prepared the person is, a court appearance in a case of a violent crime is never a benign experience. Once more, the survivor will have to see her (alleged) assailant, and this time without the shield of one-way glass through which she viewed the lineup. Moreover, both the survivor and the survivor's loved ones will find themselves in close proximity to the accused for an hour or more. So, when considering whether or not a parent, spouse, or lover should be present during a hearing or trial, it is wise to reflect on the following: this person will have to be fairly close to a person who may have violated or beaten or threatened to kill someone whom they love. The survivor must be present meanwhile, and will be expected to keep her composure and behave calmly and rationally. The family members themselves will be required to keep their emotions in check while they listen to a graphic description of exactly what was done to their loved one. Also, both they and the survivor may face harassment by the defense lawyer, the defendant, or his family or friends.

Even though a survivor's spouse, family, parents, or other relatives may believe that they can provide "moral support" by being in the courtroom with the survivor, it is unlikely that they will be able to accomplish this aim. It is more helpful if the friends and family members wait outside the courtroom while the therapist (or victim advocate) accompanies the survivor. Should the survivor feel awkward about telling the relatives or friends to wait outside, she can ask the district attorney to request that the judge close the court. This means that the proceedings will be made more private, in that the survivor can be accompanied by no more than one person. (Although this court procedure applies especially to cases in which a juvenile is the victim, many sensitive judges will make use of it in adult cases if asked to do so; or, the therapist can speak to the well-intended friends and relatives and explain why they can best help by waiting outside.)

Following the preliminary hearing, should proof against the defendant be compelling, the district attorney and the defense lawyer may conduct plea bargaining. In this procedure, a defendant may plead guilty to some of the charges. Most enlightened district attorneys will discuss that kind of maneuver with a survivor before accepting any bargain that has been offered. If the defendant does not plead guilty to some charge at this time, another waiting period will ensue before the trial occurs. Most trials for assault last from three days to two weeks; the duration varies according to how difficult jury selection is, the number of witnesses who are called, and how straightforward the case may be.

Usually a survivor is on the witness stand from one to two hours, but questioning may take longer in more complex cases, and the survivor may be called back. Being on a witness stand is very difficult in the best of circumstances, but it is far more painful in cases of sexual assault when the survivor has experienced a crime of an intensely personal nature and now must reveal disgusting, humiliating details in a room filled with strangers. The worst part is that she must be face-to-face with the person who assaulted her. A survivor of rape also should be prepared for the fact that the rapist may attempt to upset and confuse her by smiling, licking his lips, grimacing, or making gestures toward her while she is testifying. To help a survivor get ready for the trial psychologically, a clinician may wish to plan some relaxation-type exercises that she can repeat before taking the witness stand. These will differ according to the psychological needs of the woman, and they may range from breathing and muscle relaxation exercises to fantasies of the attacker being sentenced to jail, or pleasant scenes such as walking through a meadow or sitting in front of a cozy fireplace. The therapist may let her know that, if she needs time to regain her composure when on the stand, she can ask for a drink of water or to be excused for a moment to go to the restroom or because she feels ill.

If their assailants are convicted, most survivors will experience a feeling of great relief and a sense of "closure." When a trial is successful, it may represent an important symbolic event that will assist the reconstructive, therapeutic process on many levels. It amounts to a clear demonstration that there are social factors that will protect and avenge people who have been violently attacked (without their having to take revenge themselves). Above all, the survivor will have done battle with her attacker and won. Most survivors with whom we have worked, especially those who have had strong support systems, later reported that the court process was worth going through—providing the assailant was tried and convicted. Also worth noting is the fact that those who work in the criminal justice system (e.g., district attorneys, police officers, and judges) are beginning to recognize the value of providing support services to victims. These professionals realize that one possible benefit of such programs is that they may obtain a higher percentage of convictions.

What happens when an accused assailant is not convicted? This distinct possibility exists and must be confronted realistically. Yet, even though there is no conviction on the charge, there may be instead a conviction on another count, such as a lesser crime. In many cases, this kind of lesser punishment does provide some solace to the survivor, especially if it enables the survivor to overcome the helpless, passive role that many victims drift into almost inadvertently. Even if the accused person is not convicted of anything, the clinician can reaffirm that the survivor took a step toward regaining control over his or her life by attempting to right a wrong. Finally, it cannot be emphasized too much that persons who commit assault rarely stop after a single offense. The present case may provide significant evidence toward a later case that will lead to the ultimate conviction of the assailant in question.

If the person who committed the crime is neither caught nor convicted, a survivor's entire Recovery Cycle will be prolonged; as such, it may be accompanied by recurrent nightmares and strong fears of being alone, as well as fears of the assailant returning to attack once more. During this period of anxiety and fear, it is wise for a clinician, at least initially, to recognize the survivor's need not to be alone and try to strengthen the support network. In therapy, it will be a good idea to proceed slowly in a structured, stepwise manner, encouraging the survivor to attempt to do more and more on her own. Meanwhile, the clinician can persuade her to explore practical tasks that she can perform in order to ensure her personal safety and to make her home secure.

CHAPTER 16

Disaster, Loss, and the Family

The occurrence of a disaster, by definition, is trauma-producing. The effects, we believe, vary by severity but not by type: the difference is quantitative, not qualitative. We observe similar symptoms in every traumatized person, reflecting the basic means by which the psyche reacts to shock. In respect to trauma caused by disasters, we see magnified the truth of the adage: it's not what happens to you, but how you respond to it that counts.

In recent years, people have experienced many disasters, some created by nature such as the Loma Prieta Earthquake of 1989, the Northridge Earthquake of 1994, the earthquake in Turkey of 1999, the tsunami in Indonesia of 2004, and Hurricane Katrina in 2005. Other disasters were the result of human intent, such as 9/11, the Oklahoma City bombing of 1995, the Madrid train bombing of 2004, the London bombings of 2005, the earlier World Trade Center attack of 1993, and the Egyptian resort bombing of 2005.

A saving grace, in light of these catastrophes, is that human beings can be enormously resilient. When disaster strikes in a Western industrialized country, people are usually aided to recover fairly rapidly (Norris, 2002; Pennebaker, 1993). Of course, with a natural disaster in countries such as ours, people are generally better protected: they may have had warnings and consequently better preparedness, with better rescue and support services after the event than elsewhere. Moreover, after a natural disaster, there are likely to be fewer traumatic consequences if there were no elements of human malice, negligence, or neglect before the fact, or a poor rescue and relief response after the fact. If the latter occur, the trauma is worsened by human error.

Disaster and Family Trauma

When a family is embroiled in a catastrophic event of external origin, the family system may be assaulted in many ways. Individual family members may suffer emotional injuries that alter relationships between them and other members of the system. Roles may temporarily shift, whereas others may be permanently destroyed. Even though, in some cases, a traumatic event can solidify a family system as family members "pull together" (Bonanno, 2004), it also can break a family apart, setting its stunned members adrift (Figley, 1988; Everstine and Everstine, 1993; Goenjian, 1995, 2000, 2001; Maddi, 2002, 2005). Most families have a reserve of stabilizing mechanisms on which they draw during stressful times, but certain traumatic events may wreck a family's homeostatic balance and render the system nonfunctional.

Much of the literature and research on family dynamics is aimed at the treatment of pathology in the context of family therapy. For the clinician, it may not be wise to apply the same concepts in assisting families traumatized by a disaster. In many, perhaps most, families that are coping with a disaster, there is little or no underlying pathology. Services should not be labeled as "mental health," because many disaster survivors will avoid them. If pathology exists within the system, it will surface and can be addressed at that time by the therapist.

Because a potentially traumatic event transcends the normal range of human experience, it can propel one or more members of the family system into situations for which they have no readily available defenses or experiences to draw on for guidance. The first recourse of the family system may be to draw upon religious beliefs or family myths for support. If these resources, bolstered by faith, are sound, the trauma response may soon approximate stabilization. As Figley aptly has noted (1988a), when family mythology is largely affirmative it can be central to a family's recovery from trauma. Norris (2005) has confirmed how valuable the survivor's belief system can be to recovery. But, when the belief system is not a healthy one, as when some victims view disaster as God's punishment, it will be the task of the therapist to offer the family a new frame of reference. In our experience, this kind of reframing is essential to recovery in cases in which the belief system contains intrapunitive elements or is maladaptive in some other way. In fact, traumatized families—especially those that have survived a disaster—can be helped in this regard by sympathetic religious practitioners.

Some families possess resilient defenses and have contact with external resources that will help them cope with the emotions brought forth by the disaster. Others will need help in coming to terms with these emotions. Help for families traumatized by disasters will ideally be conducted on several levels. Psychologically, each family member will be trying to sort out his or her emotions and repair overworked defense mechanisms. The family system will confront questions concerning how members interacted during the event. It may have to adjust to changes in living conditions such as the loss of its home or community as well. Relations with the larger social system may have to be addressed, that is, the wake of a traumatic event may have altered the family's status within the social system, or the family may incorrectly perceive that its status has changed (i.e., real or imagined stigmatization). A clinician can help family members to perceive the situation accurately and adjust accordingly. Finally, because many traumatized families have faced and will continue to face real danger, as for example in a terrorist attack or natural disaster that could occur again, the therapist may provide educational counseling that will supply practical coping strategies for situations that potentially threaten survival in the future.

The Family and Adversity

Each family holds to beliefs and shelters myths about injury, adversity, and loss. These certitudes are, in many cases, an amalgam of religious teachings, cultural attitudes, and family history, unified by magical thinking, random reinforcement, and the logic of superstition. Some families are strongly influenced by religion, while others profess popular cultural mores such as those promulgated by television. Yet another type of family may look to family tradition as a primary source of values. In working with a traumatized family, one must comprehend and be sensitive to this belief structure. Families in traumatic turmoil often shut out those who, they perceive, do not share or respect their beliefs. This is a fundamental, self-protective, homeostatic mechanism that the family can rely on to create a sense of safety and stability in the face of potential chaos. Unfortunately, this façade can be quite maladaptive.

Most severely traumatized families lack the emotional flexibility to change their views rapidly in the wake of a disastrous event. For this reason, the clinician's intervention must reflect appreciation of the belief system of the family. The problem is that the nature of their beliefs are not always made clear by family members at the start. And, because of the tendency of a family under siege to draw together and exclude outsiders, a therapist may have to expend considerable effort in learning about the belief system and in gaining trust. This trust is a touchstone in working with traumatized families (Figley, 1988b; Rosenthal et al., 1987; Norris, 2005). Friends and relatives often form a sort of "membrane" or shield around traumatized families or their members (Green et al., 1985, p. 61). Although this protective action is intended to prevent further trauma, it can also serve to keep those who would help outside the circle. Our experience has shown that understanding and respecting a family's beliefs will help in penetrating this barrier, at the same time that it engenders requisite trust.

What Disaster Does

The unique dimensions of trauma produced by catastrophic events have been measured and catalogued by much research in recent years. Disaster survivors are affected by one or more of the following trauma-producing elements:

1. Rapid onset: Few disasters wait until potential victims are warned; exceptions include the flood that builds slowly to a critical stage, or the hurricane that marches steadily up the coast. The more sudden the event, the more devastating to survivors, a fact well understood by those who plot terrorist attacks.

2. No history of dealing with a similar event: because disasters in some areas are rare, people have to learn how to cope on the spur of the moment; information or guidance may be ill-informed or too late in coming.

3. Duration: This factor varies from case to case. For example, a flood that develops slowly may be slow to recede, but an earthquake can be as brief as a few seconds and cause lasting damage. For some victims of prolonged disasters, the traumatic effects can multiply with each

passing day if the losses and damages continue to build and the survivors remain in a state of helplessness.

4. Lack of control: One has no control over a disaster; it may be a long time after the event before a person can regain control over even the most mundane aspect of his or her daily routine. If this loss of control is felt for a protracted period, even the most competent, independent person may be traumatized severely.

5. Grief and loss: A disaster survivor may have become separated from a loved one or have lost the person by death; the worst part is probably waiting to find out how much one has lost. (The worst case of all is one in which a missing person is never found but "presumed dead.") During an event that persists in time, there may be no opportunity whatever to grieve what has been lost because one must flee to survive.

6. Permanent change: The destruction caused by a catastrophic event may be irreparable; a survivor may be faced with an entirely new and hostile environment, in which he or she must rebuild a new way of life.

7. Exposure to death: Even brief exposure to life-threatening circumstances may alter a person's personality structure and "cognitive map." Repeated brushes with death can create profound changes in adjustment level. At the very least, coming close to death may bring about an extreme existential crisis, for example, a shift in core values.

8. Moral uncertainty: A survivor of disaster may be called on to make value-laden decisions that could change his or her life—for example, whom to save, how much to risk, whom to blame, or how to explain what happened.

9. Behavior during the event: Each person would like to display "grace under pressure," but only a few can manage this. What the person did or did not do while a disastrous event was occurring may haunt him or her long after all other wounds have healed.

10. Scope of the destruction: After the catastrophe has ended, the survivor will likely be affected in some way by the impact that an event has had upon the community and its social structure. To the extent that new cultural rules or normative behavior is required by what has happened, the person may be forced to adapt or become alienated.

Each of the foregoing components of the trauma response in cases of disaster can be clarified, modified, or alleviated by support, education, and treatment. In preparing to treat a disaster survivor, the therapist should take these factors into consideration.

The Disaster Process

Not unlike the stages of grief described by Kubler-Ross (1969), the reaction to a natural disaster follows a sequential pattern. We identify six distinct stages of this form of trauma response, namely:

- Shock and disbelief
- Facing the reality of the event
- Traumatic survival mode until the event passes
- Adding up the losses
- Acceptance
- Rebuilding

Those who provide care to disaster survivors will certainly observe this process unfolding, but appropriate support can help facilitate the process.

One key to successful intervention with disaster survivors is to provide support to the family unit. Then, the primary intervention should facilitate the family members in "joining" others who have survived as well, so that they have a sense of sharing with a community that has had a horrible experience. Conceptually, this will help each person to move beyond the feeling that he or she was, somehow, "singled out" for punishment by the event. The sense of community is important because family units may have been dispersed or even decimated, and survivors left seeking new emotional bonds. A second key to assisting survivors emotionally is to encourage, as soon as possible in the counseling or support process, a practical, proactive, future-oriented outlook on the part of the survivor. We have observed that the sooner a victim is able to look ahead—realistically planning to rebuild, devising a set of precautions in readiness for a similar event in the future—the earlier he or she will begin the process of healing and recovery.

Apart from an individual person's terror, injury, and loss, there is inherent to the disaster experience a group dynamic that cannot be evaded. What a survivor did or did not do in the event may well be judged according to group values, as opposed to a private standard. Did the person "freeze?" Did the person become fixated on trivial matters? Did he or she give voice to futile anger, in such a way as to increase the anxiety of others? Did the person behave with rigid, robot-like calm, giving an insensitive or uncaring impression? Did the survivor behave according to the expectations of the group's cultural values? The clinician who works with a traumatized group would do well to look into how each group member is perceived by the others in this respect. What needs to be prevented, of course, is scapegoating of persons who did not react as nobly or appropriately as the others would have wished.

It is true that, in most disasters, including terrorist attacks for which retrospective data are available, the majority of survivors have been resilient. There are many documented instances of resolutely high functioning in the aftermath of disaster. In effect, the cognitive survival state into which people are thrust, permits him or her to do "what needs to be done." This is a highly defended state of limited cognition, focused on survival, that keeps the person going in the face of deadly peril. This cognitive survival state is not without its negative effects. There is the danger that normal channels of reasoning may temporarily become blocked or shut down. For example, a survivor who is capable of tolerating excruciating pain may adopt a single-mindedness that reaches the level of obsession. This may motivate heroic feats, but if it persists after the event has ended, it may impede recovery. A clinician who works with such a survivor may observe impairment in judgment, as well as restriction in the capacity for abstract thought. In fact, successful treatment may have to move at a slower pace until the abstract capacity is regained.

As the defenses that had been mobilized to cope with the initial stages of the trauma response are relaxed or have become exhausted, a period begins in which the survivors assess what damage has been done. In this time of counting losses, symptoms can be expected to appear in those survivors who will experience symptoms. Those who have lost loved ones will begin to grieve—excepting those who are caught up in a new crisis, such as having to find a new place to live after losing their homes. One also should not ascribe extreme emotional responses just following a disaster to underlying pathology, or as a predictor of how severe his or her emotional injuries will be. Such symptomatic or extreme behavior may be an expression of the person's intense anguish of the moment; this may dissipate fairly rapidly, once he or she becomes involved in the task of reconnecting with family and community and rebuilding a life.

We have found that a brief assessment questionnaire can be useful to make triage decisions about which person is most in need of immediate mental health care. The following is an example of a questionnaire of this kind.

Trauma Screening Protocol

Ask the person if he or she has experienced the following during the past 30 days:

- Inability to go to sleep or sleep through the night
- Nightmares about the event on a regular basis
- Thinking about the event even when not wanting to; or, flashbacks of the event on a regular basis
- Trying to avoid things that remind him or her of the event
- Often feeling fearful or anxious or being easily startled
- Feeling attacked, estranged from others or emotionally "numb"
- Feeling emotionally disconnected from people or unlike himself or herself

If a person answers "yes" to five or more of these statements, he or she should be considered at-risk for post-traumatic stress and should be referred for treatment.

It cannot be overemphasized that many people suffer profoundly during a disaster and bravely hide it for years. The very symptoms of trauma can be denied, even as they occur, or can be attributed to some other cause. This phenomenon operates by the same process that permits people to perform admirably when disaster strikes. On a mass level, it is the same process that enables some groups of people to collaborate and work together in the face of the fear and horror of disaster situations. Even so, the consequences of this suppression of feelings about a traumatic event can be pernicious.[1]

The best part of working therapeutically with disaster victims is their encouraging prognosis for recovery. After all, the vast majority were functioning well enough before the catastrophe. With time and support, most can attain their former levels of adjustment. The only counterweight to this optimistic assessment of outcome is the problem of case-finding. Some disaster victims may never have given a thought to emotional difficulties before the event and may, therefore, tend to avoid defining their newfound concerns as psychological issues. They seek advice from religious counselors, colleagues, teachers, and medical practitioners, rather than mental health professionals.[2]

For our private practice, we have created a note that can be given out to survivors shortly after a natural disaster has ended. It is adaptable for use by any agency, clinic, or practice that has an emergency response service. The text of this note is presented on the next page.

We have experienced a profoundly traumatic event together. The staff of _____ would like to let you know that we are here to help in any way we can. We are available 24 hours a day to answer questions or to meet with you; our services are confidential.

Most traumatized children only experience symptoms for brief periods. If you have a question or a concern, please feel free to call us at any time. We are here to help.

The Staff of _____.

Effects on Adults

An emotional reaction to a traumatic event is very natural. The most common responses to traumatic events are:

1. Anxiety about the possible recurrence of the event
2. Confusion, difficulty in concentration, memory problems, or an inability to estimate time accurately
3. Temporary mood swings, general changes in temperament, and irritability
4. Flashbacks of the event which may be visual or may take the form of reliving the event emotionally
5. Sleep problems or nightmares
6. A change of appetite or eating patterns
7. Emotional distress caused by events or objects that remind you of the traumatic event
8. A desire to avoid anything that might remind you of the traumatic event
9. Diminished interest in significant activities (work, social, or family)
10. Feeling depressed or detached or estranged from others
11. Shortness of temper, angry feelings, or a lack of patience with yourself or others

Effects on Children

Frightened or traumatized children (especially very young children) express their feelings about a frightening event by means of behavioral changes. This trauma reaction is expressed through behavior because most children do not possess the social, developmental, or psychological maturity to comprehend, fully, what has happened to them. In most cases, these behavioral changes are the child's way of saying that he or she was overwhelmed by something very terrifying.

After a traumatic event, it is important for parents to give extra time to their children and do extra things to reassure them. It is usually best for children and adults to resume their normal routines as soon as possible. But, if a child is frightened or behaves oddly, he or she should not be reprimanded or punished. It is also a good idea to take extra time, over the next few weeks, for the parents to talk with their child about what has happened, and to encourage the child to share his or her feelings about what happened with them. Bear in mind that a child may need to have several talks with a parent before he or she can resolve an event such as the recent one.

The following is a list of symptoms that children frequently display after traumatic events:

1. Fear is the most common initial reaction. Children are often reluctant to separate from their parents; some may actually cling to their parents and need constant physical contact or reassurance.

2. Traumatized children may have nightmares, often about scary objects other than the event. Some children may refuse to sleep alone or in the dark.

3. Some children react to a traumatic event with anger and hostility. This anger is usually an expression of the child's fear and helplessness. Temper tantrums or obstinate, unruly behavior (as well as mood swings) are common in traumatized children.

4. Reluctance to go to school is often a symptom of an unresolved trauma.

5. Many traumatized children turn their emotional pain into bodily symptoms. Many complain of tummy aches and headaches that have no physical cause. They may use these symptoms as an excuse to stay home from school. Parents should respond to such unusual physical complaints in an understanding way that is reassuring to the child.

6. Traumatized children show a wide range of phobic or avoidant behavior, such as fear of being outside, being alone, or being in closed-in areas.

7. Many traumatized children regress or temporarily engage in the behavior of an earlier developmental stage. Some children will wet their beds, lose their toilet training, suck their thumbs, or generally act like younger children.

8. Changes in eating habits are fairly common in traumatized children. Frightened children may be reluctant to eat; or, they may hoard food or go on eating binges.

9. Some children feel that the traumatic event was their fault or could somehow have been prevented from happening. Children who experience guilt feelings may need considerable reassurance from their parents.

Family Interventions

Two major systemic issues need to be factored into the treatment equation for families. First, in a disaster everyone—including the helpers—is traumatized. In the San Francisco area, after the earthquake of 1989, many helpers and rescue workers were caught in the dilemma of seeing to the needs of their own families while still performing professional duties. Second, when the event has destroyed or altered a survivor's environment in some way, the person may have lost certain support systems on which he or she relied, or familiar surroundings that provided comfort by "being there." For this reason, an intervention begun during the early stages of the postdisaster period must be practical, that is, focused on safety, survival, and coping with immediate consequences of the event. The two issues converge in this way: the clinician who takes time away from personal concerns must guard against potential countertransference feelings in which the survivors that he or she helps become substitutes for his or her own family members or friends.

Initial intervention should focus on restoring family unity as soon as possible. For example, poor planning in respect to rehousing or relocation can affect a family as an emotional aftershock. In fact, poorly conceived postdisaster relocation efforts can cause lasting damage. An instance of this occurred when a small child was sent to live with his grandparents after the family home had been lost in a flood. The child misperceived his parents' well-intentioned desire to send him to his grandparents, where he would be safe, as some form of punishment. He felt banished from his parents and older siblings for, somehow, magically causing the flood. His puzzled grandparents could not understand why this child, who was "safe" with them, developed symptoms, while his older siblings who remained with their parents at the flood site did not.

Not only should the family be urged to join together as soon as possible, but its members should be assisted to resume their normal roles as well. Children should be discouraged from adopting pseudomature or parental roles. Often, pseudomature behavior on the part of children is mistakenly perceived as a positive sign and encouraged by the parents. Even if the family is not able to return to the former home, family members should be advised to return to their normal routines and behavior patterns at the first opportunity.

In the act of drawing closer together, members of a family may follow their natural inclination to exclude strangers at a troubled time. This may be a vexing paradox for the therapist who would intervene on behalf of the family: he or she must strive that much harder to gain family trust. Even so, the path to trust may be smoother if the clinician has had first-hand experience with a disastrous event of the same kind. Having shared a similar experience may cause a therapist to be perceived as less threatening and more trustworthy. In any case, trust will be essential to obtaining the family's full commitment to participation in family therapy.

Working at the Scene of a Disaster

1. Realize that you are part of a team with a structure and a chain of command. The chain of command has been created for everyone's safety and should be respected. Being part of this team means that you take up whatever task is necessary to help the survivors by providing for their basic needs for comfort.
2. Try to make an empathetic personal contact with the people involved. Avoid giving advice at this stage; mainly listen and provide information. Help them obtain their basic needs. Let them tell their stories and validate their feelings.
3. If you give them information, they will probably remember less than half of what you say, so keep communication simple, direct, and caring.
4. Avoid giving advice: it may be misconstrued as criticism.
5. Help survivors satisfy basic needs for medical care, food, and shelter; do not forget sleep.
6. Help provide information about the location and condition of family members and loved ones.
7. Educate survivors about traumatic reactions and grief processes, helping to normalize and validate their experiences.
8. Help mediate tensions between and among people and family members and aid them to assume their normal roles and activities as soon as possible.
9. Assist local helpers and support services.

When you have just arrived at the scene of a disaster, your first thought may be to ask yourself "What can I do in the midst of this horror?" In fact, you can do a lot if you keep your focus on the basics. First, coordinate your efforts with your colleagues and remember that you are part of a team. Therapists, for the most part, work as individuals, and working in a team may be a new or unfamiliar experience. One is expected not only to cooperate with the other team members but to protect each other emotionally and lend a hand in tasks that may be physically demanding and nontraditional.

Another concept that may be new to clinicians is that of the chain of command. Most of us have worked with supervisors, but this more rigorous structure is an essential one that must be respected at the scene of a disaster. The agenda of the entire relief effort is to supply the basics: safety, shelter, sustenance, information, and, above all, human kindness.

After an earthquake, one of the authors was walking though a school building where people waiting for medical attention had been triaged as "severe but stable." All that could be done in the moment was to give them as much information as possible about where other survivors were or if they had been evacuated to an unknown location. Several aftershocks had been felt, and the school building was possibly unsafe. The clinician saw an older teenage girl lying on a cot in a cold, dimly lit hall; her face bore a look of frozen terror, as she faded in and out of consciousness. The clinician took the girl's hand and held it for a moment, telling her where she was and explaining that she was in line to be treated for her injuries. The girl said "I'm alive. Am I alive?" The clinician replied, "Yes, you are alive."

As tears rolled down the girl's face, she mumbled "I thought I was dead. I can't feel myself." The clinician replied "You are numb but you have been checked by the paramedics. You may feel very bad but your condition is stable. You will be all right." The girl lost consciousness again, and the clinician stayed with her for awhile, holding her hand. After moving on to talk with other survivors, she periodically returned to the teenager and held her hand. Occasionally, her eyes would open. Later, it was learned to which shelter location her brothers and parents had been taken. The clinician wrote the information on a piece of paper and pinned it to the girl's shirt, so she would have it with her.

About three weeks later, the clinician was seeing young people who, still in the hospital, were suffering symptoms or post-traumatic stress as a result of the disaster. The teenage girl was still there, but she did not recognize the clinician. When she was asked about the disaster, she said that she didn't remember it because she was "knocked out" by debris. The worst part, for her, was waking up cold, numb, and unable to speak in a place full of grey light, lying stiffly on a board. She was sure that she was dead and would never see her family again. It was to this cold, horrible moment of being alone that she flashed back again and again.

Then, she said that something strange had happened: "I felt a warm hand and someone talking to me and I knew I wasn't dead; I was alive." The person said I would be okay, or something like that, but it was the hand I remember—when I felt that warm hand." The clinician had the intuition not to tell her that she was the person. Rather, the entire experience of the warmth of that touch belonged to her. In this way, the experience of lying alone in a cold, gray hallway had been restructured and fear supplanted by reassurance.

Traumatic Loss

It is true that many have demonstrated resolve and perseverance in calamitous times, but the sudden death of a family member puts these qualities to the sternest test. Walsh and McGoldrick stated this fact succinctly: "Of all human experiences, death poses the most painful adaptational challenges for families" (1991, p. 25). Often, coming to terms with this kind of trauma is not simply a matter of seeing reality clearly, but requires an acceptance of reality at its ugliest. David Rieff recounts the story of the father of a woman who was killed, along with many others, when terrorists caused a plane to crash in Ireland in 1985. As the father left the morgue after identifying his daughter's body, a group of journalists surrounded him. When one asked, "What are you going to do?" the man answered with great dignity, "Do? What do you expect me to do in this dirty world?" (1991, p. 56). The journalist's inane question was not worthy of the man's answer, with its agonizing truth.

The grief process that this father experienced may have been long and tortuous, merely because death had been so unexpected. For example, the father may seldom have thought about what he might feel if his child died. Furthermore, there may have been complications in their relationship that now would never be resolved. Without warning, the story ends because the final pages of the book are missing. The father's perplexity could last a lifetime.

Loss of a loved one by natural disaster can have even more drastic effects if the event has destroyed artifacts and mementos of those who were lost. When the parents of a friend of ours were killed by the Mexico City earthquake of 1985, all of their belongings (including photos, letters, family documents) were buried in the rubble that had once been their apartment house. When our friend was staring at the wreckage, he noticed, lying at his feet, a copy of his parents' marriage certificate; this was the only verification that he could find of their existence. In a matter of seconds, they had vanished into the void.

In another scenario that is common to natural disasters (or war or other political upheaval), bodies are swept away, burned, or buried and never found. This situation, in which a loved one is declared "missing" or "presumed dead," creates its own kind of anguish—a paralysis of emotion. One can appreciate what flights of imagination are stimulated by this form of traumatic loss, in which false hopes alternate with dreadful imaginings about the victim's fate. Long after any chance for survival has passed, these yearnings may linger. (In these cases, the eventual confirmation of death holds some consolation, for it enables the survivors to deal with their loss and properly grieve.) Not only does the "presumed death" keep survivors in suspense, but it prevents them from making use of rituals such as the funeral or the wake to reach closure. They may find themselves caught in tangled legal processes concerning what is to be done with the person's property while he or she is missing. In fact, their own need to survive and carry on with life may complicate their grief, causing them to feel oddly guilty toward the lost loved one.

There is trauma, as well, when a loved one is found dead by violent means. Identification of the body is one source of excruciatingly painful emotions. It is not so much the sight of the lifeless body that arouses our sorrow, but the empathic wound we feel by imagining the pain and suffering before death. Just a verbal description of what this might have been like can excite powerful feelings of despair.

When traumatic death cuts short a young life, or when the death could obviously have been prevented, the survivors' suffering can be especially intense. For example, death caused by drunk driving is a trenchant example of an event that somehow should have been prevented. The mother who permitted her daughter to go for a ride with a boyfriend who got drunk and killed her in an accident, experiences loss that is hopelessly tangled with self-castigation.

Homicide, another form of preventable death, is often committed by a member of the victim's own family. Family members, who are already experiencing considerable grief reactions may also blame themselves for not preventing the death. Members may feel that the family has dishonored itself. Moreover, if a child has witnessed another family member kill his or her parent, the ultimate childhood trauma will surely follow (Eth & Pynoos, 1985, pp. 35–40). The most frightening thought in childhood is to contemplate a parent's death. When it happens, children cannot begin to cope with its reality, because they have no cognitive framework for the experience. The dichotomy between eternal and finite is beyond comprehension, and, as a result, the child perceives a parent's disappearance as abandonment. Often, this abandonment is construed as a form of punishment. A child may ask questions such as, "What does 'forever' mean?" or "What do people eat for breakfast when they go to heaven?" The child ponders at length such subjects as where Mommy or Daddy are right now, and why they won't come back. The child may ruminate on even more disturbing questions when trying to cope with a presumed death; for example, if there is a chance that the parent is still alive, why don't the others do more to bring him or her back? The frustration of the adults may be multiplied many-fold in the child, who wants to believe so desperately that the parent will return and that the nightmare will soon be over. In times of war or natural disaster, the situation is even more fraught with anxiety for a child, because the adults may be preoccupied more with survival needs than with answering a frightened child's questions.

Magical thinking may help sustain the child through a time of loss, but it can make matters worse. For instance, a child who has been told that a parent "just went to sleep" may develop a fear of sleeping. Even worse, the child's fantasy life can lead to the belief that something he or she has done or thought caused the parent's death. Some children form the wish to "join" a parent in death, and thus are definitely at risk of committing self-destructive acts or even suicide. In addition, there is a risk factor with adolescents who have experienced earlier, in childhood, the traumatic or unresolved death of a parent or parent-figure.

The grief reactions of children differ from those of adults both in form and intensity. A child tends to fluctuate more often between periods of intense mourning and normal behavior, than does an adult. In one case, a four-year-old girl who was attending her mother's funeral was observed to be, by turns, dumbstruck and playful. When her emotions threatened to overwhelm her, she would escape into playing with a stuffed animal that she had brought with her. The capacity of a child to grieve is regulated by the child's developmental level, in that the questions that the child wrestles with are governed by how much he or she can understand of what has happened. When a new stage of development is reached, new questions will demand answers and new issues will need to be resolved. When these matters arise, some time may have passed since the death occurred, and adults who have completed their grieving may try to suppress the child's inquiries. They may have "moved on," but the child has not. For example, a widowed parent may have found someone new to love, and may consider the child's need to reflect on his or her lost parent as an intrusion on the present relationship. The therapist needs to deal with this systemic conflict sensitively.

Some children try to compensate for the loss of a parent by incorporation, in which the child attempts to take on his or her parent's role in the family. This is not encouraged, just as it is not advisable to foster any pseudomature behavior in a child. Even so, there are many adults who seem to derive pleasure from observing this type of role-playing by children, and getting them to discourage it may require the clinician's most sensitive but persuasive powers.

Treatment for Traumatic Loss

When a family suffers the death of one of its members, the interplay of psyche and system is a continual ebb and flow. Each person struggles with the pain, conflict, and anxiety of his or her wholly individual experience of the loss. From a systemic point of view, the structure of the family may be altered, and the roles within it may need to be reorganized to cope with the loss (McGoldrick, 1991, p. 51). In addition, the family's interactions with, and place within, the greater social system may have been temporarily or permanently changed by the traumatic event.

Even though some significant traumatic losses may never be fully resolved, the family will eventually accept and adapt to them. Some families have the internal resources to make the necessary adjustments to continue as a healthy family system, whereas others will require assistance. With the more extreme cases, in which the family is devastated by more than one loss caused by a single event, there is a danger that the trauma response (although homeostatic in principle) may escalate into nonadaptive behavior and, if not treated, pathology on the part of one or more family members. Examples of nonadaptive behavior include making impulsive changes to compensate for the loss(es), such as moving away or remarrying hastily. Some parents who have lost a child will conceive a new one soon after, with the best of intentions, to provide a replacement.[3] This is another instance of making things worse by trying to make them better. Here, the changes come too soon (as with a replacement child), or are so drastic (a hasty remarriage) that the family is plunged into added turmoil.

Walsh and McGoldrick (1991, p. 16) discuss two fundamental styles of pathogenic family interaction following a traumatic loss, "enmeshment" and "disengagement." The *enmeshed* family insists that each member share in the experience of the loss; those members who do not hold a shared view or reaction to the loss are silenced or pointedly ignored. The *disengaged* family is generally incapable of tolerating a shared or interactional experience of the loss: members drift apart to experience their grief in isolation from the others. A clinician might find the enmeshed family to be quite resistive to outside intervention; that is, even when help for every member is offered, they believe that together they can do whatever is required. If the family fits in the disengaged category, the therapist will have to be flexible, meeting with the individual family members, dyads, or other subsystems; this kind of family resists meeting as a whole if an outsider will be present to observe its interactions.

Even within the family group, individual grief reactions may vary widely. For instance, women tend to focus on emotional aspects of the loss, whereas men focus on the practical aspects. The clinician should take these tendencies into account, to facilitate the understanding of each person's way of grieving by everyone in the group. No one's way is more "valid" than another's. There should be no secrets in the traumatized family—at least none about the traumatic event. The keeping of a secret from a child is particularly dangerous, for one compelling reason: most children can sense when adults have conspired to keep something from them, even when they haven't the slightest notion of what it might be. If they feel this sensation after a death, they will know what the subject of the secret is, but not its exact content. They will fill this vacuum with fantasies of all sorts, even to the point of myth-making about the lost loved one. We have observed that when a child is forced to create a myth about the cause of a death, there is invariably an element of self-blame.

For the adults of a family that has lost a loved one, the primary treatment objective is to help them resolve conflicts that were abbreviated by death. Their regret at not having "cleared things up" before it was too late is mixed with anger at being left behind, and confounded by pangs of guilt for not being able to prevent the traumatic event. Some can relieve this internal pressure by writing a "letter" to the lost person or by establishing a certain ritual that will help him or her to say goodbye. In many cases, role-playing, guided fantasy, or empty-chair work proves useful. Remember that the family's history will need to be revised as a result of what has happened. As this reflective process evolves, the family may restructure itself with new relationships and alliances and, by doing so, set a course toward a healthy future.

Below is a list of questions that we have found useful when interviewing grieving people. Often, people in the early stages of grief are so overwhelmed by the experience of loss that they may have difficulty in putting the experience into words. Because of this, a structured interview format can help grieving people organize their thoughts and feelings.

Structured Grief Questionnaire

(Instruction: circle the number of each true statement.)
1. I thought about him or her when I didn't mean to.
2. I stopped letting myself get upset when I thought about him or her or was reminded of him or her.
3. I tried not to remember him or her.

--continued

Structured Grief Questionnaire (continued)

4. I had trouble falling asleep or staying asleep because pictures or thoughts about him or her came into my mind.
5. I had strong feelings about him or her.
6. I had dreams about him or her.
7. I stayed away from things that reminded me of him or her.
8. I felt that he or she did not die or that it was make-believe.
9. I tried not to talk about him or her.
10. I kept seeing him or her over and over in my mind.
11. Other things kept making me think about him or her.
12. I had lots of feelings about him or her, but I didn't pay attention to them.
13. I tried not to think about him or her.
14. Any reminder brought back feelings about him or her.
15. I don't have feelings about him or her anymore.
16. It was easy to make me angry and upset.
17. Loud noises made me jump in surprise.
18. I would feel as though it could happen all over again.
19. I have trouble keeping my mind on what I was doing if I think of him or her.
20. Thinking about him or her made my heart beat faster.
21. Thinking about him or her made it hard for me to breathe.
22. Thinking about him or her made me sad.
23. I kept checking to make sure nothing else bad would happen.
24. I talk to him or her before I go to sleep at night.
25. I ask him or her for advice.

CHAPTER 17

Traumatic Events in the Workplace

Each day seems to bring news of people who have decided to reveal that they were physically or sexually abused as children. The percentage of the population who have been victims of, or who have witnessed, violent acts is large and on the increase. When those experiences are added to the ones caused by the unusual (e.g., natural disasters) or the commonplace (e.g., car crashes), the probability that any person is the survivor of at least one traumatic experience is even greater. Even so, many of these people have been able to mobilize their own emotional resources to overcome the effects of these events; that is, their trauma responses have reached closure. But there are many others who have not been so fortunate, in that they retain unresolved conflicts caused by trauma; worse, some are not aware of the extent to which they are affected by long-since-"buried" feelings. In terms of Freud's two sources for the etiology of problems, love and work, it is easy to see how trauma in one sphere can influence how one functions in the other. If a person brings traumatic "emotional issues" to the workplace, his or her performance on the job may be adversely affected.

One factor that contributes to this transfer of personal life to work life is that the workplace is analogous to a family system. An authority figure may be seen as the symbolic substitute for an abusive, neglectful parent by an employee who has been the victim of familial trauma. In the beginning, the employee is likely to strive hard to please this newfound "parent," in an attempt to earn the acceptance or recognition that was denied in his or her own family. When these high expectations are not met, as in many cases they are not, complications can be expected to arise. The employee who feels rejected by an authority figure who unwittingly has been cast in a parent-substitute role, will likely express his or her frustration by some form of "testing" or rebellious behavior. Misplaced scorn or resentment may rise to the surface unchecked, and become directed toward supervisors who have no idea what they have done to offend.

How often is this the underlying dynamic in cases when an employee is disciplined for "insubordination?" When the clash comes, each antagonist retaliates blindly against the other, because neither has any comprehension of what the issues are: the employee has no conscious awareness of his or her reasons for creating a substitute parent, whereas the supervisor does not know that he or she is playing a role. Each responds reflexively to the "unreasonable" behavior of the other. When they are totally polarized in their perceptions of what is happening, communication stops. From that point, emotions take over and the battle escalates.

A clinician may be asked to intervene in this kind of conflict when the employee is referred by management for "counseling," or voluntarily seeks help for what is happening to him or her at work. The best policy for a therapist is to set boundaries around clear clinical objectives, to avoid being drawn into the workplace struggle. The most practical aim is to provide suggestions about how the employee can negotiate a truce at work. A long-term goal might be to help the client understand what led to this state of affairs. That will mean bringing to the surface any episodes in the client's history that will explain his or her current maladaptive way of perceiving people. If past trauma is uncovered in this process, this will also have to be dealt with.

It is well known that personal and family problems are the major cause of employee absenteeism and impaired job performance. In sum, a past or current problem at home may surface as a problem at work. It is the task of the clinician to sort out this possible cause of workplace conflict from that caused by prior trauma, and plan treatment accordingly.

Workplaces Believed to Be Safe

When they go to work, people carry with them the same assumption that they carry when entering any public place, namely, that it is safe. Not only is it assumed that the work environment is a safe one, but also one expects that the people one encounters in the course of doing the job are reasonable and will not act negligently, abuse civil rights, or do any other harmful things. That trust notwithstanding, everyone knows of at least one instance in which a normally tranquil work environment has suddenly become traumatic. In one such instance, a receptionist in a real estate office was taking a message from a client, when, suddenly, an out-of-control car crashed through the window of the office, struck her desk, pinned her to the wall, and seriously injured her. A young attorney was working late to prepare for a case; in the next office suite, a man was showing off a gun in his collection. Two shots rang out and the bullets went through the wall, striking and nearly killing the attorney as he sat at his desk. Workers in a modern, state-of-the-art office building in a major city were seriously injured when a large piece of construction equipment at the building next door went out of control and slammed into their building. In another office building, workers were exposed to toxic fumes believed to be carcinogenic, which were produced by a fire. A 55-year-old man of an ethnic minority background walks into the office of Human Resources, in tears, and exclaims "What do I have to do to get him to stop—go 'postal'?" Simultaneously, his supervisor calls Human Resources to report his belief that this man is a workplace threat to him.

Employees look to management for support and assistance when traumatic situations occur. A sensitive approach by management can become a major force in how swiftly and thoroughly the employees will recover. Managers who take an overly defensive, aloof, or adversarial position in these matters—due often to their fear of litigation—can make the situation far worse. Sometimes, such a defensive approach will exacerbate the employee's anger and actually lead him or her toward acting-out or litigation, whereas a neutral, even-handed, caring approach will serve the best interests of all. Most traumatized employees can return to proper functioning if they are treated reasonably. This would include being given access to clinical services that can aid recovery as soon as possible. These services should be confidential and presented in a way that makes employees feel that they are genuinely meant to help them recover. Sadly, many companies, agencies, and insurance carriers are reluctant to make psychological referrals after a traumatic incident at work, fearing that each referral will lead to expanded claims against them. In our experience, exactly the converse is true.

Recommending and making psychological services available to employees who may have suffered trauma can reduce the number of stress claims (not to mention the settlement amounts), because it makes a clear statement to the employee that management is concerned about his or her well-being. Furthermore, when an employee gets help with symptom alleviation, the person is less likely to turn to drugs or alcohol as a form of self-medication, or to convert emotional distress into psychosomatic symptoms. Counseling or therapy can also serve to channel feelings—especially anger—appropriately, so that the traumatized person can vent it constructively. If not, these feelings may become displaced toward coworkers, friends, or family members.

In our view, treatment to help an employee cope with a traumatic event should be carried out by professionals who have specialized experience and training in this form of clinical work. The services offered should be designated as *relief of job-related trauma,* because people have a tendency to avoid traditional "mental health" care. The treatment services should be designed for the specific needs of each individual employee and modified to fit the specific work environment. In the ideal case, of course, the employee would be able to return to his or her regular job assignment and schedule, but when that is not possible, therapy should facilitate the employee's reassignment or retraining.

Although we are constantly impressed with the strength and resilience of the human spirit, there are those who must struggle to perform within the average range, even under ordinary circumstances. Hence, when a traumatic event strikes these people, it can render them virtually nonfunctional. Some suffer from past, unresolved trauma; others have nonfunctioning support systems or lack them completely. Employers should be advised not to assume that every previously capable worker can return to a pretrauma level of functioning, even when the traumatic incident was of moderate proportions.

The Roles of Supervisors, Managers, and Consultants

Many organizations delegate responsibility for dealing with the varied aspects of a traumatic event at the workplace to supervisors and mangers. They assume that these leaders will know what to do and will deal with the matter appropriately. Even so, with the exception of professions such as law enforcement, fire fighting, and emergency services, whose supervisory personnel are trained in interventions with employees after extreme events, few managers are better prepared to deal with a crisis situation than is the average person. It is true that there have been many cases of inspirational, even heroic, leadership in times of grave danger and acute loss, but the leaders probably behaved so admirably because of exceptional qualities that they themselves possessed. Seldom are supervisors and managers given thorough training in what specifically to do, as leaders, when employees experience a traumatic event.

Training at the managerial level should include information about the core psychological components of the trauma response. When feasible, the organization would do well to consider using outside consultants to provide this training. It is also recommended that the contract with those who do the training include a provision in which the consultants will be available to the organization when a traumatic event actually occurs; one such arrangement would be that a consultant will visit the scene of an emergency to advise supervisory personnel on the spot. When appropriate, a consultant might provide a direct service to traumatized persons; or, the consultant may concentrate attention on the larger issues of group reintegration and recovery.

As with any organizational consultation, a clinician should be sensitive toward matters concerning roles, status, and professional boundaries. In traumatic situations, tremendous pressure may be placed on a consultant to "do everything;" in addition to consulting, he or she may be asked to do employee assessments as well as therapy with employees. These requests often are made with the best of intentions by managers, who are reacting to felt needs of the moment and may not have thought through some of the inherent conflicts of this request.

As clinicians, it is essential to make clear distinctions between the tasks of *treatment* and psychological *evaluation or assessment.* In many cases, these functions serve the same purpose, but they *may* serve conflicting purposes under some circumstances. For example, a traumatized person may have taken time off from work to recuperate and may have received treatment during this time. When the person feels better and seeks to return to work, his or her supervisor may ask the therapist whether or not the employee is ready to return to work. Because the clinician has been a consultant to the organization, the employer considers the request of information to be a legitimate one, but, because of the nature of the therapeutic relationship, there is a probability that the therapist is biased in favor of the client. Hence, the therapist may not be able to offer a wholly objective evaluation of the client's fitness to return to work. In short, there is a conflict of interest.

It is important that an employer know about this possible outcome when entering into any contractual arrangement with a mental health professional as consultant. At the outset, it is useful to establish that consultation, evaluation, and treatment are distinct entities, each with its own ground rules. It may be that a clinician will contract to play only one of these roles for the organization, or that several colleagues will divide the roles among them. In any case, the organization should be made aware, in advance, of what it can expect.

Anger, Blame, and Responsibility

After a traumatic incident at a workplace, emotions usually run the gamut from numbness to terror or rage. Those directly involved in the event are probably in a state of shock or emotional paralysis, whereas those less directly involved may display their anger more freely. In time, the anger of those who were directly involved will emerge, often through the medium of speculation and information-gathering about who might bear responsibility for what happened. (In the wake of a natural disaster, this often takes the form of identifying those who should have given a warning.) It is one of the anomalies of traumatic injury that a victim's angry, acting-out behavior may emanate from a preconscious process in which the anger is expressed before the person is aware of feeling angry.

Because of the hierarchical structure of workplaces, in which people tend to defer to authority, there is often an impulse on the part of employees to think of their supervisors as being somehow responsible for a disastrous event. And even when most people perceive that what has happened was clearly an accident, there is no guarantee that certain employees will not feel resentment or that one of them will not blame "the brass" or "the company." It is characteristic of paternalistic systems that followers will cast their leaders into the role of "failed protector" when a crisis occurs. If there is considerable anger being felt toward top management, and especially when there is some degree of culpability among members of the managerial group, a clinician can play the role of peacemaker. The therapist as consultant may be able to defuse these feelings by means of individual counseling or, if there is more than one victim, group sessions. Although it is important that anger be brought to the surface, the clinician can exert an influence on an employee to express it appropriately. In this way, an employee can achieve a catharsis of feelings without losing his or her job in the bargain.

The Work Environment and Trauma

When a traumatic event occurs at a workplace, employers should take decisive steps to facilitate stabilization and recovery. For example, time should be set aside for employees to discuss and work through their reactions to the event; employees should not be forced but encouraged to participate. Psycho-educational discussion groups for this purpose can best be organized according to the employees' degree of involvement in the traumatic event. Individual psycho-educational sessions should also be offered to those who may not be comfortable in a group. In many instances, those who were directly involved view the participation of those who were not with suspicion; they suspect that the motives of the others for joining the group might vary from morbid curiosity to pity. Therefore, including those who were not directly involved should be done with considerable caution, lest their presence impede open discussion. Although some employee groups may choose to discuss the traumatic event only among themselves, it is recommended that employers enlist a trained group facilitator, to ensure that the group functions efficiently. Another reason for having professional leadership is that the professional can spot employees who may need more intensive clinical interventions.

Each employee of an organizational group or team should be encouraged to participate in the group process to some degree. It discourages stigmatizing; it fosters a sense of community and gives the employees a sense that they are valued by management. Furthermore, those who exhibit signs of trauma and are unwilling to enroll in a group should be approached privately. The indications of trauma that they have given should be brought to their attention sensitively, and then they can be referred for individual counseling. In the ideal instance, a supervisor would first consult with a mental health professional about how to discuss the problem with a resistant employee. The discussion should focus on observable, measurable behavior, as opposed to "attitudes" or mannerisms. Every effort should be made to convey a sense of genuine concern lest the discussion be misconstrued as critical or punitive. An employee who has witnessed the traumatic injury of another person also may have been traumatized by being a helpless onlooker. Hence, witnesses should be included in any program of services that the organization provides for injured employees.

After a traumatic incident, employers should give employees as much factual information as possible about the incident as well as the condition of coworkers. Often, in the confusion following a traumatic incident, misinformation and rumors abound. Although these rumors are rarely malicious in intent, they can serve to make an unfortunate situation worse. After a traumatic event, people have a deep need for information, chiefly to recapture a sense of control and to dispel the fear that random forces have been set loose. If they are not told frankly what has happened, their imaginations may run wild.

Because acquiring information is a key component of the trauma response, supplying that information is one of the important functions of the discussion groups referred to above, because they provide a structured setting in which to exchange knowledge constructively. Similarly, those employees who are recuperating at home or in a hospital should be supplied with accurate information as well. In many instances, there is a flurry of support and attention for injured coworkers immediately after a traumatic event, but as time passes, the survivors' contact with fellow employees may dwindle, causing them to feel alienated. Civilization is not so advanced that there are no longer superstitions about bad luck. In this context, it often takes the form of one worker avoiding another who was the victim of a traumatic event; the "logic" is that the victim's ill fortune could "rub off" on the one who is, so far, unscathed. This fear of contagion by people who have been singled out by fate can even lead to ostracism of the victim. And, even when the reaction is not so primitive as this, it can generate marked friction among colleagues at a workplace. These irrational sources of conflict can be defused by group meetings, led by persons trained in aspects of the trauma response.

Any intervention that an organization can provide after a traumatic event should strive to (a) channel feelings of blame, (b) dispel magical thinking (i.e., superstition), and (c) restore group cohesion. The discussion format is by no means a substitute for psychotherapy, but it can succeed in bringing back stability among the members of an organizational team.

High-Risk Careers

Professions that involve high-risk activities or constant exposure to dangerous situations—such as police work, fire-fighting, emergency medical services, and the military—warrant special consideration and care because of factors unique to these professions. The public is shielded (and shields itself) from many of the randomly violent aspects of life. Strong defenses and rich fantasies are used by the general public to insulate their thoughts from these horrors. Fortunately, there are agencies and services that take up the burden of intervening when events of this kind occur. Knowing about the existence of these protective agencies and services represent our best defense against worrying about what might go wrong. Even so, we have a tendency to take these guardians for granted, and we are quick to criticize them if they do not respond as rapidly or act as efficiently as we would like. It is easy to fall back on the commonly held notion that the people who do this kind of work enjoy the maudlin circumstances that they encounter on the job, or that they should have known what they were getting into ("It comes with the territory."). It is true that the people who work in these professions enjoy and take pride in their work. But moments such as attempting to give CPR to a dying three-year-old, holding a dying partner who has been your friend for 10 years, digging through the rubble of a fallen building to look for survivors among corpses, or seeing a buddy's arm blown off can take a toll on even the most zealous and hardened professional.

People choose high-risk careers for all manner of reasons. Many have a realistic sense of what the job entails, believe sincerely that they are well suited to the profession, and know themselves well enough to have developed good coping and defensive strategies. Some are drawn by youthful idealism to "serve and protect" but have no idea what the reality of that job holds in store for them. Some others make this choice because of low self-esteem; these people are drawn by factors such as status, glamour, and excitement. Others are propelled by a counterphobic need to "undo" past harm or past traumatic experiences, just as some people are attracted to the helping professions because they were neglected or abused as children. No one would dispute that these are legitimate reasons for making a career of protecting one's country or rescuing people in distress. But it is certainly preferable for the person to be aware of these motives than not aware.

When exposure to potential trauma is a fairly regular occurrence on a high-risk job, a professional must develop a flexible defense system that can be activated at difficult times and deactivated as needed, especially when personal life resumes at the end of the workday. This is the ideal case, but in some high-risk jobs it is viewed as unprofessional or weak to discuss feelings associated with highly charged situations or events. Workers are encouraged to be tough and, one way or another, to "stuff" their feelings. Denial is popular in this context, in that some people cannot even acknowledge that an event was emotionally painful. Nevertheless, a growing body of research testifies to the reality of trauma in "public safety" occupations (e.g., Lester, 1982, p. 1094; Levitov & Thompson, 1981, p. 167; Martin, McKean, & Veltkamp, 1986, pp. 100–101; Taylor & Fraser, 1982, pp. 8–10), even though there is still considerable resistance in these professions toward admitting its emotional toll.

Because many people who work at a high level of risk defend themselves against strong feelings routinely, they incur a further risk of entering a chronically defended state. When this occurs, they carry their work-related defense mechanisms into other spheres of their lives. And these defenses, so functional in the professional realm, can be grossly dysfunctional when extended to home and family; often, they cause considerable alienation in significant relationships. One manifestation of this state of affairs is when the worker confines his or her social interactions to fellow workers, based on the belief that only people who have shared experiences can understand or care. There has been much improvement in public awareness of the emotional hazards of professions such as these, but this glacially slow change in attitude represents a mere beginning. Of course, everyone reaches out with sympathy when a police officer, soldier, rescue worker, or firefighter dies in the line of duty. But there is still a want of sensitivity toward the everyday stresses of these protectors and restorers of community peace.

Creating an Emotionally Healthy Work Environment

The creation of an emotionally healthy work environment should begin with the employees' initial training and be enhanced by subsequent training. Taking care of oneself, emotionally, should be *promoted* as an intelligent approach toward a successful career, and not seen as a sign of weakness.

In addition to educating people about how to recognize the symptoms of stress and trauma and to accept these conditions as "normal" and not signs of weakness, the organization should actively support peer counseling services and sponsor professional counseling services as needed. Ideally, the latter services would be kept separate from the organizational structure itself (i.e., "out-house" instead of "in-house"), and should maintain absolute client confidentiality. In effect, information about the content of treatment sessions (or even their occurrence) should not be disclosed to management without the permission of the employee. Only in this way can an employee place trust in the counselor, a trust that must be established if the counseling service is to be fully utilized by employees.

Organizational sponsorship of a clinical program means more than just making it available. An organization should actively support participation by employees who are in high-stress careers. Too often, employees deny needing help themselves, mainly because they are preoccupied with helping others; or, they fear that seeking help might harm their careers.

Emergency Interventions after a Critical Incident

People who experience serious workplace trauma should be seen as soon as possible individually—if only one session—following a serious traumatic event; even those who were on the periphery of it should be seen at least once. As noted earlier, witnesses may be as traumatized as the actual participants. Individual screening of employees to find out who needs assistance the most should be carried out as soon as possible after the event.

Preferably, screening would be done by clinicians who are known and trusted by the staff, or a trained peer counselor because unknown mental health professionals may be viewed with suspicion and receive a guarded response. This derives from the fear that the person could be diagnosed or otherwise labeled, thereby acquiring a stigma in the form of a "jacket."

Group therapy following a traumatic incident can be helpful, but before forming a group, a clinician should individually screen the people who were directly involved in the incident. For some, meeting in a group may be inappropriate and contraindicated: for example, a person may be too distraught or fragile to tolerate the group process. Not everyone behaves as others think they should during an emergency and, subsequently, there may be strong negative feelings on the part of some people about how another person reacted; this, in turn, could cause the group process to become confrontational. In addition, there could be litigation that affects those who were involved, which could compromise the confidentiality privilege. If this is likely, it may be better to substitute individual counseling for those who might conceivably be affected by litigation, review, or possible investigation, because group therapy is not protected by the confidentiality privilege. Once prescreening of participants has been completed, it is a good idea to wait until the people have stabilized sufficiently before holding the first group meeting. That will permit the survivors to have some time for rest and reflection. We have found that group sessions for traumatized people proceed more smoothly when there is a "time-out" period before starting. We have found that some of the problems associated with Critical Incident Stress Debriefing programs were caused by requiring people to attend these sessions too early, without proper prescreening. The sessions may have caused the participants to reopen traumatic experiences before they were prepared to cope with them.

The focus of the group experience should not be merely on catharsis, because participants very likely will be returning to the same conditions that produced the traumatic event. In such instances, ventilation of feelings alone is seldom much help if there is only one session with no follow-up. Groups for these personnel should be organized around a clear structure that validates feelings through understanding, putting what happened into perspective, and accepting that they did the best they could under the circumstances. These strategies are aimed at achieving a measure of closure, so that the group members can take up their professional duties again as soon as possible. When feasible, the group may meet for as many as six times, depending on the severity and complexity of the traumatic situation.

The group approach can be effective with employees who are in high-risk professions because—apart from their elaborate funerals for fallen comrades, which are deeply moving—there is no standard ritual that provides for release, working-through, and resolution of feelings aroused by a traumatic incident. For example, losing and grieving for a fellow officer, firefighter, buddy, or partner is never prepared for in reality. A clinician who works with organizations such as police or fire departments or the military is often struck by how their funerals are fraught with emotion, some thinly suppressed and some overflowing. People who normally, in the course of their work, face tragedy with calm and control, may find themselves expressing feelings of which they were scarcely aware. These stately and elegant funerals offer a setting in which the unstated agenda is that it's all right to show bereavement and sorrow. They fulfill an absolute need imperfectly, and by doing so demonstrate how strong the need is. A group for traumatized personnel will be a more direct but private means to the same end, and individual counseling the most direct and private of all.

Even when someone has attended group sessions, he or she may find it useful to enter psychotherapy concurrently or after the sessions have ended. High-risk professionals may, in fact, require intensive treatment for a considerable period following a traumatic event. An advantage of therapy of this kind is that it can include members of the traumatized person's family, when appropriate.

Individual Therapy

Clinicians should be very sensitive to the fact that people who experience a serious traumatic event in the workplace may come to therapy with complaints other than those related to the traumatic event. They may seek treatment for family problems or other emotional issues such as unexplained anxiety, job dissatisfaction, depression, sleep dysfunction, or excessive drinking. Not unlike other traumatized people, they may have resisted seeking treatment because of the stigma that is associated with mental health care. Or they may have attributed their problems to "weakness." Conversely, they may see, in therapy, a direct threat to their careers.

Therapists should be prepared to find that people in high-risk professions may not be able to discuss the details of the traumatic situations in which they were involved, for several reasons: there may be an ongoing investigation, the activity may be "top secret," or he or she may have been ordered not to discuss the facts of the operation. Moreover, he or she may fear that you, the therapist, may be shocked by the details of the event. And, he or she may feel ashamed or guilty about his or her actions in the incident.

In beginning individual treatment with people in such professions, we have found it helpful to say that they do not have to tell us details of what happened. Instead, they can tell us about how they felt about what happened. Often people are enormously relieved that they do not have to "do over" or relive horrible details of the traumatic event to get help.

When beginning therapy with traumatized people, one must be extremely sensitive to issues such as guilt, shame, and responsibility. A therapist should make it very clear that it is not his or her role to judge. A therapist should not be surprised if he or she is tested by a trauma client to see if the therapist is "safe." This testing may take the form of questioning to see how much one really knows about the event, accompanied by the recounting of grisly stories or being evasive and distant.

There also will be aspects of their work that you as a therapist may not know and, in this type of situation, it is wise to let your client know what you don't know. This kind of specific information is essential if you are planning to do any form of cognitive restructuring or hypnotic work; because, if you do not understand the details of the event or even the slang used in certain high-risk situations, you may expose an encapsulated trauma without realizing what you are doing.

The following is a tragic example of such lack of knowledge. A couple came to see a couple's counselor, mainly at the wife's insistence. The wife's main complaint was that, since returning from the military, he was "different." She described him as "detached" and "cold." She believed that his military experiences, because they were harsh, brought back memories of his being abused in childhood.

After meeting with the couple, the therapist felt that it would help the husband if she utilized EMDR to help him reprocess his childhood abuse and resolve his past issues. Unfortunately, the therapist was unfamiliar with the details of his military experience. Once the EMDR process was begun, the client began to become more emotional, using unusual language and making repeated references to a small body part. The therapist did not realize the significance of his behavior, because she was not knowledgeable about the details of his war experiences.

The man began to be aggressive toward his wife, biting her on the part of the body to which he had made reference. The therapist did not now what the body part meant, but there were other moments when he was very affectionate and contrite, so the therapist thought that she was making progress. She had no idea that she was opening an encapsulated battle trauma, with no therapeutic means of support or control. One terrible night, the man attacked his wife's body part again and then suddenly ran into the bedroom, grabbed a gun, and shot himself to death in front of her, ending his torment.

The therapist had not known that the man's assignment in combat was that of an assassin. The body part with which he was obsessed was the ear; the organ was cut off the assassin's victims and kept by him as a trophy of a mission accomplished. This case study is not meant to denigrate the therapeutic process or the therapist in question; instead, it is meant to highlight the need to obtain accurate information about the encapsulated traumatic experience, and the actual combat duties of the person, before beginning to treat someone who has been in combat.

We have found it useful to learn as much information about where and when and how a military person served, and to obtain consultation from a local veteran's center. We have found these centers to be very helpful, as well as appreciative of caring therapists in the community.

Case Finding

In some cases, treatment is sought because a spouse has insisted on it; external motivation of this kind is not always a good prognostic sign. The trauma can be more complex if the person is reacting not only to a recent, known traumatic event but also to an accumulation of past traumatic situations; in such cases, a person's defenses may have been sufficiently strong to prevent a severe trauma response, but the most recent event has proven too much for those defenses. Often, when emotions from accumulated traumas do erupt, they follow a divergent path toward some "safe" aspect of the person's life, such as marriage or family; this may be why a spouse is the one asking for help. This is another instance in which the iron might of the defenses deployed earlier is a disadvantage, because the person is unable to see the connection between his current outpouring of emotions and the traumatic event. The significant others are themselves unable to perceive the connection, because the loved one convinced them, in the past, that what happened had done no harm. For their part, the outbursts that are presently occurring may not seem justified by the recent traumatic event. To them, it may seem as though "All of a sudden he just fell apart," or "She blew up for no reason."

This perplexity of the loved ones and family members of people after a traumatic event is an artificial condition that the survivor creates, in them, unwittingly. In the belief that it is best to protect them from the harsh realities of his or her trauma, the person spares them the details; some have a rule never to talk about "it" at home. This attempt to shield the loved ones is misguided in many instances, because it requires a degree of self-deception to succeed. The unspoken fear is that, by revealing how they really felt, their defenses would fail them and they might "break down." To some in these professions, the showing of emotions is still a forbidden sign of weakness.

Once an event has been accepted as trauma-producing and a survivor has acknowledged traumatic feelings, therapy to guide recovery can begin. To help the person restructure the meaning of the event by means of a cognitive/behavioral process, a major theme of the approach recommended here, providing information to the survivor is a key element. By supplying facts about what happened, and helping the person reinterpret what he or she remembers of the event, one can stimulate functional defense mechanisms into renewed activity. For example, a statement of belief such as, "I failed to save my partner" can be restructured into, "I did everything possible to save him (her)."

Exposure Therapy

Despite its purported efficiency in treating the symptoms of trauma, there has been documented resistance to the implementation of exposure therapy; for example, Cook, et al. (2004, p. 374) wrote that "Front-line clinicians in real-world settings rarely use this treatment." Some clinicians have expressed concern that complex, extreme trauma reactions, especially those resulting from events caused by human intent, cannot be adequately measured by a checklist of symptoms. There are more profound personal, even existential issues that must be considered when helping a person pass through the stages of the trauma response, on the way to recovery (see also Chapter 13).

Serious questions can be raised about a form of treatment for trauma that involves reexposure of the survivor to the details of the traumatic event. These details, for some survivors, were horrific in the original experience, and can generate as much or more horror if repeated in treatment. In short, great care must be taken not to make the injury worse.

Workplace Violence

Violent events occurring in workplaces create much sensational publicity, and the result is widespread fear and mythmaking. For example, the few instances of employees "going postal" and creating havoc in places where they work or had worked, is so firmly ingrained in the public consciousness that a new phrase has entered the language. The fact is that, among several distinct types of workplace violence, attacks by a disaffected worker are the least likely to occur.

Three major categories of workplace incidents have been identified by the California Occupational Safety and Health Administration. These types are differentiated as follows.

TYPE I

The most common and most potentially lethal form of workplace violence is committed by people who are in no way connected to the organization or business. Sixty percent of the homicides that occur in the workplace involve robberies or attempted robberies of stores or gas stations or taxi drivers.

TYPE II

Some violent incidents are committed by persons who have been the recipients of services by an organization and who may have been injured or in some way "wronged" by the person who provided the service, or are the significant others of people who were injured or killed by a service provider. Those who are at-risk of being assaulted for these reasons include police officers, correctional personnel, bus drivers or other transportation workers, health care or social service providers, teachers, and other public or private-sector employees who serve people in various capacities. Thirty percent of workplace homicides are of this origin.

TYPE III

Ten percent of workplace homicides are of the "postal" variety, usually committed by current or former employees of the organization and usually directed toward a supervisor, manager, or coworker. Unfortunately, many such incidents result in injury or death to victims chosen at random.

Clinicians should take note of the potential for workplace violence to be a consequence of marital disputes that have become abusive and may have escalated to battering. This occurs when, for example, a domestic violence perpetrator attacks a victim at his or her place of work. In such a case, a therapist should make sure that the workplace is included in the plan for the victim's safety, and as a part of any restraining order that may be obtained.

Critical Incident Stress Debriefing

One approach to helping traumatic-event survivors achieve recovery is the Mitchell Model of Critical Incident Stress Debriefing (Mitchell, 1983). Despite its lack of a thorough research background, this model has gained wide popularity because of its surface appeal and commercial success. It consists in group sessions with people who have shared an ostensibly traumatic experience; group members are encouraged to vent their trauma-based emotions, with the goal of catharsis. In the ideal case, post-traumatic reactions would be resolved in one or two group sessions. The training and certification of practitioners to conduct these sessions has been mandated by some employee assistance programs.

According to the model, a debriefing group should meet within 48 hours of the event, for a session lasting from three to four hours. Nevertheless, our experience, and that of Litz et al. (2003) and Shalev (2002), has been that people who are still reacting to the immediate impact of the event, are not capable of processing and retaining new information about the event and its effects. In this acute state, most people are susceptible to distorting information and may even be retraumatized in the process. Furthermore, the people who participate in these groups are often not screened beforehand, and are often not followed up after the treatment.

Independent study of this model has found its use questionable at best, and, in fact, its use has been discontinued by the U.S. Department of Defense, the American Red Cross, and the U.S. Department of Health and Human Services (Parry, 2001; Rose et al., 2001; Litz et al., 2002). Nevertheless, some commercial health providers still endorse it.

Postscript

Crisis work and trauma treatment naturally have much in common. Above all, they require of the clinician his or her most refined skills. They are not intellectual exercises, nor can they be appreciated or even fully comprehended in the Ivory Tower. For the most part, the more effective methods are not in the repertoires of novice therapists, simply because these methods rely heavily on experience. They are the toughest cases encountered by mental health professionals, and they offer the richest intangible rewards. There is no more gratifying outcome for the clinician than to have helped someone recover from trauma or make of crisis an opportunity.

Notes

Chapter 1

1. In this book, the terms "crisis" and "emergency" are used interchangeably. Whether or not an emergency situation has become "acute" can be inferred from context.

Chapter 6

1. American Medical Association, Diagnostic and Treatment Guidelines on Domestic Violence, 1992.
2. AMA (op. cit.)

Chapter 7

1. Adapted from Schmitt, B.D. The Physician's Evaluation (1978). In B.D. Schmitt (Ed.) *The Child Protection Team Handbook*. New York: Garland STPM Press.
2. Source: National Clearinghouse on Child Abuse and Neglect Information, U.S. Department of Health and Human Services (January, 2004).

Chapter 8

1. This chapter focuses on incest committed by a father against his daughter(s), the most prevalent type. Mother-son incest, equally heinous and pathological, is not discussed directly, but the basic principles of treatment are the same for both types.

Chapter 9

1. Lemmings are known to stampede to their deaths by drowning, not to kill themselves but because of some sort of hydrophilic compulsion to find water.
2. Within this relatively stable prevalence of suicidal deaths, it should be noted that there have been significant increases, proportional to the total, of suicides by adolescents and the elderly.
3. The object of anger can be an institution, such as "the company" or "the courts" or "the system" or an abstract concept such as "God" or "Fate."
4. The archaic term for depression, "melancholia," literally means black bile, a secretion of the liver thought to lead to disease.
5. A detailed account of the events that led to the suicide of Sylvia Plath can be found in Everstine, L. (1993) *The Anatomy of Suicide: Silence of the Heart.* Springfield, IL: Charles C. Thomas, pp. 62–70.
6. Adapted from Everstine, L. (2000) *The Meaning of Life: A practical guide to staying alive.* Philadelphia: Xlibris, pp. 78, 79.

Chapter 10

1. To say that stress (as in "post-traumatic stress disorder") is the result of a "stressor" is, of course, a tautology, adding nothing to our understanding of the phenomenon.
2. For instance, it is in this highly compromised, primitive state that brainwashing takes place.

Chapter 11

1. Adapted from the Everstine Trauma Response Index (ETRI), available from Behaviordata, Inc., Suite 100, 20833 Stevens Creek Boulevard, Cupertino, California 95014 (copyright 1988, 1989).
2. Adapted from the Everstine Trauma Response Index for Children (ETRI-Child), available from Behaviordata, Inc., Suite 100, 20833 Stevens Creek Boulevard, Cupertino, California 95014 (copyright 1988, 1989).

Chapter 14

1. National Center for PTSD Fact Sheet (August 10, 2005).

Chapter 15

1. There are many instances in which an adult male is raped by a man, and in fact the reported incidence of this crime increases yearly. That subject is not taken up in this chapter, except by analogy. The victim is assumed to be female and the assailant male.

Chapter 16

1. This is an example of mechanisms of defense that have done their work too well in protecting the person from having trauma symptoms; in effect, the mechanism has functioned out of control, as does the fibrillating heart. What is not obvious is that the person may have endured added emotional hardship throughout the years of repression, such as when problems along the way were not as easily solved because of the "unfinished business."

2. A deterrent to recovery happens in the case of people who seek help in the wrong place, for the wrong reason. A common sequel to natural disasters is that survivors present themselves at hospital emergency rooms for a variety of psychosomatic complaints, chiefly because they do not recognize or acknowledge that they are suffering trauma. This is a source of concern to medical personnel who are trying to care for the dying and wounded. Clinicians can perform a service for hospitals by training doctors and nurses to be sensitive to the needs of these people and to refer them to mental health resources.

3. This "replacement child" phenomenon has been studied extensively by the French psychologist Anne Ancelin-Schutzenberger (1998). *The ancestor syndrome: Transgenerational psychotherapy and the hidden links in the family tree*. London: Routledge. Vincent Van Gogh was such a child; he was born on the year anniversary of the stillbirth of a child who was to have been given the same name. In effect, he was born with the identity of a dead person. His ego belonged to someone else. The role confusion that this created followed him throughout his short, sad life, ending in suicide.

Chapter 17

1. From another perspective, we have observed that people who come from abusive families are often drawn toward professions that project a strong "family" image, such as the military, law enforcement, and fire-fighting (see later in this chapter).

2. Confidentiality in psychotherapy has limits, proscribed by the duty of a therapist to warn the intended victim if a client threatens to harm someone, as well as the duty to report any suspicion that child abuse has occurred. For a thorough dissection of these issues, see Everstine and Everstine (1986, *passim*).

3. At memorial gatherings of the attack on Pearl Harbor, there are many instances in which survivors demonstrate that they still have pent-up feelings from a traumatic event that occurred more than 60 years before. Probably few of these veterans sought treatment during or after their terms of service, and it is likely that few had any idea that their trauma responses had been unresolved for so long.

4. "Cal/OSHA Guidelines for Workplace Security," State of California, March 30, 1995.

References

Adams, M. S. & Neel, J. V. (1967). Children of Incest. *Pediatrics, 40*(1), 55–63.

American Psychiatric Association. (1994). *Diagnostic and stastical manual of mental disorders* (4th ed.). Washington, D.C.

Ammerman, R. T., Koilco, D. J., Kirisci, L., Blackson, T. C., & Dawes, M. A. (1999). Child abuse potential in parents with histories of substance use disorder. *Child Abuse and Neglect, 23*(12), 1225–1238.

Antonopoulou, C. (1999). Domestic violence in Greece. *American Psychologist, 54*(1), 63–64.

Arata, C. M. (1998). To tell or not to tell: Current functioning of child sexual abuse survivors who disclosed their victimization. *Child Maltreatment, 3*, 63–71.

Bard, M., & Sangrey, D. (1980). Things fall apart: Victims in crisis. *Evaluation and Change, Special Issue, 28–35.*

Barret, O. W., & La Violette, A. D. (1993). *It could happen to anyone: Why battered women stay.* Thousand Oaks, CA: Sage.

Birdwhistell, R.L. (1970). *Kinesics and context.* Philadelphia: University of Philadelphia Press.

Bonanno, G. A. (2004). Loss, trauma, and human resilience: Have we underestimated the human capacity to thrive after extremely aversive events? *American Psychologist, 59*, 20–28.

Boney-McCoy, S., & Finkelbor, D. (1998). Psychopathology associated with sexual abuse: A reply to Nash, Neimeyer, Flulsey, and Lambert (1998). *Journal of Consulting and Clinical Psychology, 66*(3), 572–573.

Briere, J. (2002). Treating survivors of severe child abuse and neglect: Further development in an integrative model. In Meyers, J. E. B., Berliner, L., Briere, J., Hemix, C. T., Reid, T., & Jenny, C. (Eds.), *The APSAC handbook on child maltreatment,* 2nd Edition. Newbury Park, CA: Sage.

Briere, J., & Spinazzola (2005) Phenomenology and psychological assessment of complex post-traumatic states. *Jounal of Traumatic Stress, 18*, 401–412.

Browning, D. H. & Boatman, B. (1977). Incest: Children at risk. *American Journal of Psychiatry*, 134, 69–72.

Burgess, A. W., & Holmstrom, L. L. (1974a). Rape trauma syndrome. *American Journal of Psychiatry*. 131(9), 981–986.

Burgess, A. W., & Holmstrom, L. L. (1974b). *Rape: Victims of Crisis*. Bowie, MD: Brady.

Cardefla, B. (2000). Hypnosis for the treatment of trauma: A probable but not yet supported efficacious intervention. *International Journal of Clinical and Experimental Hypnosis, 3*, 221–234.

Carson, D. K., Gertz, L. M., Donaldson, M. A., & Wonderlich, S. A. (1990). Family-of- origin characteristics and current family relationships of female adult incest victims. *Journal of Family Violence, 5*, 153–171.

Chalk, R. A., & King, P. A. (1998) *Violence in families: Assessing prevention and treatment programs*. Washington D. C.: National Academy Press.

Cohen, J. A., & Mannarino, A. P (1996). A treatment outcome study for sexually abused preschool children; Initial findings. *Journal of the American Academy of Child and Adolescent Psychiatry*, 35, 42–50.

Cohen, J. A., & Mannarino, A. P. (1998). Interventions for sexually abused children: Initial treatment findings. *Child Maltreatment*, 3, 17–26.

Cohen, J. A., & Mannarino, A. P. (2000). Predictors of treatment outcome in sexually abused children. *Child Abuse and Neglect*, 24, 983–994.

Cohen, J. A., & Mannarino, A. P., & Knudsen, K. (2003). Treating sexually abused children: One-year follow-up of a randomized controlled trial. Paper presented at the 156th annual meeting of the American Psychiatric Association, San Francisco.

Cournoyer, B.R. (1996). Converging themes in crisis intervention, task-centered and brief treatment approaches. In A.R. Roberts (Ed.), *Crisis Management and Brief Treatment*. Chicago: Nelson-Hall.

Courtois, C. (1999). *Recollections of sexual abuse: Treatment principles and guidelines*. New York: W. W. Norton & Co.

Courtois, C. (2004).Complex trauma, complex reactions: Assessment and treatment psychotherapy. *Theory, Research, Practice, Training*, 4 412–425.

Courtois, C. A., & Jay, J. (1998) Trauma responsive therapy: A shift in perspective. *Centering: Newsletter of The Center: Posttraumatic Disorders Program*, 3(5), pp. 1, 8.

Dale, J. (1995). Development of telephone advice in A&E: Establishing the views of staff. *Nursing Standard*, 9, 28–31.

Deblinger, E., Lippman, J., & Steer, R. (1996). Sexually abused children suffering post-traumatic stress symptoms: Initial treatment outcome findings. *Child Maltreatment*, 1, 310–321.

deChesnay, M., Marshall, E., & Clements, C. (1988). Family structure, marital power, maternal distance, and paternal alcohol consumption in father-daughter incest. *Family Systems Medicine*, 6, 453–462.

De Francis, V. (1969). *Protecting the Child Victim of Sex Crimes Committed by Adults*. Denver: American Humane Association.

Dutton, M. A. (1992). *Empowering and healing the battered woman: A model for assessment and intervention.* New York: Springer Publishing Co.

Ekman, P. & Friesen, W. V. (1969). Nonverbal leakage and clues to deception. *Psychiatry, 32,* 88–106.

Elliot, D. M., & Briére, J. (1994). Forensic sexual abuse evaluations of older children: Disclosures and symptomatology. *Behavioral Sciences & the Law,* 12(3), 261–277.

Erickson, M. H. (1980a). The nature of hypnosis and suggestion. In E. L. Rossi (Ed.), *The collected papers of Milton H. Erickson on hypnosis* (vol. 1). New York: Irvington.

Erickson, M. H. (1980b). Hypnotic alteration of sensory, perceptual and psychophysical processes. In F. L. Rossi (Ed.), *The collected papers of Milton H. Erickson on hypnosis* (vol. 2). New York: Irvington.

Erickson, M. H. (1980c). Hypnotic investigation of psychodynamic processes. In E. L. Rossi (Ed.), *The collected papers of Milton H. Erickson on hypnosis* (vol. 3). New York: Irvington.

Erickson, M. H. (1980d). Innovative hypnotherapy. In E. L. Rossi (Ed.), *The collected papers of Milton H. Erickson on hypnosis* (vol. 4). New York: Irvington.

Erickson, M. H. & Rossi, B. L. (1975). Varieties of double bind. *American Journal of Clinical Hypnosis, 17,* 143–57.

Erickson, M. H., Rossi, B. L. & Rossi, S. I. (1976). *Hypnotic realities.* New York: Irvington.

Eth, S., & Pynoos, R. S. (1985). Developmental perspective on psychic trauma in childhood. In C. R. Figley (Ed.), *Trauma and its wake* (vol. 1) (pp. 35–40). New York: Brunner/Mazel.

Everstine, D. S., & Everstine, L. (1983). *People in crisis.* New York: Brunner/Mazel.

Everstine, D. S., & Everstine, L. (1993). *The trauma response.* New York: W.W. Norton & Company.

Everstine, L., & Everstine, D. S. (Eds.) (1986). *Psychotherapy and the law.* Orlando, FL: Grune & Stratton.

Faust, J. & Katche, L. B. (2004). Treatment of children with complicated posttraumatic stress reactions. *Psychotherapy: Theory, Research, Practice, Training,* 41(4), 426–437.

Figley, C. R., (1988). Post-traumatic family therapy. In F.M. Ochberg (Ed.), *Post-traumatic therapy and victims of violence* (pp. 83–109). New York: Brunner/Mazel.

Foa, B. B., Dancu, C. V., Hembree, E. A., Jaycox, L. H., Meadows, B. A., & Street, G. P. (1999). A comparison of exposure therapy, stress inoculation training, and their combination for reducing posttraumatic stress disorder in female assault victims. *Journal of Consulting and Clinical Psychology, 67,* 194–200.

Foa, E. B., Davidson, J. R. T., & Frances, A. (1999). The expert consensus guideline series: Treatment of posttraumatic stress disorder. *Journal of Clinical Psychiatry, 60,* Supplement 16.

Foa, E. B., Keane, T. M., & Friedman, M. J. (2000). *Effective treatment for PTSD: Practice guidelines from the International Society for Traumatic Stress Studies*, New York: Guilford Press.

Freud, S. (1946). *Totem and Taboo* (1913) (A. A. Brill, Trans.). New York: Vintage.

Gebhard, P. H., Gagnon, J. H., Pomeroy, W. B. & Christenson, C. V. (1965). *Sex Offenders*. New York: Harper and Row.

Goenjian, A., Molina, L., Steinberg, A., Fairbanks, L., Alvarez, M., Goenjian, H., & Pynoos, R. (2001). Posttraumatic stress and depressive reactions among Nicaraguan adolescents after hurricane Mitch. *American Journal of Psychiatry*, 158(5), 788–794.

Goenjian, A., Yehuda, R., Pynoos, R., & Steinberg, A. (1996). Basal cortisol, dexamethasone suppression of cortisol, and MHPG in adolescents after the 1988 earthquake in Armenia. *American Journal of Psychiatry, 153*(7), 929–934.

Gold, S. N., (2000). *Not trauma alone: Therapy for child abuse survivors in family and social context*. Philadelphia: Taylor & Francis.

Gordon, L. (1986). Incest and resistance: Patterns of father–daughter incest, 1880–1930. *Social Problems*, 33, 253–267.

Green, B. L., Wilson, J. P., & Lindy, J. D. (1985). Conceptualizing post-traumatic stress disorder. A psychosocial framework. In C. R. Figley (Ed.), *Trauma and its wake* (vol. 1) (p.61). New York: Brunner/Mazel.

Greenstone, J.L. & Leviton, S.C. (1993). *Elements of crisis intervention: Crises and how to respond to them*. Pacific Grove, CA: Brooks/Cole.

Hackney, Fl. & Cormier, S. (1994). *Counseling strategies and interventions* (4th ed.). Boston: Allyn and Bacon.

Hansen, M. (Ed), & Harway, M. (Ed) (1993). *Battering and family therapy: A feminist perspective*. Thousand Oaks, CA: Sage.

Hembree, E., Street, G., Riggs, D. & Foa, E. (2004). Do assault-related variables predict response to cognitive behavioral treatment for PTSD? *Consulting and Clinical Psychology, 72*, no. 3, 53 1–534.

Hendricks, J.E. & McKean, J.B. (1995). *Crisis intervention: Contemporary issues for on- site interveners*. Springfield, IL: Charles C. Thomas Publishers.

Henry, D. B., Tolan, P. H., & Gorman-Smith, D. (2004). Have there been lasting effects associated with September 11, 2001, terrorist attacks among inner-city parents and children? *Professional Psychology: Research and Practice*, 35(5), 542–547.

Henry, J. (1997). System intervention trauma to child sexual abuse victims following disclosure. *Journal of Interpersonal Violence*, 12(4), 499–512.

Herman, J. (1992). Neuropsychology of violence. *Forensic Reports*, 5(3), 221–233.

Howard, C. A. (1993). Factors influencing a mother's response to her child's disclosure of incest. *Professional Psychology: Research and Practice*, 24(2), 176–181.

Jacobson, N. S. & Gottman, J. M. (1998). *When men batter women*. New York: Simon and Schuster.

James, R.K., & Gilliland, B.E. (2001).*Crisis intervention strategies* (4th ed.). Pacific Grove, CA: Brooks/Cole.

Kempe, C. H., Silverman, F. N., Steele, B. F., Droegemuller, W., & Silver, H. K. (1962). The battered child syndrome. *Journal of the American Medical Association*, 181, 17–24.

Knowlton, K. F., (2004). Straw house to a brick house: Constructing a strong self in an age of terrorism. *Families, Systems, & Health*, 22(1), 54–57.

Kubler-Ross, E. (1969). *On death and dying*. New York: Macmillan.

Lamb, S., & Edgar-Smith, S. (1994). Aspects of disclosure: Mediators of outcome of childhood sexual abuse. *Journal of Interpersonal Violence*, 9(3), 307–326.

Lanktree, C., Briere, J., & Zaidi, L. (1991). Incidence and impact of sexual abuse in a child outpatient sample: The role of direct inquiry. *Child Abuse & Neglect*, 15, 447–453.

Lehman, D. R., & Hemphill, K. J. (1990). Recipients' perceptions of support attempts and attributions for support attempts that fail. *Journal of Social and Personal Relationships*. 7(4), 563–574.

Lester, D. (1982). Subjective stress and sources of stress for police officers. *Psychological Reports*, 50, 1094.

Levang, C. A. (1988). Interactional communication patterns in father/daughter incest patterns. *Journal of Psychology and Human Sexuality*, 1, 53–68.

Levitov, J. E., & Thompson, B. (1981). Stress and counseling needs of police officers. *Counselor Education and Supervision*, 21, 163–168.

Lieberman, A. F. & Van Horn, P. (1998). Attachment, trauma, and domestic violence: Implications for child custody. *Child and Adolescent Clinics of North America*, 7(2), 423–443.

Liles, R. E., & Childs, D. (1986). Similarities in family dynamics of incest and alcohol abuse: Issues for clinicians. *Alcohol Health and Research World*, 11, 66–69.

Lindemann, F. (1944). Symptomatology and management of acute grief. *American Journal of Psychiatry*, 101, 141–148.

Linley, P. A. (2003). Positive adaptation to trauma: Wisdom as both process and outcome. Journal of Traumatic Stress, 16, 601–610.

Litz, B. T., Gray, M. J., Bryant, R. A., &Adler, A. B. (2002). Early intervention for trauma: Current status and future directions. *Clinical Psychology: Science and Practice*, 9, 112–134.

London, K., Bruck, M., Ceci. S. J., Shuman, D. W. (2005). Disclosure of child sexual abuse: What does the research tell us about the ways that children tell? *Psychology, Public Policy, and Law*, 11(1), 194–226.

Lustig, N., Dresser, J. W., Spellman, S. W., & Murray, T. B. (1966). Incest: A family group survival pattern. *Archives of General Psychiatry*, 14, 31–40.

Lynch, M. (1975, August). Ill health and child abuse. *Lancet, 31* 7,16.

Machotka, P. F., Pittman, F. S. & Flomenhaft, K. (1967). Incest as a family affair. *Family Process*, 6, 98–116.

Maddi, S. R. (2002). The story of hardiness: Twenty years of theorizing, research, and practice. *Consulting Psychology Journal*, 54, 173–185.

Maddi, S. R. (2005). On hardiness and other pathways to reslilience. *American Psychologist*, 60(3), 261–262.

Maisch, H. (1972). *Incest* (C. Bearne, Trans.) New York: Stein & Day.

Malinowski, B. (1927). *Sex and Repression in Savage Society.* London: Routledge & Kegan Paul.

Martin, C. A., McKean, H. E., & Veltkamp, L. J. (1986). Post-traumatic stress disorder in police and working with victims: A pilot study. *Journal of Police Science and Administration, 14*(2), 100–101.

McGoldrick, M. (1991). Echoes from the past: Helping families mourn their losses. In F. Walsh & M. McGoldrick (Ed's), *Living beyond loss* (pp. 50–78). New York: W. W. Norton.

McGrath, B. (Ed.), Keita, G. P., Strickland, B. R., & Russo, N. F. (1990). *Women and depression: Risk factors and treatment issues: Final report of the American Psychological Association's National Task Force on Women and Depression.* American Psychological Association.

Meiselman, K. C. (1978). *Incest.* San Francisco: Jossey-Bass.

Mitchell, J. T. (1983). When disaster strikes: The critical incident stress debriefing process. *Journal of Emergency Medical Services,* 1, 36–39.

Murdock, G. P. (1949). *Social Structure.* New York: Macmillan.

Myer, R.A. (2001). *Assessment for crisis intervention: A triage assessment model.* Pacific Grove, CA: Brooks/Cole.

National Victim Center (1993). *Crime and victimization in America: Statistical overview.* Arlington, VA.

Neuner, F., Schauer, M., Karunakara, U., & Elbert, T. (2004). A comparison of narrative exposure therapy, supportive counseling, and psychoeclucation for treating posttraumatic stress disorder in an African refugee settlement. *J. Consulting & Clinical Psychology, 72*(4), 579–587.

Norris, F. H. (2002) The range, magnitude and duration of effects of natural and human- caused disasters: A review of the empirical literature. A National Center for PTSD Fact Sheet.

Norris, F. H. (2005) Psychosocial resources in the aftermath of natural and human-caused disasters: A review of the empirical literature, with implications for intervention. A National Center for PTSD Fact Sheet.

Ozer, E. J., Best, S. R., Lipsey, T. L., & Weiss, D. S. (2003). Predictors of posttraumatic stress disorder and symptoms in adults: A meta-analysis. *Psychological Bulletin, 129,* 52–71.

Parry, C. (2001). *Evidence-based clinical practice guidelines for treatment choice in psychological therapies and counseling.* London, UK: Department for Health, National Health Service.

Parsons, T. (1954). The incest taboo in relation to social structure and the socialization of the child. *British Journal of Sociology,* 5, 101–117.

Pennebàker, J. & Harber, K. (1993). A social stage model of collective coping: The Loma Prieta earthquake and the Persian Gulf War. *Journal of Social Issues, 49*(4), 125–145.

Peters, J. J. (1975a). Social, legal and psychological effects of rape on the victim. *Pennsylvania Medicine, 78*(2), 34–36.

Peters, J. J. (1975b). Social psychiatric study of victims reporting rape. Paper presented at the 128th annual meeting of the American Psychiatric Association, Anaheim, California.

Pizzey, E. (1974). *Scream quietly or the neighbors will hear*. Baltimore: Penguin Books.

Prediger, D.J. (1994). Multicultural assessment standards: A compilation for counselors. *Measurement and Evaluation in Counseling and Development, 27,* 68–73.

Reiff, D. (1991, October). Victims all? *Harper's,* 49–56.

Rose, S., Bisson, J., Wessely, S. (2001). Psychological debriefing for preventing post traumatic stress disorder (PTSD) (Cochrane review). In *The Cochrane Library* Oxford, UK: Update Software.

Rosenthal, D., Sadler, A., & Edwards, W. (1987). Families and post-traumatic stress disorder. In T. C. Hansen & D. Rosenthal (Eds.), *Family Stress* (pp. 81–95).

Sas, L. D., & Cunningham, A. H. (1995). *Tipping the balance to tell the secret*. London: London Family Court Clinic, Inc.

Schmitt, B. D. (1978). The physician's evaluation. In B. D. Schmitt (Ed.), *The Child Protection Team Handbook*. New York: Garland STPM Press.

Schmitt, B. D. & Loy, L. L. (1978). Team decisions on case management. In B. D. Schmitt (Ed.), *The Child Protection Team Handbook*. New York: Garland STPM Press.

Seemanova, E. (1971). A study of children of incestuous matings. *Human Heredity, 21,* 108–128.

Shalev, A.Y. (2002). Acute stress reactions in adults. *Biological Psychiatry, 51,* 532–543.

Skowron, B., & Reinemann, D. H. 5. (2005). Psychotherapy interventions for child abuse and neglect: A meta-analysis. *Psychotherapy: Theory, Research, Practice, Training, 42*(1) 52–71.

Spiegel, D., & Cardefla, E. (1990). New uses of hypnosis in the treatment of post-traumatic stress disorder. *Journal of Clinical Psychiatry, 51,* 39–43.

Spiegel, H. (1974). *Manual for hypnotic induction profile: Eye-roll levitation method*. New York: Soni Medica, Inc.

Steinmetz, S. K., & Strauss, M. A. (Ed's) (1974). Violence in the Family. New York: Harper and Row (originally published by Dodd, Mead & Co.).

Summit, R. (1983). The child sexual abuse accommodation syndrome. *Child Abuse & Neglect, 7,* 177–193.

Sutherland, S., & Scherl, D. (1970). Patterns of response among victims of rape. *American Journal of Orthopsychiatry, 40*(3), 503–511.

Symonds, M. (1980a). The "second injury" to victims. *Evaluation and Change, Special Issue,* 36–38.

Symonds, M. (1980b). Acute responses of victims to terror. *Evaluation and Change, Special Issue,* 39–41.

Taylor, A. J. W., & Fraser, A. G. (1982). The stress of post-disaster body handling and victim identification work. *Journal of Human Stress, 8,* 4–12.

van der Hart, O., Boon, S., & Van Everdingen, G. B. (1990). Writing assignments and hypnosis in the treatment of traumatic memories. In M. L. Fass & D. Brown (Eds), *Creative mastery in hypnosis and hypnoanalysis* (pp. 231–253). Hillsdale, NJ: Erlbaum.

van der Hart, O., Brown, P., & van der Kolk, B. A. (1989). Pierre Janet's treatment of post-traumatic stress. *Journal of Traumatic Stress, 2,* 379–396.

van der Kolk, B. A. (1987). *Psychological trauma.* Washington, DC: American Psychiatric Press.

van der Kolk, B. A. (1988). The trauma spectrum: The interaction of biological and social events in the genesis of the trauma response. *Journal of Traumatic Stress, 1,* 273–290.

van der Kolk, B. A., McFarlane, A. C., & Weisaeth, L. (Ed's) (1996). *Traumatic Stress: The Effects of Overwhelming Experience on Mind, Body, and Society.* New York: Guilford Press.

Walsh, F. & McGoldrick, M. (Ed's) (1991) *Living beyond loss.* New York: W. W. Norton.

Watlzlawick, P. (1964). *An anthology of human communication;* Text and tape. Palo Alto: Science and Behavior Books.

Watzlawick, P. (1976). *How real is real? Confusion, disformation, communication.* New York: Random House.

Watzlawick, P. (1978). *The language of change.* New York: Basic Books.

Watzlawick, P. (1984). *The invented reality* (pp. 325–332). New York: W. W. Norton.

Watzlawick, P., Beavin, J. H. & Jackson, D. D. (1967). *Pragmatics of human communication: A study of interactional patterns, pathologies, and paradoxes.* New York: W. W. Norton.

Watzlawick, P., Weakland, J. H. & Fisch, R. (1974). *Change.* New York: W. W. Norton.

Wealcland, J. H. & Jackson, D. D. (1958). Patient and therapist observations on the circumstances of a schizophrenic episode. *Archives of Neurology and Psychiatty, 79,* 554–574.

Weakland, J. H., Fisch, R., Watzlawick, P. & Bodin, A. M. (1974). Brief therapy: Focused problem resolution. *Family Process, 13,* 141–168.

Weinberg, S. K. (1955). *Incest Behavior.* New York: Citadel.

Weiner, I. B. (1962). Father-daughter incest: A clinical report. *Psychiatric Quarterly, 36,* 607–632.

Widom, C. S., & Hiller-Sturmhofel, S. (2001). Alcohol abuse as a risk factor for and consequence of child abuse. *Alcohol Research and Health, 25*(1), 52–57.

Wortman, C. B., Silver, R. C., Kessler, R. C., Stroebe, M. S., Stroebe, W., & Hansson, R. O., (1993). *Handbook of bereavement: Theory, research, and intervention.* Cambridge: Cambridge University Press.

Yllo, K. A. (1993). Through a feminist lens: Gender, power, and violence. In R. J. Gelles & D. R. Loseke (Eds.), *Current controversies on family violence* (pp. 47–62). Newbury Park, CA: Sage.

Zeahnah, C. H., & Sheeringa, M. 5. (1997). The experience and effects of violence in infancy. In J. D. Osofsky (Ed.), *Children in a violent society* (pp. 97–123). New York: Guilford Press.

Index

K

Kidnapping, by stalker, 60
King, P. A., 65
Knowlton, K. F., 154, 180

L

La Violette, A. D., 65
Lamb, S., 222
Language, relationship through, 12
Lanktree, C., 129
Lester, D., 287
Lethality of traumatic event, 167–168
Levang, C. A., 121
Leviton, S. C., 24
Levitov, J. E., 287
Lieberman, A. F., 110
Life partner, as real target of suicide, 144
Liles, R. E., 123, 129
Limited intelligence, effect of, 62–64
Lindemann, F., 242
Lineups, 252–253
Linley, P. A., 180
Litz, B. T., 180, 190, 295
Location of traumatic event, 163
London, K., 120, 223
Loneliness, fear of, 71
Loss, traumatic, 272–274
Loss of sphincter control, in children after sexual assault, 225
Lost relationship, unfinished business with, 149
Lower back, injuries on, as sign of child abuse, 106–107
Lustig, N., 129

M

Machotka, P. F., 129
Maddi, S. R., 180, 260
Maisch, H., 129
Malinowski, B., 118
Man/woman team, working in, 33
Managers, role of, 282–284
Mania, in bipolar disorder, 59
Manic individuals, 6
Mannarino, A. P, 236
Martin, C. A., 287
McGoldrick, M., 272, 275

McGrath, B., 65–66
McKean, J. B., 24
Medical recovery period after trauma, 191–192
Medication in acute emergency, 7
Medication referral, following trauma, 176
Meetings with investigator, 252
Meiselman, K. C., 118–119, 121, 123, 130, 222
Mental illness, 59
Military, persons in, risks undertaken by, 286
Milton Erickson school of hypnosis, 201
Mitchell, J. T., 294
Mitchell Model of Critical Incident Stress Debriefing, 294
Molestation, child. See Child abuse
Mood swings
    after trauma, 206
    in children after sexual assault, 225
Moral uncertainty, 263
Murdock, G. P., 118
Myer, R. A., 7, 10, 14, 23–24
Myths regarding violent individuals, 58–59

N

Narcissistic personality disorder, 59
Narrative reprocessing therapy, following trauma, 176
Natural disasters, 6
Neel, J. V., 119
Neglect of children, 99–116
Neighbor, as real target of suicide, 144
Neuner, F., 204
Neurobiology of trauma, 157–159
Nightmares, 168–170, 268
    in children after sexual assault, 225
Norris, F. H., 261–262

O

Orientation of individual, 48
Origin of incest taboo, 118
Ozer, E. J., 175